JAGUAR

▸▸Contents

60
JIM CLARK'S D-TYPE
RESTORED TO RACE-WINNING SPEC

{ **F E A T U R E S** }

7	**WELCOME**
8	**JAGUAR TODAY**
14	**JAGUAR BEGINNINGS**
20	**XK120 vs C-TYPE**
30	**BROADSPORT XK120**
36	**ROWAN ATKINSON MKVII**
42	**XK120 FOUR-SEATER**
48	**HAWTHORN'S JAGUARS**
60	**JIM CLARK'S D-TYPE**
70	**DEREK BELL DRIVES MKI**
74	**XKSS**
82	**XK120, 140 AND 150**
92	**USING THE XK EVERYDAY**
94	**XK vs THE REST**
98	**USING THE MK2 EVERYDAY**

36

74

82

128

230

206   **XKR AT THE 'RING**

214   **XF FIRST DRIVE**

216   **XF SV8 vs MASERATI**

222   **JAGUAR DAIMLER HERITAGE TRUST**

226   **JDHT ON THE MILLE MIGLIA**

230   **E-TYPE SIX-CYLINDER BUYERS GUIDE**

235   **E-TYPE V12 BUYERS GUIDE**

241   **XJ6 AND 12 BUYERS GUIDE**

246   **XJS BUYERS GUIDE**

248   **EVERY JAGUAR MADE**

246

248

104   **XK140 vs E-TYPE S2**

110   **EAGLE E-TYPE**

120   **LOW DRAG E-TYPE**

128   **NEW V12 E-TYPE**

136   **XJ13 RESTORED**

146   **XJ220 ROAD AND RACE**

156   **XK120 vs E-TYPE vs XK8**

164   **XJR AT LE MANS**

166   **JP1 ON THE ROAD**

170   **PROTOTYPES**

174   **BROWNS LANE**

178   **C-TYPE REPLICA**

184   **S-TYPE R vs M5 vs RS6 vs LOTUS**

194   **XKR vs MASERATI vs 911**

204   **XKR FIRST DRIVE**

110

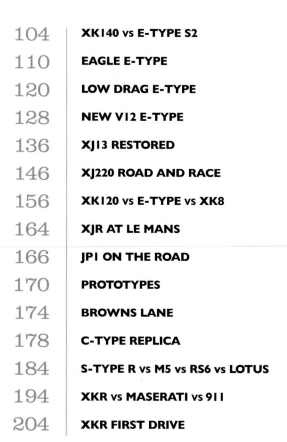
146

206

FOOTMAN JAMES

Insurance specialists. At your service.

0844 875 0592
www.footmanjames.co.uk

All our policies include the following as standard:

- Motor Legal Expenses
- 24 hour Breakdown Recovery (UK and European)
- Personal Accident to include Road Rage & Carjacking
- Limited Mileage and Multi-Vehicle options are also available.

From a XK140 to a XK60. Whatever your pride and joy, we'll get you covered.

The enthusiasts' favourite for over twenty five years, Footman James is one of the leading specialist insurance brokers.

With a UK client base of 140,000 owners of classic and vintage vehicles, Footman James consistently uses its enormous influence to arrange the best deal for you.

So whatever your pride and joy, you can be confident that with Footman James behind you, you've adopted the best policy.

Talk to us soon.

We're at your service!

FOOTMAN JAMES
Insurance specialists. At your service.

Quoteline: 0844 875 0592 www.footmanjames.co.uk

Authorised and regulated by the Financial Services Authority. Telephone calls may be monitored or recorded for your protection.

COMPETITIVE RATES on modern car, motorcycle, home and contents insurance

›› Welcome

FLAWED BUT FANTASTIC

'There's an appeal to a Jaguar that tugs at every enthusiast's heart strings'

Jaguar has had its ups and downs but it's one of those marques that you can't help but love. Many of the cars are flawed, whether through compromised initial design or quality control that was, well, we know what it was like during those British Leyland days, no need to go on about it... And yet from the SS100, through the XKs, the E-types, the Mk2 and the XJs, to the very latest XF, there's an appeal to a Jaguar that tugs at every car enthusiast's heart strings.

This publication is packed with Jaguar features from *Octane* and *evo* magazines, by some of the finest writers in the motoring world. I love the effortless knowledge imparted in Philip Porter's features, the enthusiasm of John Simister's drive of the restored XJ13 and the self-effacing genius of Rowan Atkinson's description of his MkVII drive at the Goodwood Revival. And they're just three examples in over 200 pages.

What's best, though, is that we're not having to rely on nostalgia here: the latest XK8 and XF are genuinely so good that they stand up to the strongest of rivals, from the likes of Porsche, Maserati and BMW. And they do so with style and at realistic prices – age-old Jaguar attributes.

So enjoy this celebration of Jaguar. There's plenty to read!

David Lillywhite

JAGUAR
THE COMPLETE STORY

Editorial office
Octane, 1 Tower Court, Irchester Road,
Wollaston, Northants NN29 7PJ, UK
Tel: +44 (0)207 907 6585. Fax: +44 (0)1933 663367
Email: info@octane-magazine.com
Website: www.octane-magazine.com

Advertising office
Octane Media Advertising Dept, 19 Highfield Lane,
Maidenhead, Berkshire SL6 3AN, UK
Tel: +44 (0)1628 510080. Fax: +44 (0)1628 510090
Email: ads@octane-magazine.com

Managing editor:	David Lillywhite
Art editor:	Rob Gould
Designer:	Dean Lettice
Editorial manager:	Janet Mills
Production:	Nigel Grimshaw
	Keith Adams
Advertising director:	Sanjay Seetanah
Advertising sales:	Rob Schulp
Advertising production:	Anisha Mogra
	Kerem Kolcak
Publisher	Geoff Love
Newstrade director	Martin Belson
Marketing manager	Alex Seeberg
Managing director	Ian Westwood
Group finance director	Ian Leggett
COO	Brett Reynolds
CEO	James Tye
Chairman	Felix Dennis

Jaguar: The Complete Story is published under
licence from Octane Media Ltd, a subsidiary company of Dennis
Publishing Limited, United Kingdom. All rights in the licensed
material belong to Felix Dennis, Octane Media or Dennis Publishing
and may not be reproduced, whether in whole or in part, without
their prior written consent. Octane is a registered trademark.

Repro by Octane Repro
Printed by BGP, Bicester

Distribution Seymour, 2 East Poultry Avenue,
London EC1A 9PT. Tel: +44 (0)20 7429 4000

Periodicals Postage paid @ Emigsville, PA.
Postmaster: send address corrections to Octane Media c/o 3330
Pacific Ave, Suite 404, Virginia Beach, VA 23451

Jaguar: The Complete Story ISSN 1906-3723 is published by Octane
Media Ltd.

The publisher makes every effort to ensure the magazine's contents
are correct. All material published in Jaguar: The Complete Story is
copyright and unauthorised reproduction is forbidden. The editors
and publishers of this magazine give no warranties, guarantees or
assurances and make no representations regarding any goods or
services advertised in this edition.

CONTRIBUTORS

ROBERT COUCHER
AS THE OWNER of an XK140, Robert is Jaguar through and through. He compares the XK with a Series II E-type, p104.

PHILIP PORTER
THE WHIRLWIND behind the XK Club, the E-type Club and numerous Jaguar books, Philip has six features in here.

JOHN SIMISTER
JOHN WAS LUCKY enough to help with the restoration of the XJ13, and then to test drive it – a rare privilege. See p136.

ROWAN ATKINSON
THE WORLD FAMOUS actor is also a dedicated historic racer. Here he describes his drive at the Goodwood Revival, p36.

DEREK BELL
HE'S BEST KNOWN for winning Le Mans five times, but Derek appreciates his Jaguars, and loved testing a MkI, on p70.

Jaguar TODAY

After years of uncertainty Jaguar looks ready to move forward thanks to new owners Tata – a company that understands Jaguar's heritage and which seems keen to nurture the brand's values...

Words: Keith Adams

For a company that's held in such high regard by its devotees it's hard to reconcile the turbulent history Jaguar has endured over the past 30 years. First there was BMC, then it became mired in the BL takeover; that was followed by a short period as a Public Limited Company, before falling into the clutches of Ford. And now, the leaping cat once again finds itself subject to an ownership change – the Indian manufacturing conglomerate Tata having taken the hot seat. Will Jaguar's life ever be straightforward?

When Ford purchased the company in 1989, for an eye-watering £1.6bn, it finally looked as if the future was assured. Throughout the 1990s investment from Uncle Henry poured in enabling both the factories and model range to be expanded and overhauled. Clearly the intention was to give Jaguar a fighting chance against BMW and Mercedes-Benz.

Installed as the jewel in the crown of Ford's Premier Auto Group, the four-car Jaguar range looked as if it could do no wrong… **»**

Below
Built from aluminium and styled by
Ian Callum, the svelte Jaguar XK of
2006, is a clear indicator of Jaguar's
future direction.

What makes up Jaguar?

**Jaguar and Land Rover
Shared Facilities**

Halewood, Merseyside
Jaguar X-type and Land Rover
Freelander production.
Employees: 2100

Gaydon, Warwickshire
Design and engineering, marketing,
sales and service. **Employees:** 2890

Jaguar Facilities

Castle Bromwich
Assembly plant for XF, XJ and XK.
Employees: 2200

Browns Lane
Veneer manufacturing, heritage
centre. **Employees:** 490

Whitley
Design, research and development.
Employees: 1980

Unfortunately profitability and Jaguar weren't natural bedfellows. Throughout 2006, then into 2007, Ford's US finances began to unravel which placed UK operations under close scrutiny.

On June 11, 2007 Ford confirmed what the media had been hinting at for months – it planned to sell Jaguar *and* Land Rover. The situation wasn't ideal because Land Rover was profitable and Ford would have preferred to retain it. However, both companies shared so much infrastructure that selling them as a single entity was the only option. Besides, a loss-making Jaguar – marque kudos or not – would have been near-unsaleable.

As it was, the sale dragged on far longer than anyone expected – despite Ford's advisers Goldman Sachs, Morgan Stanley and HSBC wanting to secure a quick deal. After protracted negotiations Tata of India emerged as the preferred bidder and the contract was finally inked in March 2008. With the wobbling global economy as its backdrop and the tide turning against luxury cars the $1.15bn deal was probably good news for Ford.

Financially, Tata was in a great position to take on Jaguar and Land Rover – it's a huge conglomerate that owns divisions as diverse as Corus (formerly British Steel) and Tetley Tea. In automotive terms it is one of the fastest growing brands thanks to a strong home market. The launch of its '1-lakh car', the £1250 Nano, has also put it firmly in the spotlight.

Despite all this the most interesting aspect of Ford's sale of Jaguar to Tata is actually that the current cars are the best for years, although that clearly doesn't apply to the X-type. Launched in 2001, as part of a two-pronged attack (alongside the 1998 S-type) on the BMW market, it was lambasted as nothing more than a Mondeo in drag, despite the obvious benefits of all-wheel drive and a range of V6 engines. Sales were slow to take off, but once the estate and turbodiesel versions were rolled out in 2003 things started to pick up. X-type received a light facelift in 2007, but given Tata's commitment to sports cars its future looks uncertain.

The XF is where Jaguar's future now lies – it has wooed **»**

'THE MOST INTERESTING ASPECT OF FORD'S SALE OF JAGUAR TO
TATA IS THAT THE CURRENT CARS ARE THE BEST FOR YEARS'

'THE XF IS WHERE JAGUAR'S FUTURE NOW LIES'

everyone who's driven it, and thanks to Ian Callum's brave design language, the leaping cat has gained new focus. In the UK the XF has been a huge success, with buyers queuing up.

Next comes the XK, which started Jaguar's modernist ball rolling in 2006. The aluminium-bodied coupé set new standards in terms of handling and ride, and in XK-R form with 420bhp to play with, road testers were left wondering whether the similarly-styled Aston Martin DB9 was worth the £50,000 premium. Available as a convertible or coupé, and popular in Europe and the USA, the XK is another modern Jaguar success story.

The top of the range XJ saloon is a bit of an enigma. Despite looking like a facelift of the 1990s X305 saloon, it was new from the ground up when it appeared in 2003, and boasted a featherweight aluminium structure. Unfortunately sales have been disappointing and its lack of success was probably the tipping point for Jaguar's move away from retro-led styling.

Tata has already confirmed that the future is secure and that Jaguar's Porsche Boxster-rivalling F-type sportscar development programme (due in 2013) has been confirmed, along with the XF-style rebody of the XJ saloon.

Despite the chilly financial conditions prevailing at the time of Tata's purchase of Jaguar, its future in the UK seems assured (see box out). Given Jaguar's recent troubled history this is the closest it has been to a safe and secure future in years and that surely is the best news of all.

Jaguar's new owner RATAN TATA

Is Ratan Tata a safe pair of hands for Jaguar? 'We're conscious that these brands belong to Britain,' he affirmed. 'I have to say we respect these brands and support their needs.

'Our interest in Jaguar is very much in the culture behind them. We want to be an international car company and need a window for our new technology and capabilities.' Jaguar is perfect to achieve these aims.

Since the purchase, these models have been signed-off by Tata: new XJ (Project X351, due in 2010) and F-type (Project X700, due in 2012), with the XF coupé awaiting the green light.

Tata has also confirmed that Jaguar will be pushed upmarket (leaving the X-type hanging by a thread) and super-expensive Daimler versions will be introduced.

Full range of quality parts for yesterday's, today's and tomorrow's Jaguar cars...

Jaguar BEGINNINGS

The success of Jaguar from the humblest of starts was led by one man, William Lyons

Words: David Lillywhite

'LYONS LEARNED EARLY ON HOW TO APPEAL TO THE CAR BUYING PUBLIC'

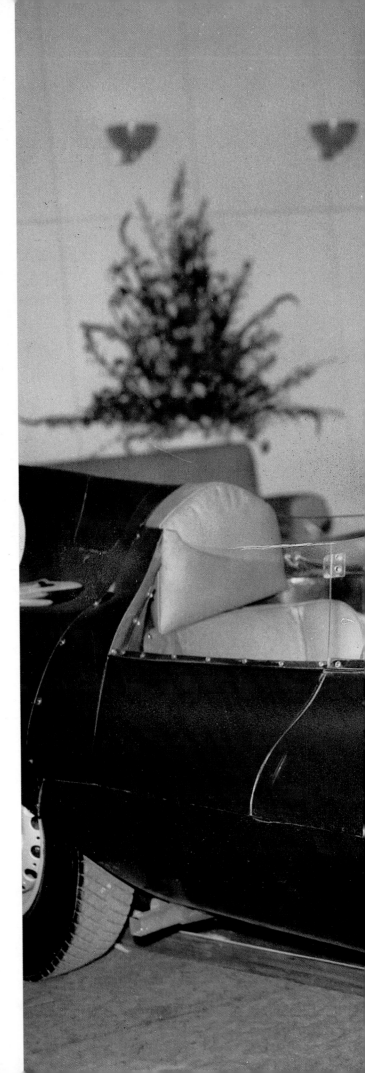

Right
Lyons shows off the
1955 Le Mans-winning
D-type on March 1956
tour of the Browns
Lane, Coventry factory.

There have been countless talented individuals involved in the success of Jaguar. But its direction and image were down to one man, William Lyons, who started out with the company that became Jaguar before he was 21, and continued until retirement at 71, in 1972.

William Lyons, later Sir, learned early on how to appeal to the car buying public, but it was as a young motorcycle enthusiast (pictured in 1920, page 14) that he made his first shrewd move: spotting the potential in a business run by one William Walmsley, who was building sidecars and fitting them to reconditioned motorcycles. It was a good product let down by poor business skills, and Lyons homed in on it.

He formed the Swallow Sidecar Company in 1922 with a bank overdraft of £1000, found basic premises in Blackpool and started to build the sidecars in partnership with Walmsley. The sidecars, built in aluminium, were among the most stylish around – something that Lyons realised was crucial in appealing to the potential buyer.

Unfortunately for Lyons and Walmsley, the strong between-the-wars sidecar market was obliterated by the introduction of the Austin Seven, which brought motoring to the masses with its low purchase price, reliability, ease of driving and modest running costs. »

Clockwise from above
The E-type cemented the Jaguar legend; Lyons with VW boss Kurt Lotz; C-type moved Jaguar into major motor sport success; but it all started with neat aluminium sidecars built by Swallow.

It was at this point that Lyons displayed the shrewd thinking that would define his management of Jaguar over the years: he understood the mentality of potential buyers, and set about creating a car that would be affordable and yet appealing to those who saw themselves as a cut above the typical Austin Seven owner.

He created a stylish two-seater aluminium body mounted on the proven Austin Seven chassis and negotiated the first of many deals with Bertie Henly, of the successful dealership Henlys, to supply 500 cars. The Austin Seven Swallow genuinely looked special, with neat lines and a polished radiator cowl, allowing its owners to live out the fantasy that they actually weren't too badly affected by the economic hardship of the 1920s and early '30s, and instead keep up appearances amongst their peers. But at £175, or £185 with a hinged hardtop, the model was only about £10 more than a typical standard Seven.

Such was the Swallow's success that the company introduced a saloon model, swiftly followed by a larger model built on the Morris Cowley chassis.

By the time of the 1929 London Motor Show, the company was exhibiting new models based on the Fiat Tipo 509A, the Swift Ten and the Standard Big Nine. The largest, the Standard Swallow, was to prove especially important, for it offered relatively extravagant styling and a range of colours that were genuinely daring and extrovert for the era.

Actually, though, Lyons felt restricted by the use of other manufacturers' chassis, but was well aware that the industry at the time was littered with failed car makers, so decided to stick with Standard running gear on a Swallow-design chassis and new body. And so the SS I and SS II sports coupes were born, in summer 1931. Lyons' obsession with building cars that were low to the ground made for a sleek-looking car, with an outrageously long bonnet that prompted one newspaper report to claim that the new model had the look of a £1000 car – and yet it was just £310.

Lyons had used simple tricks to make the SS models stand out from their more mundane (but similarly priced) rivals. Engines were mounted further back in the chassis than was normal practice at the time, and front leaf springs were mounted alongside the engine, for the lowest ride possible. The flagship SS I was the one that everyone hankered after, but the smaller, cheaper SS II was cleverly styled to bask in the SS I's reflected glory – and it sold strongly.

In 1933, Lyons demonstrated another trick that he would go on to use again and again to maximum effect: the use of his

cars in motor sport. The new Tourer version of the SS I became the first of the breed to take part in a serious competitive event, with three cars entered into the tough and prestigious Alpine Trial. Success over the following years did much to enhance the SS name.

William Walmsley, however, had lost interest and left the company in 1934, leaving Lyons to go it alone with his ambitions to improve the quality of his cars. His first steps were to appoint a chief engineer, William Heynes, and expert engine design consultant Harry Weslake. Meanwhile, the SS I Airline saloon and the SS 90 models were born, and the range was becoming comprehensive and classy enough to warrant a new, more appropriate name. Jaguar. But the company was still named SS, and the cars know as 'SS Jaguars'.

With engines tweaked by Weslake and Heynes, the SS 90 was developed into the wonderfully stylish and sporting SS 100, now the most legendary of the pre-World War Two models. Of course it was cut short by the war, during which the Jaguar plant was turned to war production, but it was during wartime firewatch shifts on the roof of the plant that Heynes sketched out the initial designs for the engine that would move the cars and the company into a new era. The engine became known as the XK, a 160bhp (higher later) six-cylinder, twin-overhead

'LYONS HAD USED SIMPLE TRICKS TO MAKE THE SS MODELS STAND OUT FROM THEIR MUNDANE RIVALS'

camshaft design that was first introduced to the public in a two-seater sports car, the XK120.

The XK120's swooping looks, stunning performance and success in motor sport, in particular at Le Mans (from 1950) made it and subsequent models a great success. From this grew C-type and D-type racing cars, the E-type and later the XK8 and XKR, plus a long line of sleek saloons and coupes that survived poor management and quality control (mostly after Lyons' retirement) to evolve into the current XK and XF range we have today. Incredibly, the XK engine lasted right up until 1994, but it's the legacy of Sir William Lyons, to produce sporty, distinctive cars that punch above their weight in terms of price, that provides the link from 1922 to the present day. △

The Legend begins

A memorable day behind the wheels of a Le Mans XK120
and Ecurie Ecosse C-type shows why Jaguar's iconic
designs redefined the post-war sports car

Words: Peter Morgan   Photography: Michael Bailie

Above and facing page
XK120 'AEN 546', en route
to 11th at Le Mans in 1951,
and as it is today.

I'm hurtling along in top at what seems like an incredible speed. The 3.4-litre straight six is settled into an easy gallop and the big Smiths tacho needle is pointing to three-thousand-five-hundred with the sureness of Big Ben announcing mid-day. Beyond the radiant Flag Metallic Blue bonnet the long straight stretches ahead, and I'm basking in seventh heaven.

An icy blast numbs my face, but I hunch down further into the cockpit and savour the warmth that is wafting over my legs like a comforting blanket.

Behind me, a golden rooster tail of fallen autumnal leaves defines the course of this car, like an arrow-straight contrail in a brilliant blue sky. Is there really anything better in life than driving a C-type Jaguar on a sunny winter's day?

All that is good and great in Britain's motor racing heritage is defined in this car. It is the Establishment – an early 1950s statement on motor sport's future by a generation who, just ten years before, had engineered Spitfires and Hurricanes.

It almost goes with the calibre of the car that it is quite tricky to drive, and you need a sympathetic touch to handle the engine and the sometimes recalcitrant gearbox. But after a few laps of the test track I'm doing OK, and enjoying this glorious celebration of 'the way it was'.

For a moment I can picture being a part of the weekend's sport in France. I grin at the thought of the drivers' Champagne-induced headaches the day after victory at La Sarthe (twice, in 1951 and 1953), and their victorious blast back to Coventry.

> 'ON SUNNY DAYS AT GOODWOOD, IT'S EASY TO FORGET WHAT THE DANGER AND HARDSHIP OF DRIVING THEM WAS REALLY LIKE'

I double-declutch and downshift to third, just for the sake of hearing again the crisp report of this seemingly unburstable engine, casting another glance around the gauges to check the Ts and Ps. And then I look at the speedo.

I'm barely doing 80mph! Suddenly, I don't feel so cock-sure of myself after all.

A voice in my head tells me to try turning off the sun, throw in a blustery rain shower and double my speed. And I imagine that it's the darkest, coldest time of the night on the loneliest place in racing – the three-and-a-tad miles of the Ligne Droit des Hunaudières.

The big Lucas headlamps, that looked so impressive in the pits, now project two hopelessly inadequate fingers of yellow light barely 30 or 40 yards ahead. And the only thing I can see in the rain-lashed beams is the strobing dashed line in the centre of the road. I'm exhausted, wet and cold, but my life depends on what my straining eyes can pick out of the murk ahead – that first glimmer of a slow red tail-light that, if I don't see and pass, could kill me.

Today, when we see cars like this on sunny summer days at Goodwood, it's easy to forget what the danger and hardship of driving them was really like. Of course, for a generation that had survived so much, that was part of the thrill. But let's not kid ourselves today that winning in these cars was easy. Look past the oil-smudged faces of drivers like Whitehead, Walker, Hamilton and Rolt and their eyes show a satisfaction in knowing they have tested themselves, not just their cars, to their limits. Their smiles are the smiles of men who appreciate the joy of just being alive.

1951 Jaguar XK120

SPECIFICATIONS

Engine
3442cc, dohc in-line six, two SU carburettors

Power
160bhp @ 5000rpm

Torque
195lb ft @ 2500rpm

Transmission
Four-speed manual, rear-wheel drive

Suspension
Front: ind, via wishbones and torsion bars, telescopic dampers, anti-roll bar. Rear: live axle, semi-elliptic springs, lever-arm dampers

Brakes
Drums all round

Weight
1321kg (2912lb)

Performance
Top speed 125-132mph

Value
Cost new £1263
Value now c£200,000

1952 C-type
SPECIFICATIONS

Engine
3442cc, dohc in-line six,
two SU carburettors

Power
200bhp @ 5800rpm

Torque
220lb ft @ 3900rpm
Transmission
Four-speed manual,
rear-wheel drive

Suspension
Front: ind, via
wishbones and torsion
bars, telescopic
dampers, anti-roll bar.
Rear: live axle
suspended on trailing
links, transverse torsion
bar, Panhard rod,
telescopic dampers

Brakes
Originally drums all
round
Weight
1016kg (2240lb)

Performance
Top speed c150mph

Value
Cost new £2327
Value now c£800,000

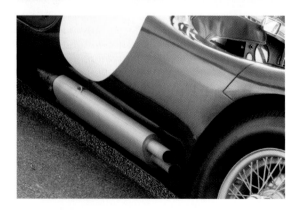

Below
Ian Stewart takes
the chequered flag in
XKC006's first race:
Jersey, 1952.

The C-type was Jaguar's first Le Mans winner. A product of a wartime dream to build, first, a world-beating engine and then, in a resurgent world of motorsport, a car that could put the Jaguar name right at the top of every driver's most-wanted list.

The straight-six that William Lyons' team developed is one of the great automobile engines of all time. Called the XK, the long-legged 3.4-litre had an alloy head with double overhead camshafts and initially produced a maximum of 160bhp. And when they realised they had no suitable car that would fully demonstrate the performance of their new engine, the men at Jaguar built a new chassis.

At the 1948 Motor Show, the new XK120 was a sensation. The '120' stood for the car's maximum speed – a remarkable figure for a production car at that time. To silence sceptics, Jaguar took a car to a stretch of motorway at Jabbeke in Belgium and recorded no less than 126mph. And with the windscreen removed, they achieved 133mph!

Nevertheless, they didn't expect a car like the '120' to sell that strongly: they planned to make just 200, aiming them at the competition world. But once the word was out the XK120 did indeed sell like fresh, hot cakes.

Meanwhile, the competition successes began to build. The first major victory came in the Dundrod Tourist Trophy, when a promising youngster named Stirling Moss discovered the new car's rich potential.

The first steps on the international stage were taken with an exploratory visit to Le Mans in 1950. Success eluded the three specially prepared XKs, but many lessons were learned. Jaguar's engineers knew that what they really needed was a purpose-built racing car.

'FAST LAPS ARE ALL ABOUT ACCEPTING THAT THE HARD DUNLOP RACING TYRES WORK BEST WHEN THEY ARE SLIDING'

At Le Mans in 1951, the team turned out with the new XK120C – which quickly became known to all as the C-type. It was lighter and more slippery than the production car, and it proved to be a winning formula. Although two of the three factory cars unfortunately retired, the Peters Whitehead and Walker claimed victory.

A second and far more emphatic victory at Le Mans would follow in 1953. By this time the 24 Hours had taken on very significant importance for any manufacturer hoping to appeal to the burgeoning world sports car market. The opposition was stiff, and included competitive entries from Ferrari, Alfa Romeo and Cunningham.

Nonetheless, what tipped the balance for the C-types was not only the solid reliability of the XK engine but a perfect unfair advantage in the form of Dunlop's new disc brake. For lap after fade-free lap the C-types were able to leave their braking into the sharp Mulsanne corner much later than the other, drum-braked, cars.

Major Tony Rolt and Duncan Hamilton won that year's race at an average speed of nearly 106mph, with the Moss/Walker car second and Whitehead and Ian Stewart fourth. The C-type passed into motor racing legend and the Jaguar XK became the sports car every driver coveted.

The Pastel Green XK120 featured here finished 11th at Le Mans in 1951, the highest-placed XK120, in the hands of Bob Lawrie and Ivan Waller. They averaged over 84mph for the 24 hours and completed 1992 miles to the finish – 265 miles behind the winning C-type. The story goes that the more accomplished Waller drove fully 18 hours himself.

Current owner Guy Broad's family has known this car, on and off, since » the early 1970s. Despite its factory preparation for the 1951 24 Hours, he says that there are no really significant differences between this and a regular production example – including a typical 160bhp from the engine. But there are many fascinating details that set it apart.

The bonnet has three neat circles cut into it, giving teasing glimpses of the highly polished twin-cam head. The openings allowed faster oil and water top-ups and helped cool the engine bay. I also note the delicate hollow copper beading finishing the rear wheelarches, which on the production car would have been covered by fully enclosed spats. And perhaps recalling a lost 1930s zest for life are the delicate swirls of the fast fuel filler and the streamlined, bowled lenses of the special Marchal headlamps.

Factory prepping for the 1951 race gave this car a huge 40-gallon fuel tank (the same size as the C-type's) and wire wheels – the latter an option that did not become available on the production cars until the following year. This XK doesn't, though, have disc brakes. These were available only after 1953 and its successive owners have resisted the temptation to customise this otherwise largely original 1951 example.

'On' rather than 'in' seems to be the appropriate description for how you sit in the well-finished cockpit. The simply trimmed bucket seats have both driver and passenger sitting out in the airstream in period style.

Starting is a matter of twisting the ignition key and pressing the button. Some energetic pumping of the accelerator coaxes petrol from the twin SUs into the cylinders and, seemingly in its own good time, the big six rumbles into life.

'THE SIX-CYLINDER'S FREE-REVVING SPIRIT MUST HAVE BEEN A REVELATION TO THOSE BROUGHT UP ON A DIET OF BENTLEYS'

The slow-acting four-speed gearbox could be described as the Achilles' heel of the early XKs, but the clutch action is weighted well and there's a mechanical thumbwheel device on this car for blocking accidental selection of reverse gear. There is synchromesh – theoretically – but I find the only way I can get a clean downshift is to double declutch and use a generous boot of throttle to spin the engine up.

Nevertheless, the XK120 is as docile as a lamb – and a beauty to drive. It pulls well from as little as 1500rpm and has a wonderful hard edge to its exhaust above 2500. The acceleration is brisk, and I love it all the more because I'm so close to the engine's noise and, of course, to nature.

The six-cylinder's free-revving spirit must have been a revelation to those bought up on a diet of slow-turning Bentleys. Front torsion bar independent suspension means the ride is also far more confident than that of pre-war British sports cars.

Nevertheless, after some 15 minutes behind the wheel, I'm getting tired. At low speeds the steering is monumentally heavy (by today's standards) and to haul this car through the tighter corners demands a lot of effort. When I stop, I'm cold enough that my speech is slurring, my arms are aching and my legs feel like jelly. I'm wondering what Messrs Lawrie and Waller did for stamina.

So it is with some trepidation that I clamber into the compact cockpit of the C-type. All around me is bare aluminium sheet and the sturdy tubes of the spaceframe chassis. A set of spare spark plugs wait for their moment by my right elbow and, like the whole of the dash area, the outsized Bakelite steering wheel is finished in a functional black.

'WHAT TIPPED THE BALANCE FOR THE C-TYPE WAS NOT ONLY THE SOLID RELIABILITY OF THE XK ENGINE BUT A PERFECT UNFAIR ADVANTAGE IN THE FORM OF DUNLOP'S NEW DISC BRAKE'

Above
Owner-driver Bob Lawrie stands proudly with his XK, Le Mans '51.

C-type is lighter, more powerful and faster than XK – but they're both wonderful to drive.

While the engine retained its original 3442cc capacity it was given a higher compression ratio, higher-lift camshafts, larger exhaust valves and bigger carburettors, lifting the maximum power to between 220 and 230bhp. A lighter, stiffer spaceframe replaced the XK120's very conventional twin box-section chassis. There were torsion bars front and rear (the 120 has leaf springs on the rear) and a rack and pinion replaced the less precise recirculating ball steering.

This is a car for life's players, and few would dispute that this one has played in a few important games. By 1952, the C-type had established itself as the next step up for successful XK120 drivers. After a promising first season in 1951, this was the path taken by Ecurie Ecosse team owner David Murray. The team's first C-type was this car, chassis XKC006, initially purchased and driven by Ian Stewart in July 1952.

Stewart drove the brand new JWS 353, resplendent in British Racing Green, straight from the factory to the Jersey road races and won, very first time out.

Subsequently, Stewart took wins at Charterhall and Crimond and followed Moss and Hamilton home third at Turnberry. He was first in the Wakefield Trophy at the Curragh and later at Castle Combe. Perhaps one of the more satisfying wins came once more at Charterhall, where he set fastest lap to Stirling Moss in XKC005 and Roy Salvadori's Ferrari.

For 1953, the car was painted in the Ecosse team's Flag Metallic Blue colours, with white recognition stripes on the front. Future Le Mans winner Ninian Sanderson drove the car to sixth place in that year's Goodwood Easter Handicap, while Stewart himself continued with a consistent string of wins and placings.

The C-type was sold to Hans Davids in Holland at the end of the year. The Dutch driver won at Spa and Zandvoort before selling it on to Bryan Corser of Shrewsbury. The car later went to the USA and only came back to the UK in 1974, when Lynx Engineering restored it for owner Bill Lake.

Even before I start the engine, this feels like a well-sorted racer. My body

'AT LOW SPEEDS THERE IS A FEELING THAT THIS CAR IS LIKE A COILED SPRING, AN ATHLETE WALKING TO THE STARTLINE'

is tucked away deep inside that aerodynamic body and the controls fall to hand and foot without effort. Maybe the importance of reducing the driver's fatigue levels was more understood by 1953.

Nevertheless, at low speeds there is a feeling that the car is like a coiled spring, an athlete walking to the startline. And when I press the throttle hard, the engine note takes on a glorious-sounding roar and the car forces its way forward.

Guy Broad had told me earlier that the only way to drive these cars half decently was to hang out their tails and steer them on the throttle. Fast laps are all about cornering balance and accepting that the hard Dunlop Racing tyres work best when they are sliding.

With the Ecosse car conservatively valued at around £800,000 by auctioneer Christie's, I wasn't about to test that theory, but I could certainly admire the level of car control that drivers took for granted in the 1950s.

I marvel at the difference between the 120's drum brakes and the discs of this C-type. I can imagine the likes of Rolt and Hamilton positively grinning like Cheshire cats as they flew past the red cars going over the brow into Mulsanne.

There were just 54 C-types built and, to quote the late Andrew Whyte in his definitive volume Jaguar, the Sports Racing and Works Competition Cars to 1953, 'an authentic C-type is a thing of great value'.

That value is based on more than just rarity or aesthetics. There's also a priceless worth that can only be sensed behind the steering wheel. It's in the cockpit, with the tacho needle edging round the dial, that you also grasp the quality of the people that drove these cars. △

» Thanks to Christie's (www.christies.com) and Guy Broad Parts (www.guybroad.co.uk), and to Aviation Leathercraft/Moto-Lita Ltd (www.flying-jacket.com, www.moto-lita.co.uk) for the period clothing.

Modern romance

Words: David Lillywhite
Photography: Charlie Magee

Jaguar's XK120 was revolutionary. It gave great handling, saloon-car standards of ride and decent performance at an astonishing price. And it was, and is, beautiful.

But this XK120 deviates from the original's wonderful design. Yes it looks the same but under the skin the mechanicals have been tweaked and improved. The car has more power, better handling and braking and even more interior space than the original. In fact, it's virtually a brand-new car in most respects, a typical example of the latest Broadsport XKs that are custom-built by Guy Broad Parts.

But why mess with an icon, when William Lyons' team of engineers – including William Heynes, Walter Hassan, Bob Knight and Claude Baily – did such a great job in the first place? It's because that's what »

'IT WAS A DELIBERATE CHOICE
THAT BROAD AND HIS TEAM,
NOT THE CUSTOMER, DECIDED
MUCH OF THE CAR'S SPEC'

Right
Just 323km show on the
clock, but this isn't the
result of clicking past
100,000 miles or some
dodgy back-yard
'modification'. The
Broadsport is at least
90% new, and deserves to
start afresh.

Above
XK cooling is limited
by the tall, narrow
grille, but the
Broadsport cars use
two neat intakes
either side of the
grille to duct cold air
to the engine bay, air
box and front disc
brakes. The bonnet
louvres are to let out
engine bay heat.

Guy Broad's customers demand. They want to be able to drive
their Jaguar XKs long distances, at high speed, with complete faith
in their car's reliability. They want to be comfortable. They want
the best.

The car featured (Broadsport number 12, if you're interested), is
destined for Germany, for a customer who initially wanted a road-
rally specification XK but gradually changed his plans to encompass
trans-European touring and a lot more luxury than a typical rally
car would have given him.

Curiously, the car, which has emerged from the Coventry
workshops of Guy Broad Parts (within sports exhaust-hearing
distance of the Jaguar plant), has a distinctly Germanic feel to it.
Perhaps it's the lack of bumpers, the extra air intakes or even just
the slightly smaller diameter and increased width of those chrome
wire wheels. Or maybe it's just the colour, a pleasant surprise after
the more usual Silver, Old English White, or British Racing Green of
the typical XK.

Just as curiously, it was Guy Broad and his team, not the
customer, that decided much of the car's specification – a
deliberate decision to let the experts build the best car for the
requested uses. Guy even chose the colour.

This car started out as a rough donor XK, needing thousands
spent on it just to turn it into a vaguely driveable machine. Instead,
it returned to Coventry, where it was stripped and analysed until

all the rotten bits had been thrown out. That left the running gear,
the bonnet and the roof...

It's true, all those beautifully curved panels were binned.
Destroyed. Well, bear in mind that they were dreadfully rotten.

So in place of the original steel is beautifully crafted aluminium
alloy. This isn't as odd as it sounds because the first 240 XK120s
(all roadsters) were aluminium-bodied. They were built as much
as publicity vehicles for Jaguar's new XK engine as to become new
models, the lines of the now familiar swooping bodywork penned
quickly and easily by William Lyons, and aluminium chosen for its
relative ease of low-volume production. Only once Lyons had been
convinced of the 120's public acceptance did he allow the factory
to tool up for steel body production.

The Guy Broad workshop uses aluminium for the same reasons
that William Lyons chose the material for the first XK120s. As the
panels are built from scratch, it's possible to build in a few subtle
modifications. The most obvious are the air intakes either side of
that characteristically tall, narrow front grille – so tall and narrow
that little air tends to find its way through for engine cooling.
Hence those new intakes.

Then there are the wheelarches. Fear not, they haven't been
flared, simply made slightly deeper to ensure the new, 15in
diameter wheels gel more pleasantly with the bodywork. This is a
controversial point, because many will argue that the XK looks

better with its original 16in diameter wheels, and we're inclined to agree. But if you want a decent choice of high performance tyres without having to resort to inappropriately low profiles, then you need 15in wheels nowadays.

Is the gain in grip worth the aesthetic and originality sacrifices? The Broadsport's interior beckons.

Remember, this could have been a rally car. The Wilton carpet, the richly polished wooden door cappings, the combined CD player and satellite navigation unit (no, really), the modern heater unit, the overall air of well-being... there wouldn't have been a place for any of that.

So instead, Guy Broad's team have kitted out their 12th Broadsport build with an all-leather interior in biscuit brown, using the company's own replicas of the original competition bucket seats used in XKs in their racing and rallying heyday.

Unlike those original seats, which would have been firmly bolted to the floor, the Broadsport replicas are mounted on runners. Will they slide back far enough to overcome the notoriously limited legroom of the XK120? Well, yes and no.

In fact, there's no way that mere seat movement will overcome what was simply a minor design fault in the vertically challenged post-war years. But there's no legroom problem in this particular Jaguar XK120, thanks to serious surgery at the hands of Guy Broad and co.

Basically, they cut a window out of the metal of the bulkhead, at the end of the driver's side footwell, then bolt an extension piece to the bulkhead to extend the footwell. Into that extension piece goes a set of aftermarket pedals and, at last, legroom is sufficient for a six-footer. It's a great relief.

And so, with legs stretched luxuriously forward, you go for a drive. That famous six-cylinder engine roars away up front, never as smoothly or quietly as legend (or rose-tinted road tests) suggest but feeling much more sophisticated than most engines of the era.

This one's a 3.8-litre, the perfect size of XK engine, even though XK120s only ever came as 3.4s. While the later 3.8 weighs virtually the same, its wider bores and identical stroke make for a more freely revving, powerful and torquey unit. It's the choice of most serious Guy Broad customers, simply because it looks and feels right – after all, the XK150s were factory-fitted with 3.8 units.

The Broadsport engines are special, though. They're rebuilt to closer tolerances than the originals (sadly not difficult) to the point that they truly deserve the much-misused description of being 'blueprinted'. With a 9.5:1 compression ratio, way higher than the XK engines of yore (fuel's better now, surprisingly), a fast road/ rally camshaft and lightened flywheel, the internals aren't significantly altered, just optimised. This one, like most hot XK engines, breathes through triple 2in SU carburettors.

»

The result, in numbers, is power of 285bhp (most XK120s managed 160bhp) and torque of 290lb-ft (originally 195lb-ft). In real terms, we're talking instant pick-up, startling acceleration and, most importantly, the ability to increase speed dramatically in any situation. There's so much more to this kind of performance than mere 0-60mph figures but, well, we all like to know, don't we. This car's 0-60 should be around six seconds, a full four seconds quicker than a typical XK120.

Originally, the top speed of the XK120 was an impressive 120mph-plus, as proven by Jaguar's legendary Jabbeke highway speed run in 1949. Aerodynamics dictate that even the Broadsport car won't significantly better such top-end performance, but its five-speed gearbox conversion ensures that the engine is significantly calmer as it's heading that way. The 'box is a modern Getrag: slick changing, quiet and strong. It's driven via a competition clutch.

So there's serious engineering behind the butch Dick Dastardly looks of Broadsport number 12 and it's no surprise to find that the underpinnings are just as comprehensively reworked as the fabulous engine.

The original XK120 chassis was developed from the basics of the MkV and MkVII saloon chassis, which in turn were similar to the chassis of the pre-war Jaguar saloon. By cutting out 18in, and adding deeper box section side sections for better torsional stiffness, the XK120 received its underpinnings for little expense or design time.

It was a decent chassis for the time, too. The Broadsport uses a Guy Broad remanufactured chassis to the same design. A simple addition is the well-designed roll hoop that passes through the Broadsport's floor and bolts onto the chassis in four places; the weakest area – over the axle – is neatly triangulated for some extra strength.

The roll hoop is unusual in that it bolts into place, so it can be removed if necessary (many XK hoops have been welded in). The way it's done is by building pedestals onto the chassis to meet with the underside of the cabin floor, so the foremost roll hoop mounts can bolt straight through the floor, while the diagonals head for the rear damper mounting points.

Usefully, the torsion bar front suspension of the XK and its saloon stablemates also strengthens the chassis, but there are other parts of the running gear that suffer when a Broadsport's rather more powerful engine and uprated brakes are used to their fullest extent. Driveshafts, front axle stubs and even the spokes of standard wire wheels can all give under the new-found strains of extra torque and braking forces gained by swapping the 120's drum brakes for discs all-round. In fact, when Jaguar introduced the disc-braked XK150, stub axles occasionally sheared as a result of the change.

So Broadsport cars have powerful brakes with stub axles and wheels to match. At the front, there are the common-or-garden Girling discs and three-pot calipers that Jaguar used throughout the 1970s. This is a big step on from the troublesome Dunlop

Above
As the Broadsport rips past, the exhaust note sounds sporty but impressively smooth. Smaller diameter wheels (15in instead of 16s) allow a wider choice of tyres – the wheelarches are deeper to fill the resulting gap between bodywork and wheels.

'THIS CAR'S 0-60 SHOULD BE AROUND SIX SECONDS, A FULL FOUR SECONDS FASTER THAN A TYPICAL XK120'

Broadsport Jaguar XK120
SPECIFICATIONS

Engine
3781cc, 6-cylinder, dohc, triple SU carbs

Power
285bhp @ 5800rpm

Transmission
5-speed Getrag, lsd, uprated driveshafts

Suspension
Front: torsion bars, adjustable track control arms, Spax adjustable dampers; rear: leaf springs, four link location, Spax adjustable dampers

Brakes
front discs, three-pot calipers; rear discs, two-pot calipers. Servo assistance to front, bias adjustment

Performance
0-60mph 6.0secs; top spees 135mph

calipers of XK150s and MkIIs that used to be a popular conversion on 120s. At the rear, they're XJS items. A servo gives 3:1 assistance to the front brakes, while a twin-cylinder bias box allows fine tuning of the front-to-rear balance.

The driveshafts are stronger than standard and, as for the wheels, they're 15x6in competition offset wires, built for strength. The Pirelli P4000 205/70x15s tyres don't look too modern but offer modern grip.

Don't kid yourself, a Broadsport XK won't combine a perfect ride with exemplary handling – that isn't possible on 1940s separate chassis, leaf spring technology. But it's not a bone breaker and it sure does grip. Turn-in is sharper (negative camber helps) and it stays in line through bumpy corners, courtesy of the four-link located rear axle.

The other big difference is the steering. There's no play. It's by no means light but it's certainly not unmanageably heavy. And it's pin-sharp. The secret is a rack and pinion conversion to replace the old worm and nut steering box.

It's a massive improvement on the heavy, low-geared and slop-prone steering of the original, arguably the worst feature of a standard XK120 (along with the lack of legroom). But this new-found competence doesn't feel incongruous; to be honest, the Broadsport feels deliciously sporty and rather characterful.

There's no denying that the hefty price tag and the deviations from the original specification will put off many XK fans. But the Broadsport is a great way to enjoy the best sides of one of the greatest ever English sports cars, without having to suffer many of the disadvantages that come with an original car. △

Rowan
goes forth...

...and finishes sixth on aggregate in his Jaguar MkVII. Here's how
he acted as both Pro and Am driver at the Goodwood Revival

Photography: Jeff Bloxham, John Colley, Steve Havelock, Mike Johnson
Words: Rowan Atkinson

I've written so much about this funny old car in the past year, that I shrink from opining any more on the subject. *Octane* aficionados might remember me wibbling on in my column about its restoration, the agony over its colour choice and failure to appear on the Tour Auto, so if those readers want to skip the opening paragraphs, I will understand completely. However, I should perhaps recap the basics for any Johnny-cum-Latelys to the *Octane* fold.

This is a 1952 Jaguar MkVII. It's a big, fat, Bentley-sized object built by Jaguar on a stretched XK120 chassis with a 3.4-litre version of the XK engine. It may look rather grand but it was never that expensive, just one of those Jaguar saloons of the 1950s and 1960s which represented remarkable value for money. They all exuded more than a hint of Flash Cash from a Diana Dors/East End/Great Train Robbery kind of world, but the MkVII was nevertheless a quite

outstanding sports saloon for its day and Jaguar raced it from the very first year of its production.

The big annual event of the era was the Silverstone Production Car Race and the MkVII's victory in the event of 1952 was the first of no less than five consecutive victories. I can hear some of you chortling when I point out that its closest rivals were the Austin Westminster and the Daimler Conquest, but I don't think that takes much away from William Lyons' achievement with the MkVII. It dominated those races because it had an excellent chassis allied to a fabulous engine in the XK unit.

It not only enjoyed success as a racing saloon. Even more astonishing for a vehicle of this weight and size was its prowess as a rally car, culminating in its most improbable achievement: an outright win on the Monte Carlo Rally of 1956. I've tried to form a picture in my mind of this leviathan slithering down ice-

laden Alpine passes, but I'm afraid the image remains fuzzy and ill-defined.

In 1954, Jaguar began to experiment with the manufacture of light alloy body panels for the MkVII in an attempt to ensure its continued dominance of racing and rallying. The racing department took Sir William Lyons' personal car, an early steel MkVII of 1952, and replaced its body with an entire structure pressed from magnesium alloy.

This car was intended to be one of the Jaguar entries for the Production Car race of 1954 but, for whatever reason, it never appeared. A partly-alloy car did win the 1955 race in the capable hands of Mike Hawthorn, though.

Once the Mk1 Jaguar was introduced in 1956, (don't ask me to explain the mathematical incongruity of Jaguar's numbering!) the MkVII's competition days were over and that original one-off Works car, constructed entirely of magnesium but never raced, was dumped right at the

Below
Jaguar MkVII has serious presence on the starting grid, making it hard to creep up on other drivers and catch them unawares.

'THE RACING DEPARTMENT TOOK SIR WILLIAM LYONS' PERSONAL CAR, AN EARLY STEEL MKVII, AND REPLACED ITS BODY WITH AN ENTIRE STRUCTURE PRESSED FROM MAGNESIUM ALLOY'

back of the Racing Department with big yellow crosses all over it indicating its 'scrapped' status.

It was then spotted by young Jaguar PR director and occasional racing driver Bob Berry. He bought it for £250, fitted pre-production versions of the then-innovative disc brakes and what he described as a 'wet sump D-type engine' and took it racing. He only raced it for a year before selling off all the D-type bits and reverting to the then-new 3.8-litre road engine.

In 1963, Berry sold it to dental student Christopher Sturridge, in whose family the car remained for nearly 40 years. I then bought it in 2001, restored it and drove at the Goodwood Revival Meeting this year.

It was intended that I should drive the car in the St Mary's Trophy for 1950s saloons (a 30 car grid), sharing with Sir Stirling Moss, the blissful symmetry of his involvement being that not only did he win the first race of any kind staged at Goodwood in 1948, he was also the man who gave the MkVII its first race win in that Production Car race of 1952. Sadly he was having back trouble and was unable to drive. However, he did attend the meeting as a spectator – I don't think you could keep him away from Goodwood if you nailed his feet to the floor.

At Goodwood, the St Mary's Trophy had the 'Pro-Am' driver structure of previous years but consisted now of two races, one for the old Pros on Saturday and another for the amateur owners on the Sunday morning. Overall result was to be the aggregate of the two, but the cloud of disappointment surrounding Sir Stirling's absence had a modest silver lining for me viz, I got to do two races instead of one.

And so, deputizing for El Maestro, I presented myself at the Old Pros' drivers' briefing before qualifying on Friday in some extremely exalted company. Derek Bell, Tiff Needell, Patrick Tambay, Gerry Marshall, Perry McCarthy, Rene Arnoux and Dickie Attwood amongst them and others who may have been Pro but were not remotely old: current Audi sportscar star Allan McNish and 19-year-old hotshoe Nelson Piquet Junior.

Because of a bit of a faux-pas by my preparation bods, my car turned up sporting the wrong tyres and so I set off for qualifying on an enforced spanking new set of Dunlops. Still, the length of the practice session (25 mins) seemed to give me ample time to scrub the new tyres in for a few laps, come into the pits for a look round by the mechanics and then go out for some times.

Big mistake. The first of a few throughout the weekend which showed the gulf between the Pro and the Am. My thinking was totally Am. Initially it went to plan: the tyres had no grip at first, but were nicely warmed and scrubbed by my pit-stop and I set off for some hot laps. Half a tepid lap later, red flags came out. A car broken down in the wrong place, meeting running late, end of qualifying session. Aaargh!

Modified Jaguar MkVII

SPECIFICATIONS

Engine
3781cc, six-cylinder,
twin overhead cam,
three twin-choke
Webers

Power
260bhp@5500rpm

Torque
270lb ft@3500rpm

Transmission
Four-speed manual

Suspension
Front: wishbones,
torsion bars and
hydraulic dampers.
Rear: semi-elliptic
leaf springs and
hydraulic dampers.

Brakes
Servo-assisted discs
Top Speed
135mph (est)

Value
£55,000

Amateur, you see. A Pro would have thought: 'You never know how long a session is going to last. As soon as the tyres are able, give them hell and get some good times under your belt. Only then should you think about dropping into the pits for a cup of tea and a cream puff.'

I qualified 15th, pretty poor I thought, with a lap time of 1min.55secs. Tiff Needell in another (steel) MkVII was around 1.50. But the session for the owners' race went much better: tyres were good, we ran less fuel, I'd gained confidence and the times came tumbling down. I managed a 1.49 and qualified ninth: altogether rather more pleasing.

Although knocking six seconds off might seem impressive, I think that again it was only revealing of the amateur within and how slow I am to build up confidence in a car and in a track. At the totally delightful Goodwood cricket match on Thursday, I was discussing with the writer Doug Nye the differences between a proper racing driver and an enthusiast. He then asked whether I could remember my lap times from the last time I raced the MkVII at Goodwood. I confessed that I couldn't. 'Enthusiast!' he cried, jabbing an accusing finger at me like Hercule Poirot. And he was so right.

Knowing the margin by which my times had improved, it was with some optimism that I formed up for the Pros' race on a beautifully sunny Saturday afternoon. My grid position was in the midst of a number of smaller but less powerful cars (Standard Ten, Riley 1.5) that I thought were probably better at cornering than accelerating. And so it turned out to be. I made a good start at the drop of the Union Jack and had gained several places at the end of the first lap. I then lost one or two as a couple of smaller cars made up for their start line laggardness, but things seemed to go well until the engine in Jackie Oliver's Austin A35 had a bit of a turn for the worse and dropped oil at Lavant.

The entry to this double right-hander just before the main straight is always a little greasy, but Jackie's extra lubrication made a little off-piste exploration inevitable. I managed to avoid the gravel trap, so my spin wasn't too time consuming. But there was more Extra Virgin Oliver Oil at the end of the straight and I drove like a wuss through those areas until race end. I did finish ninth, though, just behind Tiff and Mike Salmon in the other two MkVIIs.

Sunday dawned, another blissful but even hotter day for the Am race. In this, I made a blistering start, exploiting the Jag's grunt and gaining several places. I was feeling a trifle smug and, of course, it's always at moments like that that the race is stopped. A Ford Zodiac had rolled at Madgwick (in a suitably gentle, balletic fashion) and we had a restart. Scheisse! as Austin Powers would say.

Did OK on the restart, but those in front were ready for me this time and it's never easy to take people unawares in a MkVII.

'HECK IF I DIDN'T SPIN IN EXACTLY THE SAME PLACE AS THE FIRST RACE BUT WITHOUT ANY EXCUSE OR EXPLANATION THIS TIME, OTHER THAN THAT I AM A CACK-HANDED WALLY'

After a lot of give and take, I settled into a comfy seventh and things felt pretty good until the last lap, when heck if I didn't spin in exactly the same place as the first race but without any excuse or explanation this time, other than that I am a cack-handed wally. I know that a Pro wouldn't have done it, simply because he would have known he was on the last lap and not taken any chances. Ditsy old me hadn't a clue what lap I was on, I just drive until someone says 'stop'. So I finished tenth, three positions shy of where I could have been but with an aggregate position of sixth. Which, all things considered, felt like a satisfyingly good result.

It was a great weekend, as Goodwood always is. The Jag went really well, and being allowed to race at such a special race track in such a special event remains a huge privilege. However, I came away with

the funny feeling that I didn't want to race the Jag too often. I had thought that I might want to race it a lot in historic club racing, but on reflection the car feels too special to subject to regular abuse. Apart from the fact that it is a totally delightful touring road car, I don't want to modify it to the extent that would be necessary to keep it competitive in historic racing. It may be modified as MkVIIs go, but all its modifications essentially were carried out before 1961 and I'm not inclined to drag it screaming into the 21st century.

My dilemma is a common one for those with historic cars. It stems from the fact that the phrase 'Historic Racing' is essentially an oxymoron. It's nice to think that people might just get out their old cars and drive them round in circles. But motor racing is and has always been about one thing: going faster next time than you

did last time. Serious historic racers spend fantastic sums of money on their cars to achieve just that and, as a result, many historic cars are virtually 'silhouette' racers that have been developed internally beyond all recognition.

With, it must be said, some exciting results. The St Mary's Trophy was a case in point. There was on-track equivalence between cars that wouldn't even have been on the same lap if competing in their day but whose close rivalry, courtesy of some extravagant development, made for some very exciting racing.

You've just got to decide what you want to do with your car. I think I'm clear as far as the Jaguar is concerned: I'm going to allow the old dear out occasionally, but she's not allowed to go clubbing and she's definitely never allowed to wear a skimpy top. ⚠

Clockwise
from above 3.8-litre XK engine was fitted in the early 1960s; the calm before the racing storm; running wide at the Chicane; following the racing line; A35 and Mk I enjoy race-long tussle.

H+OLY O+RDER

Farnham-based coachbuilder Abbott did much more than body Ford estate cars. This four-seater XK120 is from its golden age

Words: Mark Dixon Photography: Studiopress

Anniversaries are usually a good excuse
for a celebration but 2007 marked the 35th year since a rather sad event: the demise of traditional coachbuilder Abbott in 1972.

These days Abbott is most often remembered for the estate car conversions it built on big Fords during the 1950s and '60s, which were marketed under the Farnham name (Abbott was based near Farnham in Surrey). The company's history encompasses many more glamorous names than Henry's, however. Atalanta, Allard, Bentley, Bristol, Frazer Nash-BMW, Lagonda and Rolls-Royce were just a few of the marques bodied by Abbott – and that's discounting the one-off bodies created for many other makes of chassis.

Such as this Jaguar XK120, for example. Supplied as a rolling chassis by Jaguar to Abbott in 1951, it was commissioned with an all-new four-seater body by a New Zealand businessman and has been in the Antipodes ever since. Now fully restored by NZ-based Upper Classics, it's a unique Jaguar – but a typical example of British coachbuilding from an era when not all *carrozzeria* were Italian. »

The motor trade is an incestuous business. In the April 2007 issue of *Octane* our big 'studio' feature covered the DB Aston Martins: well, the man who sold Aston Martin to David Brown in 1947, Gordon Sutherland, went on to buy Abbott in 1950.

ED Abbott was founded in October 1929 but its origins go back much further. In fact, the company has its roots in the very beginnings of the motor industry, when coachbuilders were just that – makers of horse-drawn vehicles who saw which way the wind was blowing and adapted their skills for motor cars.

The man who started the Abbott lineage was a coachpainter called Arthur Page. Made redundant from his job with a local Farnham coachbuilding firm after WW1, he went into partnership with an ex-army officer and set up Page and Hunt Ltd in 1920.

The new company proved much more successful than the old and was soon clothing substantial chassis from the likes of Buick, Cadillac and Daimler. A high point was bodying the 20hp Rolls-Royce presented to Scout movement founder Lord Baden-Powell in 1929. Subscriptions from scout troops all over the world paid for the car, which Page and Hunt built as a four-door saloon; instead of a Spirit of Ecstasy radiator mascot, it carried a replica of the scouts' trefoil motif.

Unfortunately this high point was offset by a rather more serious low – voluntary liquidation for Page and Hunt in September 1929. Arthur Page went off to run a bus company but his former business would survive: enter Edward Dixon Abbott.

ED Abbott was a Page and Hunt salesman and a former WW1 Royal Navy pilot, who inbetween served an apprenticeship at Wolseley. The late-1920s were not an ideal time to be offering bespoke coachwork for luxury cars – potential buyers were more likely to be deciding which window to jump out of as the Depression bit – so, when Abbott bought Page and Hunt, he immediately diversified into bodying commercial vehicles, and into agencies for selling various makes of car.

These shrewd moves paid off and soon the company was back on its feet. A major contract came in from Lagonda, to build the standard coachwork for its new Rapier, and this was followed by other regular work from Frazer Nash-BMW and Talbot. Its high-profile customers included ex-prime minister David Lloyd George and writer Rudyard Kipling, who both ordered Abbott-bodied Rolls-Royces, and it even dabbled briefly with aviation – Abbott built a number of gliders, some replica vintage aircraft for film work and a handful of the infamous Flying Fleas.

'THE RESULT IS SURPRISINGLY HARMONIOUS, ARGUABLY AN IMPROVEMENT ON JAGUAR'S OWN DROPHEAD'

These ultra-light aircraft developed a reputation for killing their pilots in the mid-1930s and, while Edward Abbott knew their inherent design flaw could be solved, he was obliged for PR reasons to stop making them. He offered his unfinished machines to the workforce at sixpence each, and it's said that a number subsequently languished in Farnham suburban gardens until they either rotted or blew away.

Fortunately for Abbott, the motor industry provided a more reliable source of income and he was able to retire in 1950 a wealthy man. Into his shoes stepped Gordon Sutherland who, since selling Aston Martin in 1947, had been at a loose end. Sutherland brought some fresh blood into the company and went after new contracts; Healey (saloons) and Bristol (405 dropheads) would provide multiple orders, but the Jaguar XK120 featured here seems to have been a one-off.

Despatched from Jaguar on July 13, 1951, chassis number 660750 was bodied from scratch by Abbott in alloy over a wooden frame. The car has many detail changes compared with a regular XK120 – the windscreen is flat rather than vee-shaped, the tail lights have been repositioned, bonnet hinges are non-standard and so on – and the body is completely different from the doors back. Most significantly, it has been subtly lengthened to free up extra room for the additional rear seats, which are slightly raised to clear the back axle.

The result is surprisingly harmonious, arguably an improvement on Jaguar's own XK120 drophead – which was only a two-seater, of course. Even Abbott's craftsmen couldn't find a way of equipping the XK's cut-away doors with wind-up windows, however, so the Abbott drophead was supplied with sidescreens which, by the 1950s, were distinctly old-fashioned for a car of this price-bracket. Maybe this

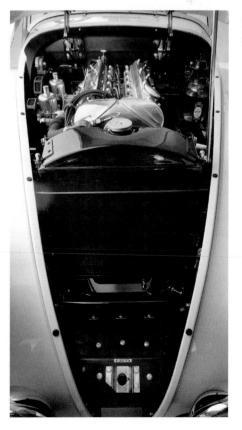

Above
Rear legroom isn't a strong point, but the Abbott XK120 does at least have a proper rear seat.

»

'AFTER LEADING A PRETTY HARD LIFE, THIS JAGUAR HAS ENJOYED A REVIVAL. ABBOTT WEREN'T SO LUCKY'

compromise is one reason why the car seems not to have been greatly loved for the majority of its life.

'The list of former owners shows about 30 names, half of whom were car dealers,' says Maarten Bubbert, proprietor of restoration company Upper Classics. 'And it had been stored in a barn for 25 years when we found it, about five years ago! It had been left there after blowing a head gasket on the way from Christchurch to Queenstown on the South Island. The owner asked someone to restore it but then changed his mind, so it just sat there partly dismantled and stripped of paint.'

Maarten admits that when one of his staff first tipped him off about the car, he hadn't a clue what an 'Abbott Jaguar' was – but when he started getting phone calls from other dealers who were sniffing around, he realised it was 'not just a backyard job'.

First impressions weren't very cheerful. The aluminium body was battered with age and had clearly been modified over the years, involving the fitment of a later XK140 bootlid. The hood frame was twisted and the interior trim had been changed more than once. On the bright side, everything was there, scattered around the barn in Queenstown – even the sidescreens.

'We took the car literally to pieces and started to rebuild it using the old panels and wood frame as templates,' continues Maarten. 'Unfortunately, very little of the original alloy could be saved because it had become too brittle to repair. The rear wings, the doors, the lower halves of the front wings and the bonnet all had to be remade, and the back end was remodelled

to return it to its original shape, working from what we had and from the pictures in several books on Jaguar.

'Fortunately, most of the minor parts are early XK120 and were therefore easy to replace if necessary, but the door locks turned out to be SS90 or SS100. The dash layout is different from an XK120's and so are the boot stays.'

No expense was spared by Upper Classics, which has restored several unique or low-production SS models and Jaguars. All the soft trim was hand made and the brightwork triple-plated, while discreet mechanical upgrades – forged pistons, high-capacity radiator, electronic ignition and electric fuel pump – are intended to optimise reliability while not compromising originality.

After leading a pretty hard life, even by New Zealand standards, this Jaguar has survived to enjoy a revival. Abbott Coachbuilders themselves weren't so lucky.

Abbott enjoyed a very successful career in the 1950s and '60s building estate car conversions, producing around 13,000 vehicles in 18 years, but the introduction in 1972 of the new Ford Consul and Granada – and with them, estate cars built by Ford in-house – removed its main source of income. The company closed shortly afterwards, just two years after Sutherland had sold his remaining interest in it. ⚠

» Thanks to Maarten Bubbert at Upper Classics, www.upperclassics. com, +64 (0)3 338 5079, and to Guy van Grinsven at Studiopress.

Above
Dashboard, bonnet hinges, boot stays and other details are all different from a regular XK's.

Office: (01621) 879579 *Facsimile:* (01621) 850370 *Mobile:* (07850) 966005

CURRENT STOCK LIST

JAGUAR COMPETITION CARS, please call for current stock of genuine competition cars.

SS100 - Please call for further details of our current stock of genuine 3.5 litres and 2.5 litre cars.

JAGUAR XK 140, ROADSTER, RHD - British Racing Green/Green hide and carpets, dark green hood, 16" chromed wire wheels. Subject of a total chassis off restoration, updates include tuned C-type engine, sandcast carbs, 5 speed gearbox, power steering, disc brakes etc etc. Superb example.

JAGUAR XK 140 DROPHEAD RHD - British Racing Green / Green hide and carpets, black hood, 16 chromed wire wheels. Subject of a total chassis off restoration 6 years ago to the highest standards, 5 speed gearbox, disc brakes, etc. Superb example.

JAGUAR XK 140 DROPHEAD M.C. LHD - Imperial Maroon / Beige hide and carpets, Beige hood, 16" chromed wire wheels, C Type cylinder head, overdrive gearbox, matching numbers. Subject of a total chassis off restoration 3 years ago. Excellent example.

JAGUAR XK 150'S' 3.8 LITRE ROADSTER, LHD - Mist Grey/Red hide and carpets, Black hood. 16" chromed wire wheels, total chassis off restoration to the highest standards. Full matching numbers and original colour specification. Very, very rare.

JAGUAR XK 150 'S' 3.8 LITRE ROADSTER, RHD - Sherwood Green / Green hide and carpets, Fawn hood, 16" colour coded wire wheels. 9,400 miles from new, yes 9,400 miles. The most original example I have seen in 25 years.

JAGUAR XK 150'S' 3.8 LITRE DROPHEAD, RHD - Dark Blue / Grey hide and carpets, dark blue hood 16" chromed wire wheels, original UK supplied car, total chassis off restoration to the highest standards. The rarest XK Drophead.

JAGUAR XK 150 'S' 3.8 LITRE DROPHEAD, LHD - Black/Red hide and carpets, Black Hood. 16" chromed wire wheels, matching numbers, subject of a total chassis off restoration to the highest standards. Exceptionally rare example, very little use since completion. Please contact for full specification.

JAGUAR XK 150 3.8 LITRE JD SPORT DROPHEAD, RHD - Dark Blue/Grey hide and carpets, Dark Blue hood, wide rimmed chromed wire wheels, total chassis off restoration to latest JD Sport specification, tuned and fully balanced engine, fuel injection, 5 speed gearbox, JD rear axle, full JD Sport brake system with AP brake calipers, full JD Sport suspension, burr walnut dashboard and door cappings, JD Sport electric power adjustable steering, etc. etc. etc. Highest specification JD Sport XK150 built to date. Please call for further details.

JAGUAR XK 150 3.8 LITRE DROPHEAD, RHD - Dark Blue / Dark Blue hide and carpets, Dark Blue hood, 16" chromed wide rim wire wheels. Subject of a total J.D. Restoration, specification includes, tuned engine, handmade stainless steel exhaust system, 5 speed gearbox, adjustable suspension, uprated brake system etc etc. Built to the highest standards.

JAGUAR XK 150 3.8 LITRE DROPHEAD, RHD - Cream / Red hide and carpets, Black hood. 16" chromed wire wheels, matching numbers, subject of a total chassis off restoration to a very high standard, J.D Sport power steering. Superb example.

JAGUAR XK 150 3.4 LITRE DROPHEAD, RHD - Cotswold Blue / Beige hide and carpets, Black hood, 16" chromed wire wheels, 2 owners from new, full history including documented service history. Subject of a total chassis off restoration, 5 speed gearbox, power steering, J.D Classic full detailing just completed. Excellent example.

JAGUAR XK 150 3.4 LITRE DROPHEAD, LHD - British Racing Green/Beige hide and carpets, black hood, 16"chromed wire wheels, subject of a total chassis off restoration 3 years ago, 2500 miles covered since, updated brakes. Superb example.

JAGUAR XK 150 'S' 3.4 LITRE FIXED HEAD COUPE, RHD - Red/Red hide and carpets, 16" chromed wire wheels, original UK matching number car subject of a total chassis off restoration 3 years ago. Final detailing just completed by ourselves. Excellent example.

JAGUAR XK 150 'S' 3.8 LITRE FIXED HEAD COUPE, RHD - Red/Beige hide and carpets, chromed wire wheels, matching number original UK car, subject of a total restoration in the 1990's good useable car, one of 50 right hand drive cars built.

THE J.D. SPORT JAGUARS - Developed and hand-built by J.D. Classics for modern motoring, with a little old-fashioned excitement! Colour specification to your choice, J.D. Classics sports front seats, complete leather interior, including door panels, parcel shelf etc., inertia reel belts to front and rear, our own unique walnut veneered centre dash to match your choice of woodwork, CD/music etc. to your choice. Highest specification, completely rebuilt sports engine, choice of either 3.4 or 3.8 litre, 4.7 litre fuel injection. 3.4 to 4.7 litre engines are gas flowed, lightened and balanced, unleaded fuel head, electronic ignition, fast road camshafts. 2'' stainless steel manifolds and exhaust system, catalytic converter, rack and pinion power steering, remote adjustable sports suspension, competition wire wheels, sports braking system, VR tires, choice of gearbox, air-conditioning, etc. Our work is carried out to an impeccable finish, and we will build to your individual specification if you wish. The world is blessed with 'look-alike', efficient, luxury vehicles. But are you excited? Boredom can be very expensive! The "J.D. Sport" is exclusive. It is a car that will express your taste. You may even get excited, again...! We do not put restrictions on the level of individuality that can be achieved 'Please contact us for a brochure'

JAGUAR MKII 3.8 LITRE SALOON MANUAL WITH OVERDRIVE, RHD - British Racing Green / Tan hide and carpets, chromed wire wheels, matching numbers and original colour specification, subject of a total restoration to the highest standards.

JAGUAR MKII 3.8 LITRE SALOON, RHD - Opalescent Silver Grey / Red hide and carpets, 16" competition stainless steel wire wheels, subject of a total restoration 3 years ago and recently updated by ourselves, JD sport power steering, 5 speed gearbox, brake system, suspension, interior, etc. Superb example.

JAGUAR MKII 3.8 LITRE SALOON, RHD - Opalescent Light Blue/Dark Blue hide and carpets, competition stainless steel wire wheels, subject of a full JD body restoration and bare metal re-paint, full JD engine bay bare metal re-paint and detailing. J.D engine overhaul, 5 speed JD gearbox, J.D power steering and brakes handmade J.D stainless steel exhaust manifold, J.D front seats, full J.D interior trim including new burr walnut woodwork, re-chromed etc

JAGUAR MKII 3.8 LITRE SALOON MANUAL WITH OVERDRIVE, RHD - Opalescent Maroon/Beige hide and carpets, colour coded wire wheels, Webasto folding sunroof, two owners from new, original car in time warp condition. Very hard to find in this condition.

JAGUAR MKII 4.2 LITRE SALOON, LHD - British Racng Green / Black hide and carpets, Racing Green wide rim wire wheels. Total restoration recently completed, fuel injection, uprated cooling system, 5 speed gearbox, power steering, modified suspension, uprated seating. Superb example.

JAGUAR S TYPE 3.8 LITRE SALOON, RHD - Opalescent Silver Grey / Dark Blue hide and carpets, wide rim chromed wire wheels. Total restoration to JD Sport specification completed 3 years ago, updates include high torque engine, 5 speed gearbox, rack and pinion power steering, updated suspension and brakes. JD Sport exhaust system, etc etc. One of a handful of JD Sport S Types built, please call for full specification.

JAGUAR E-TYPE SERIES 1 4.2 LITRE FIXED HEAD, RHD - Opalescent Silver Grey/Red hide and carpets. Competition chromed wire wheels. Matching numbers. One owner from new. Performance modifications from new. Superb original interior. Vehicle has just undergone a full JD Classics restoration.

JAGUAR E TYPE SERIES 2 4.2 LITRE FIXED HEAD, RHD - British Racing Green/green hide and carpets, Competition chromed wire wheels, subject of a total restoration to full JD Sport specification including, J.D. 5 speed gearbox, high torque engine, uprated brakes and cooling system, etc,etc. Superb example, please contact us for full specification.

WE HAVE FULL SERVICING AND RESTORATION FACILITIES TO THE HIGHEST STANDARDS, YOU ARE WELCOME TO VISIT OUR FACILITY AT ANY TIME

We urgently require for stock, more Classic Jaguars of the highest quality, particularly 'Genuine Competiton Cars' and XKs. If you own a superb Jaguar, and are thinking about selling, please contact us with an accurate description of your vehicle.

IF THE CAR YOU ARE LOOKING FOR IS NOT LISTED ABOVE, PLEASE TALK TO US ABOUT IT. WE ARE HAPPY TO DISCUSS EVERY ASPECT OF CLASSIC CAR OWNERSHIP INCLUDING CLASSIC CAR FINANCE, AND TO GIVE YOU OUR BEST ADVICE.

WEB SITE: www.jdclassics.co.uk
EMAIL: jdclassics@btconnect.com
OFFICE: (01621) 879579 **FACSIMILE:** (01621) 850370
MOBILE NUMBER: (07850) 966005 or (07834) 320030

WYCKE HILL BUSINESS PARK, WYCKE HILL, MALDON, ESSEX CM9 6UZ, U.K.

This is a story with several strands. It's about one man's passion for a famous marque. It's about two race cars that wear that marque's badge, in those days built and developed by the factory. It's about the engineer who tested and fettled the two cars in search of an advantage over the rest. Half a century down the track, he's still around, still sharp and still able to say why he made them like he did. And it's about the world champion who drove them both to victory. The common link which unites them all. What was he like to work with. How did he approach the job?

The last detail is something I've wondered many times. Since I've been driving historic race cars, I have often wanted to know why the drivers of the day didn't ask for some things to be changed. Tyres and suspension we can put down to the benefit of hindsight, but there were other things, like seats and belts. Many of the drivers were flyers, used to bucket seats and full harness belts and yet they had none for their racers.

We'll get to that, but first the passion and the cars. The two dark green Jaguars you see in the pictures are D-type XKD 505, and a 1957 3.4 litre Mk1 saloon, registration »

HAWTHORN'S JAGUARS

The D-type that Mike Hawthorn raced and a painstaking copy of his Jaguar Mk1 road car are a fitting tribute to the memory of Britain's first world champion

Words: Mark Hales **Photography:** Paul Harmer

number 881 VDU. The first is real, driven to victory in the tragic 1955 Le Mans by blond-haired, pipe-smoking darling of the British media Mike Hawthorn, and sports car regular Ivor Bueb, the second is a painstakingly accurate copy by arch-enthusiast Nigel Webb. It is identical in appearance and specification to the car which Jaguar provided for Hawthorn to use on road and track and which he drove to several victories in 1958. That was sadly also the car in which he suffered that fatal accident on the Guildford by-pass. Were he still here to check out Nigel's car, he would probably spot only the registration. The original was registered VDU 881 but the DVLA refused to release the number. It's about the only thing that Webb couldn't replace.

The engineer is Norman Dewis. Now 84 and yet still fit enough to clamber into a D-type and give rides at charity events, he was an extremely important ingredient in Jaguar's production process. Just as it has been for so long with Ferrari and Dario Benuzzi, every road and race car that left the Jaguar factory was subject to evaluation and modification according to Dewis' opinion. In his 36 years with the company, Dewis signed off no fewer than 25 models, one of which was XKD 505, also now restored to correct Hawthorn trim and wearing his favourite four-spoke wooden rimmed steering wheel and the correct Coventry trade plate number, 774 RW. These cost the princely sum of £25 at the local vehicle taxation office and allowed an unregistered car to be driven on the roads for test and evaluation – or for delivery to Le Mans. Not only did the cars undergo some 1700 miles of testing beforehand, but they were sometimes driven all the way from Coventry to La Sarthe and then raced for 24 hours. Imagine that happening now...

No matter how often you see it, the Jaguar D-type's features never fail to strike you. The dramatic lines of the aluminium body styled by former aircraft engineer Malcolm Sayer and which, like the cat in the badge, look cuddly enough to stroke but powerful enough to kill. The huge fin which smoothed the air cleaved by the driver's head and which, I now find, contains a cubby to stow tools and spares. The deep, rivetted sheet metal monocoque tub which lay beneath it all, sitting the driver low down and beneath the buffet of wind, stiffer and stronger than any tube frame could be. Aeroplanes had been rivetted together from sheets since before the war, so the car world had already taken its time to plagiarise. But it would be a few years yet before John Cooper and Colin Chapman stunned the Grand Prix world with similar monocoque tubs.

There were the disc brakes too, with remote servo assistance, inside cast aluminium instead of spoked wire wheels. And there was the aircraft style rubber bag fuel tank that was suspended inside the tail and wouldn't split in a crash. All hugely innovative features which are now accepted as the norm. »

Below
The registration 774 RW was originally a Jaguar trade plate, but a previous owner of XKD 505 found the series issue attached to a MkI Sprite. It wasn't cheap.

'The D-type's features never fail to strike you. The dramatic lines, like the cat in the badge, look cuddly enough to stroke and powerful enough to kill'

Right and below
Engine could push
D-type to 192mph;
trademark tailfin
was needed to
reduce high speed
instability.

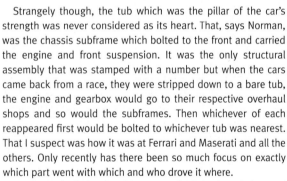

Strangely though, the tub which was the pillar of the car's strength was never considered as its heart. That, says Norman, was the chassis subframe which bolted to the front and carried the engine and front suspension. It was the only structural assembly that was stamped with a number but when the cars came back from a race, they were stripped down to a bare tub, the engine and gearbox would go to their respective overhaul shops and so would the subframes. Then whichever of each reappeared first would be bolted to whichever tub was nearest. That I suspect was how it was at Ferrari and Maserati and all the others. Only recently has there been so much focus on exactly which part went with which and who drove it where.

Dewis worked closely with Sayer – both in the wind tunnel during the development of the D and then later during the test phase when the two men would chat about the day's programme then simply go out and try it. The recently redundant Linley aerodrome near Hinckley had yet to become the Motor Industry Research Association but Dewis remembers attaching tufts of wool to a D-type and driving down the main runway with Sayer alongside in another car, studying how the wool moved. It was Dewis who subsequently complained of high speed instability when the long nose of the Le Mans C-type was tried in search of more straight line speed. The extra 7 inches at the front, he says, certainly made the car faster but it had become spooky during high-speed slalom tests. Sayer came up with the fin which cured it. Dewis and Sayer also researched the windscreen height, which was carefully optimised for speed down Les Hunaudieres.

Then when they got to La Sarthe for the 1955 event, all but one of the drivers wanted it cut down. 'They said they wouldn't be able to see when it rained,' says Dewis. 'I told them that rain doesn't stay on the screen when you are moving and for every inch they took off, it would cost them 2mph, but they wouldn't listen.' Norman is only a little guy and was always going to be below any perspex but as he and Sayer expected, his D-type would pull five-eight or even 6000rpm along the straight in top gear. That amounted to 192mph whereas Bueb and Hawthorn could only see 5500 and 180mph. 'Then,' says Norman, 'they complained about the engines...'

There was also chassis and brake work across the range which as Norman explains was rather different for Jaguar because there were precious few standard production cars which could reach 120mph, let alone exceed it. For the D, it was his job to carry out the 30 stops from 100mph at 45 second intervals and add the brake ducts to make it repeatable. And it was his job to work with Girling on the shock absorbers. 'I had a bloke from Girling attached exclusively to me,' he says, 'and I could go out and try the car, then come back and ask for the valving to be changed there and then. We could maybe get two or three variations into a day.' It sounds very modern indeed, but Dewis says Jaguar had a similarly good back door relationship with all its suppliers. Cooling too, he says, was a major concentration. My memory of cars of that era was that they would overheat whenever they got the chance and Jaguar was keen that this shouldn't happen at the races. Dewis would take one of the sheet metal men from the

SPECIFICATION
**1955 Jaguar
XKD 505**
Engine
3442cc straight six.
Double overhead cams,
two valves per cylinder.
Three twin-choke Weber
carburettors
Power
250bhp @ 5750rpm
(works Le Mans cars
with wide angle head,
275bhp @6000rpm)
Torque
240lb ft @ 3000rpm
Transmission
Four-speed manual
Suspension
Front: independent
wishbones
Rear: live axle and
trailing links
Brakes
Dunlop discs all round
Performance
0-60mph 4.7sec
Top speed: 162mph (Le
Mans cars 180-190mph)
Value
Cost £3878 in 1954
valued now anywhere
between £500,000 and
£2 million.

'Dewis would take one of the sheet metal men from the shop and cut and shut louvres and scoops until they found something that worked'

Right
Neil Webb's Mk1 is
a faithful recreation
of Hawthorn's car.
The registration 881
VDU is the mirror
image of the
original VDU 881.

'The Mk1 looks an unlikely racer until you see pictures of
the competition. Jaguar had built a 2.4 for Paul Frère
who won at Spa, which rather forced their hand'

shop and they would head off to Linley with a set of snips, a drill and some rivets and cut and shut louvres and scoops until they found something that worked. Then Dewis would take the pieces to the drawing office, ask them to put the shape on paper and make it official. 'Lots of things were done that way at Jaguar,' he says.

Listening to the account, it seemed that the concentration was on stability, ease of handling and stamina as much as speed – Dewis uses terms like 'smoothness' and 'stability' to describe the handling he liked – which, when combined with a car that doesn't overheat oil, water or brakes, is how you win long distance races. He says he preferred a touch of oversteer too because he felt that made the car controllable, but maybe this broad-brush approach stemmed from the fact Jaguar was a factory as well as a race team and the engineers who helped design and develop the cars were doing the bulk of the testing rather than the racers. 'If the car broke down, I would feel I hadn't done my job,' says Dewis, 'and I'd get a bollocking from the boss into the bargain. The Old Man would want to know why I hadn't tested whatever it was.' The Old Man was Jaguar chief William Lyons, yet to acquire his knighthood.

I managed a few laps in the D-type at a damp Chobham and the strengths that those men strove to create 50 years ago are immediately apparent. XKD 505 is a little stiffer than it was – probably about 30%, which is a lot less than most modern historic racers – but it is so much easier to drive than many. The steering feel is perfect, unassisted yet fingertip light, and you can feel the effort slackening exactly as the skinny Dunlops sniff out the slippery patches. Then provided you are sparing with the power, the balance stays with a gentle and progressive push at the nose. Always the comfortable option but comparatively rare in a powerful car with limited overall grip.

Balance across all four wheels then becomes the key to it all and you do have the option to revise this at any time by tickling the pedal. The push slowly recedes until finally the tail begins to take the lead and swing to whichever side. A bigger bootful will always turn the neutral condition swiftly into a lurid tail-out slide, but it is still so very easy to manage, not least because of the lazy way the engine pours out its 280bhp potential. Very smooth and very progressive across a wide range and sounding like only a straight-six can. Meanwhile the bespoke all-synchromesh four-speed Jaguar gearbox is slick, wind buffet in the cockpit is next to nil and the tub makes for the closest thing to a bucket seat. They may not have asked for one, but they can't have been unaware of its benefits. This might be a better place than many to spend 12 hours out of 24.

And so to the Mk1, which looks like an unlikely racer until you see pictures of the competition. Dewis says Jaguar originally had no plans to make the car into a racer – although they had done something with the huge Mk7 – but that they eventually responded to pleas from, he thinks, mainly Tommy Sopwith who felt the car could be a winner. They had also built a 2.4 for Paul Frère to race at Spa where he was also driving in the Belgian Grand Prix. Frère won the race which rather forced Jaguar's hand

SPECIFICATION
**1957
Jaguar Mk1
'Hawthorn-
spec' saloon**
Engine
3442cc straight six. Double
overhead cams, two valves
per cylinder. Twin SU 2in
carburettors as per C-type.
Power
220bhp @ 5800rpm
Torque
190lb ft @ 3000rpm
Transmission
Four speed manual,
limited slip differential
Suspension
Front: double wishbones
and coil springs, telescopic
dampers. Rear: beam axle,
quarter elliptic leaf springs.
Panhard rod.
Brakes
Disc brakes front and rear.
Vacuum servo.
Performance
0-60mph 9.1 sec
Top speed: 120mph
Value
In 1957, the standard car
cost £1114 plus £558 7s
purchase tax.

»

'How they ever drove home on the same set of tyres I can't imagine. Just a few laps of Chobham's outer loop and the front left RS5 was just beginning to scuff its outside edge'

and so Dewis, chassis man Bob Knight and engine expert Claude Bailey were duly tasked with a set of modifications.

Meanwhile Jaguar showed an early example of product placement. Wages for their contracted sports car drivers like Moss and Hawthorn were modest by modern standards so they were, as Dewis puts it, 'paid in kind' with cars. And if they made the cars quicker, then the likes of Hawthorn would race them. Free PR – or perhaps they didn't think like that in those days.

Nigel Webb whose labour of love (and not a small sum of money) this was, says that the Mk1 shell is the stiffest of the lot, partly he thinks because of old fashioned construction techniques, but also because the window apertures were smaller. The changes Dewis made at the time and which have also been faithfully replicated rather than taken further, involved all the usual stuff and will be familiar to anybody who's ever raced a production car. The Jaguar was already something of an optimum (Ford was a year away from the MacPherson strut which ended up on a billion cars) and double wishbones and coil springs suspended the front, while the big beam back axle (fitted with the optional limited-slip differential which was then tightened still further) was hung on quarter elliptic springs with a Panhard rod for lateral location.

Rubber bushes in the moving parts were replaced wherever

possible with phosphor bronze, anti-roll bars were thickened and springs and dampers were stiffened. Brake pad material was changed (discs were already fitted to all four wheels), a close-ratio gearbox with a competition overdrive (faster operation, lower ratio) was also fitted. Then the engines were fettled. The top national saloon car competition was for 'production cars' and Dewis recalls how the officials complained about the SU carburettors and inlet manifold that had been borrowed from an XK140. So the production line versions had to be refitted but, with attention to cams and pistons, the 3.4-litre engine pushed out about 220bhp.

Norman says they could have found more (D-types started at about 260) but they didn't want to go too far. The original engine spec has been replicated too, by specialist Ron Beatty, complete with a pair of period sand-cast SU carburettors. Inside, the big plastic rimmed four-spoke wheel remains but there are a pair of diminutive bucket seats, trimmed in matching green leather, which was exactly what the originals had.

Hawthorn had taken over his father's Tourist Trophy Garage in Guildford and his mechanics made a couple of extra changes which have since added to the folklore. Managing the engine's temperature was still a tricky issue and the bypass hose between head and block was blanked off, then a radiator blind was

Above
One is a race car used on the road, the other a road car used on the track. Both were winners for Hawthorn.

Above

Norman Dewis did 80-odd laps in this D-type recently, giving rides at a charity day. Says he can't do 10 hot laps these days, but he can do maybe three. He also talks about when he 'passed Kling in the Mercedes at Le Mans' and says 'Taz (Nuvolari) was a charming man'. Not many people can say things like that.

added, operated by a chain which dangled from the dash. You simply raised or lowered it according to the temperature gauge. After the accident, the swinging chain fuelled allegations that Hawthorn had fitted a hand throttle, although why a racing driver should do that would be a mystery to any keen driver. Hawthorn also added his BRDC badge to the front and a TT garage motif to the glove box, but that was about it. Offset wire wheels went a short way to redress the Mk1's strangely narrow rear track and wore a set of Dunlop RS5 crossplies (Webb managed to find a supply of these too) and that was it. Hawthorn would drive to the track, paint the numbers on with whitewash, go out and race, then head back to wherever for a night out.

If all that seems extraordinary, then the sense of re-creation is nothing less. The starter clatters and rings like a Jaguar does, then the engine is uncannily smooth and instantly revvy to the touch of a pedal. Steering is heavy and, after the D-type, feels as if there's a rubber joint somewhere on the column which winds up to be solid with about a quarter turn of lock. The throw of the gearshift feels long – the lever must move through an arc of 90° between first and second – and the synchros won't be hurried. Then as you head towards the track there's that unmistakable whine from the gears which overlays the crackling baritone from the twin exhausts and the slight shimmy and shake from the big shell over the ridges and ruts in the concrete. Up the speed and the way the car tackles the corners is like a form of automotive skiing. The lean is incredible – exactly as it was in the archive pictures where the front wheel all but disappears into the arch – and the yaw is almost as extreme. Fail to take enough speed into the corner and the car will scrabble at the front wheels, but add some Hawthorn-style commitment and the car drifts itself ▶▶

'There were times when Mike's lap times were poor. Lofty would ask what the problem was and Mike always said not to worry, he'd pick it up during the race. And he would'

for you, to the point where the inside rear wheel starts to loosen and unstick the revs. Meanwhile the steering, although still springy, has sharpened up and you can just massage it to keep the car on line. It's completely addictive and completely unlike the similar models you see at Goodwood which will have been fitted with springs at least 200% stiffer than these.

Coming back from a drift to change direction, the car straightens up, sits up, leans the other way and takes up the opposing angle. Wonderful, and a slow motion exercise in energy management. Mind you, how they ever drove home on the same set of tyres I can't imagine. Just a few laps of Chobham's outer loop and the front left RS5 was just beginning to scuff on its outside edge. Meanwhile, the engine brays under power, crackles and pops on the overrun. Another ingredient in a mix which transports you back to a different age.

I still wanted to know what it was like to work with Hawthorn and Moss and the rest, but surprisingly, this turns out to be the shortest part of the tale. 'I never really thought about them,' says Dewis. 'I just did what I wanted and my work was pretty much done before we got to the races. Then I always reported to Lofty England, but the drivers would just turn up and drive.' Just like that, I say, they wouldn't ask for anything? 'No, not really,' says

Norman. 'They might have a fad, and Rolt and Hamilton might complain a bit, but Lofty would make it clear that we'd done all the testing and that was the best it could be. If they wanted a change, it would spoil something somewhere else, like the windscreen episode.' I still can't let it go.

What about Moss, I ask. Surely he was more technical. 'Perhaps a bit,' says Norman. 'He liked a bit of oversteer, but then so did I.' And Hawthorn? 'Oh, Mike would just drive. Never asked, never complained. I remember one day, Lofty had asked Mike to test the D at Silverstone. He turns up and says to Lofty, "Why am I here? I don't want to drive it." He points at me and says, "He's the guy. If he's happy, then so am I." He got back in his plane and flew off. I think he was there a quarter of an hour.'

'There were times though,' adds Dewis, 'when Mike's lap times were poor. I wouldn't say anything to him, but Lofty would go and ask what the problem was. Mike would always say not to worry and he'd pick it up during the race. And he would. On his day, there was nothing between him and Moss. They were the two quickest, no doubt about that.' △

» Thanks to Nigel Webb and his team and to Norman Dewis.

Fuelling the passion

Octane
MAGAZINE

FREE ISSUE OFFER

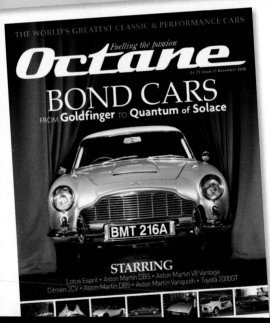

Discover the world of Octane, with a **FREE COPY** of the world's fastest growing classic car magazine.

Featuring the best from the last 100 years in motoring, Octane brings you the excitement of events from all over the world. With unrivalled track and road tests, and stunning photography of the most revered classics – Octane puts you in the driving seat of the world's finest cars.

What's more, Octane is practical, with news analysis, a comprehensive diary of events and 1000's of classic cars for sale each month.

Find out for yourself that Octane really is essential reading!

CALL NOW and we'll send you the latest copy of Octane worth £4.20, **ABSOLUTELY FREE!**

CALL FOR YOUR FREE ISSUE

0845 357 9000

Calls cost up to 2p /min plus a 6p set up fee from a BT landline. Mobile and other providers' charges may vary. UK offer only. Limited to one per household.

Quote reference:
Free Issue: JAGBKZ

WHITE LIGHTNING
THE STORY OF TKF 9 – JIM CLARK'S D-TYPE JAGUAR

What started out green, changed to white, back to green and is now white again?
The answer is D-type Jaguar chassis number XKD517, best known as the 'Border
Reivers, Jim Clark D-type', which has just emerged from a stunning rebuild

Words & archive photography: Graham Gauld Studio photography: Simon Clay

Some years ago I was in conversation with noted collector and historic racer Neil Corner, who has always selected the best cars available to him. At one time he owned an ex-Ecurie Ecosse D-type (and loved the car) but eventually it was sold to help buy the farmhouse in which he now lives.

He explained at the time that his son Nigel was not really interested in his cars but then, after the D-type was sold, he became more of an enthusiast than his father. The one car Nigel longed for was a Jaguar D-type and, as Neil remarked, sadly: 'There are only about three D-type Jaguars worth buying and they are all owned by people unlikely to sell them.' One of these was the Border Reivers car. Nigel was to wait many years before it eventually came into his hands.

Back in 1956, Henlys the Coventry Jaguar distributor had a customer for XKD517, a 41-year-old motor trader from Liverpool called Gilbert 'Gillie' Tyrer who had been a regular post-war racer. He was an early agent for Frazer Nash cars and built a Special using a BMW 328 sports car with the wings sawn off. He then got his hands on one of the streamlined 1940 Mille Miglia BMWs, and this helped make him one of the most successful North of England sports car drivers in the 1950s.

Gillie first dipped his toe in the Jaguar pond when he bought XKC038, one of the 1953 Jaguar C-type factory cars built for Le Mans. It did not actually race at Le Mans that year as it was the reserve and was then prepared for a planned visit by Jaguar to the Mexican Road Race, but this never took place. Obviously Gillie was now bitten by the Jaguar bug and made plans to get himself a D-type, hence the Henlys order placed by Tyrer's garage, Litherland Motors.

Jaguar XKD517 was a straightforward short-nose customer car and was one of three D-types sold by Henlys around that time. It had sold XKD515 to Col. Ronnie Hoare of Maranello Concessionaires and XKD518 to Peter Blond – the only D-type originally painted in red! The Tyrer model was fitted with engine number E2026-9 and the colour was described as Pastel Green rather than British Racing Green.

Tyrer did very little with the car save recording 131.58mph at the Chester Motor Club's Queensferry Sprint, before it was sold on to his friend Alex McMillan, who owned the Futura Rubber Company. Again, the Jaguar was used mainly for club race meetings for the rest of the year.

At the end of the 1956 racing season the D-type was offered for sale by Alex McMillan. He was approached by Bud Murkett, whose family owned the Jaguar dealership for the Bedford and Peterborough area.

'THIS WAS THE FIRST SPORTS CAR TO AVERAGE SPEED OF OVER 100MPH

The plan was that Bud's nephew, Tony Murkett, would race the car in the 1957 season.

The short-nose D-type might have been a relatively easy vehicle to drive but when you got it up to racing speeds it needed considerable skill to handle. Tony Murkett found this out the hard way: he had a big accident on the Silverstone Club Circuit and, on the advice of the insurance company, it was decided that someone else should race the car. Bud Murkett remembered that a local farmer friend, Charles Taylor, had a son who was a racing driver and asked if he would like to contest the D-type. The son was Henry Taylor and the car virtually took Henry out of British club racing and into International racing.

Henry Taylor was born in 1932 in Bedfordshire. He was mad about cars and started rallying but found it boring. At the age of 22 he bought his first racing car, a MkIV Cooper 500 with a Vincent 500cc vee-twin, which was not exactly the most competitive engine.

Then his father stepped in and told him that if he was serious about racing he should have the right equipment, and so Henry bought Bob Gerard's MkVIII Cooper and told his dad he could probably get a secondhand JAP engine for £30. However, his father insisted that they buy two brand-new JAP units, which Vic Martin tuned for him. In 1955 Henry had 52 wins in all sorts of events, but changed the JAP engine for a Norton and became *Autosport* Champion. Another season in 500s led »

Far left and above
Gilbert 'Gillie' Tyrer, the D-type's first owner; farmer's son Henry Taylor at Silverstone, duelling with Sears' Lister-Bristol.

LAP ANY CIRCUIT IN BRITAIN AT AN
— JIM CLARK WAS ON HIS WAY UP!

to the offer to drive the D-type. Up to that time he had only driven little 500s and now he was in a big sports car. 'I loved the D-type and found it very easy to drive, particularly with the tail out – and I was a tail-out kind of driver.'

His first race with the car was the British Empire Trophy at Oulton Park, which was run in three heats and a final. Here he was up against Britain's top drivers, including Archie Scott Brown and Roy Salvadori, and acquitted himself well, finishing eighth overall. This was despite a little incident at the notorious Cascades corner.

'I arrived much too fast in the wet,' Henry explained, 'spun the car and it shot off the road. I was conscious of the Oulton Park lake coming towards me fast but managed to stop the D from going into the water on a small patch of grass almost exactly the size of the D-type.'

At the end of the race Henry returned to the paddock damp, but warm from the heat in the cockpit, only to find his wife Peggy and mechanic Ray Lane soaking wet and blue with the cold.

'I took one look at them and realised it would be awful to try and push the car back into the transporter, so I suggested they get into that and drive it back and I would drive the D-type home to Bedford. So I left the circuit, turned on to the A5 and drove it all the way back on my set of Dunlop green spot tyres, which were pretty good in the wet.'

His first International was the Nürburgring 1000km race on May 26,

1957, when the Murkett Brothers entered the car for Henry Taylor and Archie Scott Brown. This was also scheduled to be Archie Scott Brown's first continental race. Archie was quickest of all the D-types in practice, ahead of the Ecurie Ecosse cars, but he did not get a chance to race the car, as Henry crashed heavily on the fourth lap and hit a tree.

He had better luck at Spa, where he finished third overall in the sports car race that supported the Belgian Grand Prix. It was a wet event and Henry, who was always good in the wet, initially led the all-conquering factory Aston Martin DBR1s of Brooks and Salvadori.

Henry took another eighth place in the Sussex Trophy at Goodwood and had one or two other runs in the car before his best performance of the year at Goodwood on September 28. Here he was lined up with people like Jack Brabham in the new Tojeiro-Jaguar and Archie Scott Brown in the Lister-Jaguar. Henry managed to hold off a determined Roy Salvadori in a factory Lotus Eleven and take third place, but what pleased him most was defeating Duncan Hamilton in another D-type.

By now the season was coming to an end and the Murkett Brothers had no intention of keeping the D-type. Word of this got to Scotland, where Jock McBain was keen to get the Border Reivers team back into serious motor racing. Egged on by the enthusiastic Ian Scott Watson, they made the decision to buy the D-type from the Murketts and run it in 1958 with regular BR driver Jimmy Sommervail and newcomer Jim Clark.

Clark had raced nothing more powerful than Scott Watson's Porsche 1600 Super, so a test day was booked at Charterhall, their local circuit, and the potential drivers turned up. Ian Scott Watson was one such racer but found that on the main straight it was difficult to see through his glasses, as the wind affected his eyesight. Then Jimmy Somervail went out and lapped quickly with the car, but it was Jim Clark who was the most impressive. He sat down, relaxed, and drove to perfection.

Though Jimmy Somervail was to race the car on a couple of occasions in 1958 he, like the gentleman he is to this day, announced that he would retire from motor racing because Jim Clark was clearly a driver of great ability who could make best use of the D-type.

Scott Watson now set to work organising a programme for Border Reivers, and it so happened the first race meeting of the 1958 season was almost on their doorstep, at Full Sutton in North Yorkshire. This ex-US Air Force airfield was used for the first time on April 5, 1958.

The next problem was how to get the D-type to Full Sutton. Jim Clark suggested his own farm lorry, which he kept parked out in a barn. Though April, it was still very cold in the Borders and so the D-type was loaded on the truck on the Friday evening for an early start the next morning. Jim

Above, left to right
Rare colour shot of Jim Clark at Crimond in 1958 helped with positioning of race numbers; Crimond again, and Clark leans on D-type with author Graham Gauld, Ian Scott Watson and farmer Oswald Brewis; Willie Tuckett in the now-green D-type, 1998 GP Historique de Monaco.

looked outside at the weather and decided to empty the radiator of the lorry just in case it froze overnight. Unfortunately, unknown to Jim, his farm manager had the same idea and later he also turned the tap underneath the radiator – only what he was doing was actually closing the empty radiator!

Next morning Jim was up bright and early, went to the barn, 'closed' the tap and filled up the radiator with water. However, all the liquid ran out of the bottom onto some straw, so he didn't hear it. After he had put what he thought was enough water into the radiator, he prepared to leave. The lorry travelled about three miles before the engine seized due to overheating. There was nothing else to do but unload the D-type.

Jim wrapped himself up in a heavy jacket and scarf, and then drove the car down the A1 to Full Sutton. At this meeting he not only won the sports car race but set the initial lap record for the circuit at over 100mph. This was the first sports car to lap *any* racing circuit in Britain at an average speed of more than 100mph – Jim Clark was on his way up!

Remember, too, that Jim had only ever run five races in his life before that day. On the Sunday morning he decided to get up early and drive the D-type back up the A1 to Chirnside. I remember him telling me how quick »

'SPA WAS FAST AND HERE WAS CLARK, FACED WITH THIS DAUNTING CIRCUIT IN ONLY HIS FOURTH RACE IN THE D-TYPE'

'JIM COULDN'T BELIEVE HIS EYES WHEN HE SAW ANOTHER D-TYPE COMING DOWN THE OTHER CARRIAGEWAY TOWARDS HIM'

the D-type was – and on that road journey back he was in for another surprise. Around eight o'clock in the morning, on a section of dual-carriageway, Jim couldn't believe his eyes when he saw another D-type coming down the other carriageway towards him. Both drivers braked hard and had a chat. The other D-type was owned by Sir Robert Ropner, who was a great friend of Bill Lyons of Jaguar and who had already owned a C-type but was now exercising his road-registered D-type.

Following the Full Sutton success, Ian Scott Watson was spinning like a top with big plans for the team. He announced that Border Reivers had been given an entry for the Spa 1000km race the following month and that they would go there...

Spa was fast in those days and here was Clark, faced with this daunting circuit in only his fourth race with the D-type. At the track, veteran British driver Jack Fairman took pity on Clark and drove him round the circuit in his rented Volkswagen Beetle to show him the corners. Clark was overawed when Fairman told him the speed he would have to take some of those corners, but rose to the challenge. His first shock came when the race leader, Masten Gregory in the Ecurie Ecosse Lister-Jaguar, passed him. A week later, when he told me of the experience, he was still in awe of the speed Gregory was going and opined that he thought he would never be able to drive as fast as that (sic).

Clark was to finish eighth in that race but the accident in the same race, which cost Archie Scott Brown his life, stayed with Clark for the rest of his life and from that moment he hated the circuit. Indeed, many years later he remarked, 'Why is it that I love Monaco and have never won the Monaco Grand Prix, but I hate Spa and have won it four times...'

Jim Clark had many wins with the car, and on one occasion at Charterhall the young Duke of Kent visited the track as a guest of Jock McBain, who ran Border Reivers. Jock took the Duke round the track a couple of times and then the Duke took the wheel, so becoming probably the only Duke to test a D-type Jaguar on a race circuit.

When the season ended Jim Clark had logged a remarkable 12 wins out of the 20 races he raced TKF 9 for Border Reivers. The team sold the

D-type and bought a Lister-Jaguar for 1959 – and by now Jim Clark had come under the spell of Colin Chapman.

The man who bought XKD517 was Alan Ensoll, an enthusiast from the north of England, who also owned an ex-Ecurie Ecosse C-type Jaguar. His plan was to convert the D-type into a full road car but he never completed the job. When the makers of the film *The Green Helmet* were looking for racing sports cars Alan loaned the D-type to them. Then he sold it to Irishman Bob Duncan, who had seen the car during the making of the film and later raced it at Kirkistown. It then returned to the mainland in the hands of Bryan Corser. Corser was the founder of the Loton Park hillclimb and he used the D-type as his course car. By now the car had been painted green and it was to remain green until the present owner bought it in 2006.

Corser sold XKD517 to American Jaguar collector Walter Hill, but Hill kept the car in England in the hands of Martin Morris and did not take it back to the States, as he felt it added nothing to his already impressive collection of Jaguars.

Eventually, in 1979, Hill sold the D-type to former Chevron racing driver and Devonian estate agent Willie Tuckett. Willie had first seen the car at Martin Morris's workshops and said that if it ever came up for sale he would like to buy it. Willie met Walter Hill at the Rembrandt Hotel in London, where Hill personally gave him the bill of sale. At the time Henry Taylor also wanted to buy the D-type as a souvenir of his early racing days but Willie Tuckett beat him to the punch. As a result, Taylor had a replica of TKF 9 made and used it on a number of touring events.

Willie Tuckett raced XKD517 on many occasions in historic events, ran it on many motoring tours and thoroughly enjoyed it. During Willie's tenure the car had a heavy racing accident at Silverstone and Martin Morris made a new bonnet section but retained the damaged original.

Tuckett won the Coy's '50s sports car race at the Nürburgring in 1990 and in 1995 finished third in the 1000km event at the same venue, sharing the car with his friend David Piper. His last race with it was the Magny Cours Historic in 1999.

Meanwhile Nigel Corner, who had by now carved a name for himself in » historic racing, had been badgering his friend Adrian Hamilton about this D-type. In turn, Hamilton urged Willie Tuckett to sell the car but the deal all hinged on Nigel Corner selling his Lightweight E-type Jaguar. Once this was sold, the way was clear to buy TKF 9. Nigel used it for a number of historic tours but his wife Harriet found it uncomfortable to travel in. During this time Nigel Corner added a tailfin to the car, something it had never had, and replaced the original gearbox.

Eventually Corner sold the D-type to the present owner early in 2006. The car was then sent to Chris Keith-Lucas at CKL Developments for a very sympathetic rebuild. The tailfin was removed and Chris was able to retain the integrity of the bodywork with the minimum amount of new metal, including the replacement of the original nose, easily recognisable by the domed rivets from a hasty Border Reivers repair. Also, the original gearbox has been totally rebuilt and TKF 9 has once again returned to the creamy-white of the Murkett Brothers/ Border Reivers days, with the latter's original logo of a Border Reiver on his horse – taken from a statue in Hawick in the Scottish Borders.

Today XKD 517 looks exactly as it did the first time I saw it in pristine condition in the paddock at Oulton Park 50 years ago. Jaguar enthusiasts can be assured that the car is in very good hands, with an owner who wants to preserve it as one of the finest D-type Jaguars in the world.

» Thanks to all at historic Jaguar and racing specialists CKL Developments, East Sussex, +44 (0)1424 838250, www.ckldevelopments.co.uk

'THE TAILFIN WAS REMOVED AND CHRIS WAS ABLE TO RETAIN THE INTEGRITY OF THE BODYWORK WITH THE MINIMUM OF NEW METAL'

Below
Repaired original bonnet, seemingly crumpled beyond repair, returned the D-type to Clark-era specification.

2003's Goodwood Revival meeting was enormous fun. I joined the Welsh father and son team, Anthony and Grant Williams, to share the drive with Grant in their outrageously extrovert 1958 Jaguar MkI in the 20-lap, two-driver St Mary's Trophy race for production saloons. Although their Jaguar is a 1950s car, it was accepted into this race because the Goodwood organisers really wanted it to be there. And it is usually a front-runner.

Grant Williams has become a star attraction at the Revival meetings, racing this important Jaguar with real gusto. His car control is perfect and he absolutely relishes his time behind the wheel. He really plays to the crowd, sliding the Jaguar through the corners at leary angles. Grant is a superb driver and I'm surprised he has not yet been offered a Touring Car drive, or something of that level.

This Jaguar MkI is a bit special. It was one of only three initially built as a Jaguar works car to Group 3 specification. This meant that the factory could fit all the best bits from other Jaguars, so it has an XK150 S head with three SU carbs, the brakes are from a MkIX and the doors, bonnet and boot lid are constructed of lightweight aluminium. The rear hubs were wider, from an XK150, to overcome the narrow rear track and its inherent handling limitations (this Jaguar now runs a MkII rear end). Ivor Bueb, John Coombs and Briggs Cunningham each took delivery of the first cars in 1958. This is the Coombs car, campaigned by John Coombs and raced by Roy Salvadori wearing the famous BUY 1 number plate.

Anthony William's father, 'Gordon F', was friendly with Lofty England and close to the Jaguar factory, so he had the chance to buy the car in 1962 and then race it for a number of years. Then his son Anthony took over racing it before laying the MkI up until the Goodwood Circuit revival was instigated in 1998. Anthony then prepared the car once again but found that his grandson, the young Grant Williams, was almost as quick as him first time out. Since then Grant has been pedalling BUY 1 to good effect.

DEREK BELL DRIVES
JAGUAR MKI

Salvadori's old MkI has become a star attraction at Goodwood, largely thanks to the exuberance of driver Grant Williams. In 2003 Derek Bell was co-driver to the oversteering Welshman **Photography:** John Colley, Steve Havelock

I have always had great affection for Jaguars. My father had the first E-type in East Sussex and he was the first to crash an E-type there too. It was the same car and the crash occurred after an exuberant lunch. After that he always drove Jaguar saloons. Years later I raced the 'Big Cat for' TWR (the XJ12C), which was a real handful, so my Jaguar background is half-reasonable. As you can imagine, I was looking forward to racing this MkI in the St Mary's Trophy with Grant, with mechanical back up by his father Anthony.

We almost had a disaster during the Friday practice when a halfshaft broke. Anthony immediately set about stripping the rear end when a spectator, who had driven to the circuit in his Jaguar MkII, rushed into the pits and offered all the components from his car in the parking lot! Can you believe it? The man was so keen to help ensure BUY 1 was able to race he was prepared to offer his perfectly innocent car as a parts donor. But Anthony decided to pack all the bits and pieces into the back of his van and roar off back to the workshop in Wales to fix the problem. After an all-nighter the car was ready to go again the next morning. What a good effort.

During official practice on Saturday I took the Jaguar out only to find that it had hardly any brakes at all. Grant and Anthony did not seem in the slightest perturbed. 'Just pump the pedal a few times. The rear disc is a bit out of true because of the halfshaft breaking so it's pushing the pads back into the caliper. No real problem, though.'

I must say, I am not fond of racing cars without effective brakes but I just had to get on with it. We qualified sixth and I got my lap time down to 1 minute 36 seconds. Grant's fastest was 1min 35sec so we were pretty close. My driving style is a little neater than Grant's. I would have been a second or so quicker if the brakes had worked and Grant would have improved by about the same if he had stopped having such fun going sideways.

I started the race and got up to

fourth place, having a great dice with Norman Grimshaw who was driving the Mini-Cooper S really well. We wanted to have a race with Leo Voyazides and Andy Bacon in the fast Ford Falcon. The Jaguar has a 3.8-litre engine (Anthony reckons it's putting out about 280bhp) but we were still giving away 100bhp and a lot of weight to the Falcon. Although the Jaguar is a racing car, it is very original and is fully trimmed. It's even road legal.

But the Williams' are a bit crazy and the Jaguar is set up for serious oversteer. Once you get the hang of its 'pointy' nature it is great fun. There is a lot of momentum and you do have to hurl the car at the corners, which requires a different approach to the much more sophisticated

Porsches and things I have raced over the years.

Once the car is 'in' you then steer on the throttle; a good thing as there is vast movement from one lock to the other. You have to make two bites at the tighter corners and this means that if the car gets away from you, your hands are in the wrong place on the wheel to catch it. I had a few hairy moments but that's historic motor racing for you.

The Jaguar is good through the fast corners at Madgwick and Woodcote. I used third and top, with a quick down change into second for the Chicane. Fordwater can be tricky as the car goes light on the brow; just when you feel you should back off you must keep the power down. The Jaguar is terrific sliding through Lavant, where the line is not too vital but speed is all.

Anyway, after my stint, I came into the pits to hand over to Grant. I had undone the safety harness and was ready for a quick driver change. I have only ever climbed in and out of this car on two occasions, so I yanked the door handle towards me. I think this locked the door so Grant could not get in. Eventually we got it open, strapped him in and he shot out of the pits. He did his fabulous dance routine around the circuit and got the Jaguar up to second, just behind the Falcon. He closed a six second gap down to about a second when the chequered flag dropped. That pit stop cost us the win.

Driving a beautiful Jaguar that has been raced by Salvadori and three generations of lovely if slightly mad Welshmen was very special. A memorable occasion. △

Derek Bell
Five-times Le Mans and twice Daytona winner Derek is now an Octane test driver.

'A SPECTATOR RUSHED INTO THE PITS AND OFFERED THE COMPONENTS FROM HIS MKII IN THE PARKING LOT'

1958 Jaguar MkI
Engine: 3.8-litre dohc, straight six, triple SU carburettors
Power (estimated): 280bhp @ 6000rpm
Chassis: monocoque
Suspension: front – independent;
rear – live axle with limited-slip diff

Left
Revcounter is twisted around so that redline is at the top (an old racing trick); no need to rely on the original bonnet catch; is Derek grinning for the camera or because of the car?

XK *Excess*

Take a Le Mans winner and offer it in a roadgoing version.
Impossible? Not so. Jaguar did it with the XKSS in 1957

Words: Philip Porter   **Photography:** Jason Furnari

XKS 5

You could argue it was the world's first supercar. It had prodigious performance, was rare, utterly impractical and one was owned by Steve McQueen. Sounds like a pretty good definition of a 'supercar'!

The stunning D-type, for most of us the definitive 1950s sports racing car, had succeeded the C-type in 1954. The three-car factory team, led by Stirling Moss and Peter Walker, were unlucky not to seal a debut victory at Le Mans when Duncan Hamilton and Tony Rolt finished second by a mere 105 seconds after 24 gruelling hours of racing. The following year Hawthorn and Bueb took the first of the D-type's three Le Mans wins, but it was not one to celebrate as this was the year of the awful accident that cost over 80 lives.

In '56 two of the factory D-types crashed on the second lap and Hawthorn's car was delayed by problems with its fuel injection. However, those gallant Scottish privateers, Ecurie Ecosse, came to the rescue and took a memorable win with their lone D-type, a feat they repeated the following year when D-types finished first, second, third, fourth and sixth. There was no disputing the heritage.

In 1952 Jaguar had started building 'production' C-types, which were acquired by a number of the XK120 racers in the UK and the States. Similarly, the factory laid down a small assembly line for 'production' D-types in 1955.

As the legendary Team Manager, 'Lofty' England once told me: 'The reason for building 50 C-types and later 50 D-types, was that when entering a prototype at Le Mans, the manufacturers had to give a certificate that the car entered was the prototype of a car of which at least 50 examples would be built. I think we were the only company that in fact made 50!'

Ironically, Jaguar thought the D-type was not capable of winning Le Mans again in 1957 and so, in October 1956, announced their retirement from motor racing. The intention was to take a year out before returning with a team of E-types in 1958. Most unfortunately, life did not pan out like that. The ludicrously small team of engineers had to turn their efforts with some urgency to the aging range of real production cars, the saloons and road-going sports cars. Furthermore, a near-disastrous fire had broken out at the Browns Lane factory in February, 1957. As 'Lofty' says: 'It was more important to keep

'We got so much publicity from the fire that we didn't need to go motor racing – it was much cheaper to burn the works down!'

'When Jaguar announced their retirement, some 42 production D-types had been supplied. But demand, believe it or not, had dried up, leaving 25 cars unsold'

the works going than go motor racing. In fact, we got so much publicity from the fire that we didn't need to go motor racing – it was much cheaper to burn the works down!'

When Jaguar made their announcement about retiring, some 42 production D-types had been supplied. But demand, believe it or not, had dried up, leaving 25 of the original batch of 67 unsold. Someone then had the brilliant idea of creating road cars out of the residue. I say 'someone' because several people subsequently claimed credit for the inspiration and an air of mystery surrounds the real motives for conceiving what became known as the XKSS.

Duncan Hamilton, a wonderful larger-than-life character, claimed he started the spark of an idea when he converted his ex-works car OKV 1, the 'D' he had shared at Le Mans with Rolt in '54, into a road car for Australian 'Jumbo' Goddard.

Another theory that has been peddled widely over many years is that the D-types were lying around going rusty and the XKSS was a desperate attempt to get rid of them. It is a small point, but aluminium does not rust!

When I wrote my book, 'Jaguar Sports Racing Cars', Lofty gave me a great deal of help and debunked all these theories, saying: 'One of the important things in America, especially to Briggs Cunningham, was the Sports Car Club of America [SCCA], which ran production sports car races. They should have accepted the

D-type because it was used as a road car, but they didn't. So we decided to make the D-type acceptable to the SCCA, and had to build 50 examples of this revised car. We did use the remaining stock of D-types, but always planned to make more because we didn't have 50 D-types lying around.'

Briggs Cunningham was, of course, the great American sportsman whose ambition had been to win Le Mans with one of his own cars but, having failed to do so, began racing Jaguars in his colours and at the same time became Jaguar's New York dealer. So he had a vested interest in promoting Jaguar apart from the pure sport.

Another American, Bob Blake, played a major role in actually creating the prototype XKSS. Blake was a brilliant panel beater who had worked for Cunningham and claimed to have built every single Cunningham sports racer. When Briggs ceased building his own cars, Blake, who had a British wife, moved to England and joined the Experimental Department at Jaguar.

Lofty picks up the story again: 'Plans to convert to the XKSS were discussed by Sir William Lyons with Bill Heynes [Jaguar's engineering chief], and in turn with Phil Weaver [superintendent of the Competition Department], who got a D-type over to the competition shop. There Bob Blake carried out the prototype work. Sir William naturally went to the shop to see and approve the prototype work.'

»

'All 16 XKSS cars actually produced have both their original D-type chassis number too. Twelve went to the USA, two to Canada, one to Hong Kong and one remained in Britain'

Above
The SS name is believed to stand for 'Super Sports' but this was never clarified at the time.

The changes made to the D-types to create the XKSS largely consisted of additions. The most significant changes to the bodywork, and none were of major structural importance, were the removal of the head fairing, the cutting out of the central division between the driver and passenger, and the provision of a door for the passenger on the lefthand side. A full-width, framed, wraparound windscreen was fitted, as were a pair of wipers. As the spare wheel lived in a compartment in the tail in what was the closest the D-type got to a boot, a luggage rack was mounted on the rear deck.

A rudimentary hood was provided and Blake sketched his ideas for the hood frame in an old exercise book. 'I made all the frames and bits and pieces,' he told me, 'including all the little wooden tools to make everything from. I made the front set of bumpers by cutting down the big old wide bumper, using the top radius and the bottom radius, cutting the flute out and welding the two pieces together. The back bumper went into production as a casting, quite thick but hollow in the back with bosses so that it could be bolted on – all made from my original.' These ideas led to the delicate bumper blades we would see on the E-type when it appeared four years later.

Tragically, the small production run of XKSS cars was cut short by the traumatic factory fire, which supposedly destroyed vital tooling. All 16 of the XKSS models actually produced have both their original D-type chassis number and an XKSS one as well. Twelve went to the USA, two to Canada, one to Hong Kong and one remained in Britain. At least a couple of the cars had actually been completed as D-types before being converted to XKSS variants. This was so of XKSS 728, which was first displayed at the Barcelona Fair in 1956 as a 'D' and 769 which was on show at Appleyards, the Leeds Jaguar dealership. Stored by its long-term owner in the US for several decades, 728 emerged in 1998 in a wonderful time-warp state and today belongs to Gary Bartlett.

XKSS 757 (there was no apparent logic to the sequential numbering) went to Hong Kong where it covered 1400 miles on the road and subsequently won the Macau GP on two occasions. The original owner of 707 was killed before he could take delivery and the second owner was killed at Laguna Seca a few months later. Number 766 was sold to a Cuban living in New York who then raced it extensively in Cuba prior to the Castro revolution in '59. In the 1980s, dealer Colin Crabbe discovered this car and 725 in Cuba and shipped them back to the UK.

XKSS 710 has been, in more recent years, converted first to a 'standard' D-type and then a full Works long-nose specification, but all the original XKSS parts have been retained. 713 was owned by a succession of high profile Californians, including rising movie star Steve McQueen. In 1967 he made a 'sale of convenience' to the Harrah Collection but, after a legal battle, managed to buy it back in 1978, keeping it until his death.

Of the Canadian cars, 716 was raced and hillclimbed with success and, many years later, converted into a D-type by Lynx. Two D-types were also officially converted by the factory into XKSS models, though not given XKSS numbers. XKD 533, originally raced as a 'D' in France, was returned to the factory in 1958 for conversion and remained in France for some years. Today I believe it is owned by Ralph Lauren.

As to the other example, XKD 540, the factory chassis records mysteriously state 'redundant after experiment'. It was sold to Coombs of Guildford for £2100. (The XKSS would be priced at £3878, so this sounded like a good deal.) Coombs later sold it to hillclimber Phil Scragg who sent it back to the factory for conversion in the winter of '58/59. That these two cars could be converted by the factory more than a year after the factory fire had supposedly destroyed vital jigs and tooling, thereby terminating XKSS production, rather seems to dispel that myth!

The example featured here started life as XKD 555 and was the first to be converted and was logically numbered XKSS 701, the seven standing for the year. Its initial role was as the New York demonstrator, but 701 was also raced by the Vice President of Jaguar USA, one C. Gordon Benett who finished first at Mansfield, Louisiana. It was road-tested by *Road & Track* for their August issue and they concluded it was no dual-purpose car, but they did say it was a truly tremendous machine. Interestingly, they considered the ride was soft compared with the spine-jarring ride of Italian road-race machinery.

The car continued to be raced in the States by its original owner, Robert Stonedale, who later removed the screen, bumpers and boot rack, and added a roll-over bar. In September he finished fifth in a race at Oklahoma Airport with his left leg in plaster! The car then had a succession of subsequent owners and in the early '60s suffered the period misfortune of having a Chevrolet V8 engine grafted in, which necessitated some altering of the frame. After an aborted attempt at restoration in the 1970s, the car went to Lynx where, under the guidance of Chris Keith- ➤➤

'You get into a C-type, but you put a D-type on. The impression, whether sitting in or driving, is of a car tailored to you'

1957 Jaguar XKSS

SPECIFICATIONS

Engine
3442cc, 6-cylinder twin overhead cam XK engine with triple Weber 45 DC3 carburettors. Dry sump lubrication

Power
250bhp @5750rpm
242lb ft @ 4000rpm

Transmission
Jaguar 4-speed close ratio all-synchro box

Suspension
Front: Independent incorporating upper and lower wishbones with torsion bars. Rear: transverse torsion bar, lower trailing arm and upper parallel trailing arms attached to live axle.

Brakes
Dunlop disc brakes all-round, triple pad front and twin pad rear.

Weight
1800lb (817kg)

Performance
0-100mph 13.6 secs. Top speed: 149mph. Standing quarter mile: 14.3 secs.

Value
Around £750,000

Lucas, it was rebuilt for its Japanese owner as a D-type. Later they converted it back into full XKSS specification.

In early 2001 the car was acquired by Jaguar and TVR specialists Racing Green, who are based near Guildford. The car was thoroughly overhauled mechanically for the Mille Miglia and shared on the event by Racing Green Chairman Graham Love and Mike Salmon, who raced D-types extensively in the 1960s. After a perfect, trouble-free run, Salmon commented that this was the best driving D-type he had ever experienced.

Certainly an XKSS still feels a very quick car. The steering is delightfully precise and the whole car feels very taut indeed. Thanks to the famous Jaguar torque, acceleration is vivid in any gear and, given the space and conditions, you could cruise at unprintably-high speeds with complete confidence. The superb brakes add to that feeling and I found the road-holding very predictable, allowing you to use the throttle to steer the rear end round the track we used for a very exciting day's driving.

Mechanically, the D-type and the XKSS are identical. The major difference you notice is the 'sophistication' of the full width screen. The 'D' on the road is a pure, raw sports car, whereas the XKSS is a tad more civilised. It is said that C-types have recently become as soughtafter (and thus as valuable) as D-types because they are more usable on the road. But the XKSS seems pretty happy pottering through suburbia, although is obviously at its most deliriously exciting on the open road.

The D-type was such a massive step forward from the C-type. I was forcefully reminded of this when, returning to Racing Green's impressive premises, I climbed aboard a highly authentic C-type 'recreation' that they also market. You get into a C-type, but you put a D-type on. The whole impression, whether sitting in or driving, is of a car tailored to you. Do I agree with *Road & Track* that it is not a dual-purpose car? Actually, I do not!

There may be virtually no space for the shopping, But it's the perfect, and maybe only, excuse to go shopping more often! △

JAGUAR XK

**As Jaguar enthusiasts celebrate 60 years of the XK range,
marque expert and founder of The XK Club** Philip Porter
describes why these cars created such a stir – and still do

Photography: Michael Bailie

OFE 977

JV

Sixty years ago, the Jaguar XK120 Super Sports Open Two-Seater took the Earls Court Show and the motoring world by storm. Combining performance that had previously been enjoyed only by racing cars and a few examples of rarefied exotica with ultra-modern styling and relative sophistication, the XK120 really was a landmark.

The XK burst into a very grey world that was still recovering from the ravages of World War Two, and which served only to heighten the drama of the car's entrance. Famously intended just as a testbed for the new engine that had been designed for a fresh range of saloons, the clamour for the sensational new sports car, in spite of some scepticism about its claimed performance, was overwhelming. Jaguar stuttered into production over the 1949-'50 period, in the process switching from the initial aluminium and ash frame construction to pressed steel panels.

'The XK120 was a real wind-in-the-hair sports car, yet it proved that sports cars did not need to be for masochists only'

**Jaguar
XK120 Open
Two-Seater**

SPECIFICATIONS

Engine
3442cc in-line dohc six,
iron block, alloy head,
twin SU carburettors

Power
160bhp @ 5000rpm

Torque
195lb ft @ 2500rpm

Transmission
Four-speed manual,
rear-wheel drive

Suspension
Front: independent via
wishbone and torsion
bar, anti-roll bar, lever-
arm dampers. Rear:
live axle, semi-elliptics,
lever-arm dampers

Brakes
Hydraulic drums

Performance
0-60mph 10sec
Top speed 124mph

With 'Export Or Die' the dictat from Government, the 120 led the way into America, both symbolically and commercially. The stars of Hollywood embraced the Jag-wah. An unambiguous demonstration of the car's genuine performance in front of the press at Jabbeke in Belgium and a fairytale win in the model's first race at Silverstone (admittedly against some pretty average opposition) only served to lengthen the order books. A tentative entry at Le Mans nearly resulted in unexpected glory.

A very young man who had impressed everyone vastly in little motor-cycle-engined single-seater racers was looking to make the step up and make the crucial breakthrough. He managed to borrow one of the six works-prepared 120s (Jaguar was not amused) and, with a masterly display in appalling conditions, Stirling Moss took a brilliant victory in the classic Tourist Trophy.

Combine all this with record-breaking and Ian Appleyard's unprecedented success in international rallying with another of the six (NUB 120), and the 120 could do no wrong. What was its secret? The heart of the car was the new twin-overhead-cam engine that William Lyons had the courage to put into production. Believed to be too complex for a road car, the engine, with its hemispherical aluminium head, gave excellent performance, terrific torque and, above all, had massive reserves for future development. One of the greatest engines of all time, it would remain in production for almost 40 years and power everything from world-beating sports racers to silent executive saloons, from tanks to the equally sensational E-type.

The 120 Roadster, as the Open Two-Seater became known, was a traditional sports car in some senses and radically different in others. It had a rudimentary soft-top, crude sidescreens and standard seats that were something of a joke when cornering hard. It was a real wind-in-the-hair sports car, of the type beloved pre-war. Yet it shocked some of those diehards because it had 'boulevard' suspension. With a massively over-engineered chassis, inherited from the new Mark V saloon, and suspension that was rather soft by traditional sports car standards, the 120 found a wider audience and proved that sports cars did not need to be for masochists only. And if anyone said the XK was a softy, just look at what it achieved in motor sport, where there are no compromises.

Having said that, the 120 was far from perfect. The brakes had not kept pace with the increased level of performance, an area Jaguar needed to address. Some felt the position of the steering wheel as it was presented to the driver, and its heaviness, were truck-like. Lights were marginal for the virtually unheard-of performance. The gearbox was slow and agricultural, even if it was very tough. In general, the car was no lightweight.

The XK120 gave the Jaguar marque what today we would call the 'halo effect'. The new Mark VII saloon basked in the reflected glory of its sporting sibling, and victory at Le Mans with a competition version of the XK120, the C-type, brought untold publicity for the little British company, putting it on the map worldwide.

Great car though the 120 was, it could not be considered that practical in

Below and right
First of the XKs, this particular 120 is in fact the very first steel-bodied Roadster produced.

»

'XK140 Coupés were given two rear seats that could be occupied by children or by fully-grown pygmies'

1955 Jaguar XK140 Drop Head Coupé
SPECIFICATIONS

Engine
3442cc in-line dohc six, iron block, alloy head, twin SU carburettors

Power
190bhp @ 5500rpm (this car SE spec: 210bhp @ 5750rpm)

Torque
210lb ft @ 2500rpm (213lb ft @ 4000rpm)

Transmission
Four-speed manual (SE spec with overdrive), rear-wheel drive

Suspension
Front: independent via wishbone and torsion bar, anti-roll bar, telescopic dampers. Rear: live axle, semi-elliptics, telescopic dampers

Brakes
Hydraulic drums

Performance
0-60mph 11sec
Top speed 129mph

climates less friendly than California, and Jaguar responded with the introduction of the XK120 Fixed Head Coupé in 1951. The styling was another Lyons masterpiece: though he had simply crafted a roof onto the basic Roadster shape, no-one could have known it was as simple as that. Highly revered today, the FHC had definite undertones of Jean Bugatti's work and is pure sculpture.

The new Coupé was actually a very different animal to its stablemate in a number of ways. It was, if you like, a tamed Jaguar. Gone was the devil-may-care character of the Roadster and instead here was a car that was highly sophisticated. It combined the essence of the performance with pre-war levels of opulence. The luxury of wind-up windows was complemented by the decadence of a veneered dashboard and door cappings.

While rather more practical than the Roadster, the Coupé's interior space was actually at more of a premium and its boot space very similar. But for these compromises, the 120 FHC would have been a true Grand Tourer. It was, though, a fabulous long-distance car for those who travelled light!

Announced as being for export only, it seems you had to be someone to obtain a right-hand-drive example, and, with less than 200 built, these are exceedingly rare cars today. The list of original owners includes Ecurie Ecosse racer Ian Stewart; Neville Duke, the famous test pilot; 'Gentleman' Jack Sears, who raced his; Jack Hallay, who rallied his; and Sir Jackie's brother, the late Jim Stewart, who drove for Ecosse and the Works.

The Roadster and Fixed Head represented two extremes. There was room for

yet another version that bridged the two, a car that had the FHC's sophistication but could also offer open-air motoring. The solution was what the Americans called a convertible and what Jaguar christened the Drop Head Coupé (DHC). Aping the opulence of the FHC with its interior fittings, it was graced with a luxurious, fully-lined, folding top. Once again the model found favour in the vital US market and gave Jaguar superlative coverage of the higher performance sports car sector.

As with all Lyons's cars, the XKs were incredible value for money, which further fuelled demand. This was achieved by relatively long production runs, by saving money on sophisticated tooling and, sadly, by compromising on quality in certain areas.

By 1954 it was time to 'refresh' the XK range, and also address some of the slight shortcomings. The result was the evolutionary XK140.

The 140 essentially retained the 120's style, and the Coupé interiors were the areas most altered; both these models were given two seats in the rear that could be occupied by children or fully-grown pygmies. Today they are used by most owners for extra luggage and such like, and are thus rather more practical. To achieve the extra space, the batteries, which had previously enjoyed the privilege of being adjacent to the interior, were demoted to positions under the front wings.

Externally, the DHC model was little changed in terms of overall shape. The FHC, though, came in for rather more radical surgery. To potentially house one's

Below and right
The XK140 was mechanically better than the 120, but full-width bumpers did nothing for looks.

little horrors in the back, the roofline was extended rearwards, making this model easily distinguishable. Furthermore, the front footwells were lengthened either side of the engine and the screen moved forward. All of this added up to considerably more generous interior space and better suited those 120 FHC owners who tended to suffer from claustrophobia.

Mechanically, the 140s were given the uprated engines that had previously been offered in Special Equipment versions of the 120 and the brakes were improved a little. Handling was assisted by moving the engine forward and swapping the ancient lever-arm rear shockers for telescopic chaps. Rack-and-pinion steering made this department lighter and the generous provision of a UJ in the column altered the angle of the steering wheel.

Externally, there were some detailed but very obvious changes. To save money the delicate grille of soldered, fluted vanes was replaced by a rather crude cast replica. The trade commission at the British Embassy in Washington had highlighted in a report that the imported UK cars were inadequately protected front and rear from the vast and seriously heavy Detroit sedans. Hence the 140 was blessed with proper bumpers, as opposed to the ornaments on the 120, but these did little for the aesthetics.

The Roadster model, still known as the Open Two-Seater (OTS), shared most of these changes apart from the provision of the 'nipper seats' and remained delightfully selfish. This variant was really intended for the warmer climes of the world, and almost all were exported. They proved, like the

Below and left
For comfort and power, the XK150 is by far the best of the range, but the shape isn't as sensuous.

other models, to be extremely successful for Jaguar and Britain.

Retrospectively, at least, views have diverged on whether the 140 was an improvement or not. Traditionalists felt the 140 had gone soft, and preferred the more he-man character of the 120. Others found the 140 considerably more pleasant to drive.

The 140 had evolved and, in parallel, the competition world had moved on; it was no longer possible to turn up with your 120, pump up the tyres, remove the spare and enjoy a hearty club race. Jaguar had itself played a part in that progression with the C-type, which had been designed as a dedicated sports racing car: a rather new breed of animal. Hence the 140s did not sample, or enjoy, the same level of competition activity as their predecessors, which perhaps helps account for their softer image.

By 1957, the XK range needed an injection of updating to keep Jaguar at the forefront of sports car design. With the ludicrously small team of engineers having devoted most of their time to designing and developing the new 'small' saloon range and the fabulous D-types, which followed the C-type's two Le Mans victories with three more, Jaguar was unable to introduce a completely new sports car at this stage.

Modernised in many ways, the 150 was the ultimate iteration of the XK theme and itself would sire various versions. The big step forward for the 150 was the adoption of disc brakes, which Jaguar had developed with Dunlop and had used very effectively on the later Cs and the Ds. This feature gave the 150 technical

1960 Jaguar XK150 3.8S Fixed Head Coupé

SPECIFICATIONS

Engine
3781cc in-line dohc six, iron block, alloy head, three SU carburettors

Power
265bhp @ 5500rpm

Torque
260lb ft @ 4000rpm

Transmission
Four-speed manual plus overdrive, rear-wheel drive

Suspension
Front: independent via wishbone and torsion bar, anti-roll bar, telescopic dampers. Rear: live axle, semi-elliptics, telescopic dampers

Brakes
Dunlop discs

Performance
0-60mph 7.6sec
Top speed 136mph

'Disc brakes gave the XK150 technical credibility and, apart from the low-volume Jensen, a feature the competition lacked'

»

'The XK150 has been better revered in recent years as the ultimate example of the XK range'

credibility and, apart from the very low-volume Jensen, a feature the competition lacked. A new B-type cylinder head increased power, which had progressed from the 120's 180bhp to the 140's 190bhp, to 210bhp.

Visually, the 150 was far more changed than the 140 had been over the 120. The old two-piece flat windscreen was looking very dated now and it was replaced by a wraparound one-piece item. The dramatic fall and rise of the wing line was considerably straightened and the cabin widened. This was achieved by putting the doors on a diet; the slimmer versions benefited the interior space considerably. Initially launched in Fixed Head and Drop Head Coupé form only, the range was augmented in late 1958 by the OTS.

Coincident with the launch of the 150 roadster, Jaguar made an additional 'S' version available for the Coupé models in early '59. With a so-called straight-port head and triple two-inch SUs, power was raised to a claimed 250bhp. The horsepower race was on in the States and to compete Jaguar added XK engines enlarged from 3.4 to 3.8 litres, and offered an 'S' variant of the 3.8 which, supposedly, produced 265bhp (actually much nearer 200bhp!). There were thus 12 different XK150s available before production tailed off in late 1960, in readiness for the launch of the E-type.

The XK150 has probably been better revered in more recent years, when it could be judged as a stand-alone car rather than compared alongside its peers in period. The concept was, not surprisingly, ageing by the end of the decade, but it was the ultimate example of the incredible XK range. ⚠

» Thanks to Derek Hood of JD Classics for the loan of these magnificent Jaguar XKs. www.jdclassics.co.uk, +44 (0)1621 879579.

Above
Three iterations of XK; three very different characters; each one highly desirable to today's collectors.

Using a
JAGUAR XK
everyday

Some of the Jaguar XK series of cars are now 60 years old, and even the last-of-line XK150 is 47 years of age. So is it possible to use these elderly classics on a regular basis in the modern world?

Words: Robert Coucher   Photography: Paul Harmer, Ian Dawson

The answer is yes, for a number of reasons. First, modern traffic has slowed over the last decade due to the increase in traffic and ever more prevalent electronic speed detection. These days few cars cruise at much over 85mph on British motorways, and speed limits in busy areas are, rightfully, rigorously enforced. In these conditions, all XKs are more than able to keep up with the flow of traffic. They are still quick cars.

Classic Jaguars are very popular on the Continent, in America, Australia and Britain, so a huge specialist and parts industry has grown up internationally. With a long production run – particularly of the venerable XK engine, which continued in production until the '80s – almost all parts are available at realistic prices.

Jaguar XKs are tough old beasts and are simple to maintain. Unlike a fragile, rust-prone, monocoque E-type, the XK has a sturdy chassis, and with the 140 and 150 you get massive bumpers to cope with 'touch parking'. Imagine a low-slung E-type bonnet being met with a reversing 4x4. An expensive crunch will ensue. Specialists such as Martin Robey and Contour Autocraft supply many replacement body panels.

If you intend to drive an XK on a regular basis, some subtle mods are advisable. Of course you can go all the way and effectively turn one into a modern car which looks like a classic, but that's not the point. XKs are great to drive in near-original spec, as is evident on many historic rallies and tours, let alone on the race track.

The first thing to fit is an electric fan. Jaguars have always suffered from cooling problems, which are most pronounced in the C-type and 120s, and in today's conditions effective cooling is essential. It's worth replacing all hoses as well. If you drive in London or other very built-up areas, a modified alloy radiator and expansion tank are a good idea, as this improvement makes the cars totally traffic proof. XKs Unlimited in California carries all the required parts.

Tyres are probably the next items to look at because original-spec ones are old tech and need to be at their best. Tyres are pretty much over and out after five years of age, so check them; the heavy XK needs good boots. Some of our American and German friends tend to change the wire wheels from 16 to 15in, then fit fat

XK contacts

Beacham Jaguar
www.beacham-jaguar.co.nz
Blockley Tyre Company
www.blockleytyre.com
Burlen Fuel Systems
www.burlen.co.uk
Classic Autosports
www.classicautosports.com
Classic Showcase
www.classicshowcase.com
CMC Classic Motor Cars
www.classic-motor-cars.co.uk
Contour Autocraft
www.contourautocraft.co.uk
David Manners
www.jagspares.co.uk
Doc's Jags
www.docsjags.com
E-type UK
www.etypeuk.co.uk
Guy Broad Parts
www.guybroad.co.uk
JD Classics
www.jdclassics.co.uk
Jeremy Wade
+44 (0)1630 657502
Longstone Tyres
www.longstonetyres.co.uk
Martin Robey
www.martinrobey.com
Racing Green Cars
www.racinggreencars.com
SNG Barratt
www.sngbarratt.com
Spax
www.spax.co.uk
Twyford Moors
www.jagxk.com
Upper Classics
www.upperclassics.com
Vredestein
www.vredestein.com
XKs Unlimited
www.xks.com
Zwakman Jaguar
www.zwakmanjaguar.com

205/65-series modern rubber. This upsets the gearing, makes the steering incredibly heavy (power steering is next!) and ruins the ride. But more and more drivers are realising the original 16-inch wheels are best to maintain the Jaguar's handling and composure. Tyre manufacturers are now producing decent boots of the correct size: Blockley has some high-performance crossplies which are great fun on the road or track, Vredestein has some affordable radials as used by the XK racing series, and Longstone Tyres has recently added Pirelli Cinturatos to its wide range.

Brakes are next. Original drums are fine for normal motoring and weekend jaunts, but they have to work hard and need to be in good fettle. The 150s have disc brakes which, in good condition, are excellent – even if the rear discs can be a nightmare to remove.

If you are not after FIA papers, a sensible improvement is front disc brakes. Many specialists provide upgrade kits and David Manners and SNG Barratt have most of the braking components you will need. And while the brakes are being done, fit a fresh set of dampers. They will make a huge difference; Spax and Koni are well-proven brands. If you want to throw the XK around a bit, have the front suspension poly bushed – this makes a noticeable difference to the handling and response. Racing Green Cars has the kit.

The one problem with classic Jaguars is that the cars were built down to a price, so many original components are not of the best quality. Fortunately the XK engine (especially the early ones, as used in XKs) is a masterpiece, but jokes about the Lucas Prince of Darkness electrics aren't entirely unmerited. These days improved ancillaries are available from specialists such as CMC. It is advisable to ensure the electrics have been sorted out, and an alternator conversion and electronic ignition system are worthwhile. Also, buy a fresh Lucas fuel pump from Burlen Fuel Systems and, even if you don't fit it, carry it in the boot.

A Jaguar XK with these and other improvements makes for a fast, comfortable, relaxing and effective tourer. Guy Broad can tailor a car to your exact requirements and the many excellent Jaguar specialists out there have all you need. These lovely old cars deserve to run well, and to be driven as often as possible. △

The case for the Jaguar XK

Jaguar man Philip Porter **writes with tongue slightly in cheek, in an attempt to convince you of the superiority of the XKs over some of their rivals. He treads on a few toes, maligns some revered names and expects to be shot at, if not shot down**

Over the last 30 years I have known many car enthusiasts start with Jaguar XKs, thoroughly enjoy the 'classic car experience' and then move on to those makes perceived as more exotic – Ferrari, Aston Martin, Maserati and Porsche, for example. Are they really rarer? Are they actually faster and more alluring?

Above all, are they usable? Because the most beautiful car in the world is not much good to anybody if it continually lets you down, is hellishly expensive for major work and is rarely on the road. That spells frustration and disillusion. Many of those who started with XKs have gone full circle back to them. I know one collector who had 100 examples of all the grande marque cars – vintage Alfas, Bugattis, Bentleys, Rolls-Royces, Hispanos, Delages, Delahayes and more 'modern' machinery such as Cobras and McLarens. He now has just two XKs.

Nigel Dawes is renowned for having created some very special XK120 Coupés in recent years. We have been friends for a quarter-century and he has owned every classic Aston, from DB3S through DB4GT to Project 215; he's had a variety of Ferraris, the odd Porsche and much else. Yet he ended up specialising in, and owning, XKs.

Let's tackle rarity first. The general view is that XKs are common. But are they? Bear in mind XKs were made for 12 years and the 120s, 140s and 150s are rather different cars, as are the three versions of each – Roadster, Drop Head and Fixed Head. Porsche made 68,000 356s and hundreds of thousands of 911s. Maserati built 2000 3500GTs. Some 64,000 Corvettes were produced between '56 and '59. Little Aston Martin built only a relative handful of cars? Well, they manufactured 411 DB2s, more than 1300 DB2/4s, 1100 DB4s, 1020 DB5s and about 1800 DB6s. Mercedes made over

3000 300SLs (1400 Gullwings and 1858 Roadsters). Nothing in comparison with the tens of thousands of XKs built?

In fact, only 2790 140 DHCs were produced, including just 470 right-hand-drive examples. Some 1767 120 DHCs were constructed, including a tiny 295 rhd cars. For the 150 DHCs, the respective figures for total production and rhd are 2672 (including 3.4, 3.8, 3.4S and 3.8S) and 663.

So how do the Fixed Heads stack-up? Of the 120s, some 2672 were made in total, of which a mere 195 were rhd cars. For the 140s, the figures were 2798 and 839, and for 150s, 4445 and 1367.

Finally, what of the Roadsters? Some 7606 examples of the classic 120 OTS were built, of which 1170 were rhd. A total of 3349 140 roadsters left the factory and a minuscule 74 of those were rhd cars. As to 150s, the figures were 2265 and a minute 93. All pretty rare models then, and some exceptionally so.

How about running costs? Well, figures will vary from specialist to specialist, but these are based on a cross-section of those with whom I have spoken. An annual service for a DB4/5/6 is quoted at £1400 (including VAT), with a similar figure for a Ferrari 250GT and 275GTB, Mercedes-Benz 190SL and 'pagoda' SL. A Maserati is £250 more and the Dino is also £1650. A Porsche 356 averages around £750 but early 911s are about £1000. Jaguar specialist Classic Motor Cars (CMC) charges £530 for an XK 12,000-mile or annual service.

To prepare for the worst, it is prudent to be aware of engine rebuild costs. The DB2/4 series costs £12,000-15,000 and the DB 4/5/6s £15,000-20,000. Marque specialist Chris Shenton tells me that one in four DB5/6 blocks are cracked. A new one is £8000, while a crank is £3000. He says that most DB2/4 blocks need replacing. The consensus for Ferrari engines seems to be £1000 a cylinder, but for the little Dino the total cost is £12,500-20,000. The earlier Porsche 356s are about £4500 and the early 911s around £9000.

'XKS ARE QUITE RARE, RELIABLE, MECHANICALLY SOPHISTICATED IN KEY AREAS, BUT ARE CHEAP TO RUN'

Left and right
Multi-cylinder Italian engines look and sound great, but can't compare with the XK for low running costs and reliability.

CMC recently rebuilt a Maserati Mexico which took 350 hours at £44 per hour and thus equates to £15,500.

For an XK engine rebuild, CMC charges around £4400, and VSE which does nothing but XK, and Jaguar V12, engines are closer to £2000.

Parts availability for XKs is particularly good because a healthy proportion are in use. Because they are so usable they cover a comparatively high mileage, meaning there is a good demand for spares. This, together with the fact that there is a large number of specialists competing for the business, keeps parts and labour costs in check. It's a win, win, win situation.

In contrast, the perceived exotica does not get used so much, because of the greater maintenance required, the sometimes questionable reliability and higher running costs. Because there were fewer made, many parts are just not available or the costs are astronomical due to low demand. With less use, fewer specialists and lower demand for parts, it's a lose, lose, lose situation!

'Porter is biased,' I hear you saying. Perhaps I am, so to seek impartial views I have spoken with friends and specialists for their random comments on the subject.

Mike Barker, who has owned and looked after some incredible motor cars in the last 30-40 years, comments that Astons are a bit fragile and that it would be a brave, or foolish, man who did his own servicing.

Iain Tyrrell and his company, Cheshire Classic Cars, work on most of the models that we are talking of. As to V12 Ferraris of the '50s and '60s, Iain comments that the engines are very straightforward and robust. The only item for fairly constant maintenance was the valve gear on the earlier motors. A full engine tune-up – checking points, setting ignition timing, valve clearances, etc – takes 20 hours at £55 per hour plus VAT, which is £1300.

As to Astons, one of the major concerns is corrosion of the aluminium blocks. Excessive coolant loss is a sign that the cast iron cylinder liner to aluminium cylinder block seal is starting to breach. Full engine rebuild needed. 'It's a hardy

Parts prices

(Figures quoted are ballpark prices, excluding VAT)

Rear light lens
Maserati Mexico £145
Porsche 911 £70
XK £9

Windscreen
Maserati Mexico £1100
Aston DB2/4 n/a
DB4/5 £469
DB6 £570
Ferrari Dino £600-1000 (secondhand)
E-type £250
XK150 £210
XK120/140 £110

Exhaust system
Ferrari V12 up to £3000
Porsche 911 £1200
Ferrari Dino £1000
Maserati Mexico £900
Aston DB2/4 £350
DB4/5 £530
DB6 £650
XK £375

Rotor arm
Maserati Mexico £30
Aston DB5 £15
XK £3

Clutch kit
Maserati Mexico £673
Porsche 911 £300
Ferrari Dino £300
Aston DB5 £287
XK £200

engine when it's going well, but an expensive engine to rebuild,' states Tyrrell. Jeremy Wade reckons you can abuse an XK more than an Aston, and pre-'75 Porsches can rust. Nick Goldthorp of CMC is very rude about Italian build quality and the Russian steel used: 'You can hear them rust!'

Regarding Porsches, Tyrrell says that because the 356 is air-cooled it reduces maintenance, although it is crucial to adjust the tappets every 3000 miles (to prevent burning the valves). Iain states that the 911's tappets need adjusting '...every 12,000 miles come what may. The timing chain tensioners can fail. Because the car is rear-engined, and because the chains are at the very back, you can't hear when the tensioner has gone and the chain actually grinds away the inside of the timing cases on the engine.

'The XK is a very underrated motor. Tappet adjustment on the likes of Ferraris is a major, time-consuming area. Time is money. On the XK, once the tappets are set, they'll stay at that for 30,000-50,000 miles.'

The subject of values could occupy another whole article. Suffice to say that most of the so-called exotica is over £100,000, with many Astons and Ferraris well over £200k. Paul Abadjian of Retro Classics says that good usable XKs start at £25-30k for 140 and 150 FHCs, through £30-35k for 120 DHCs, £33-38k for classic 120 OTSs, with the 140 and 150 Roadsters and DHCs £38-50k. The rarer cars are £80k-plus and upgraded XKs can fetch £200k or more.

To sum up XKs are quite rare and in rhd form some are extremely rare. They are very reliable, mechanically sophisticated but require relatively little maintenance, are cheap to run, assisted by low parts prices. And a Jaguar XK is one of the most beautiful cars on the road... △

» Thanks must go to CMC, www.classic-motor-cars.co.uk; Guy Broad Parts, www.guybroad.co.uk; Jeremy Wade, +44 (0)1630 657502; Retro Classics, +44 (0)1258 837276; Autofarm, www.autofarm.co.uk; Nick Cartwright Specialist Cars, www.nickcartwright.com; Chris Shenton Engineering, +44 (0)1782 643159; and, finally, Cheshire Classic Cars, www.cheshireclassiccars.co.uk.

CLASSIC MOTOR CARS
LIMITED

RESTORING JAGUAR'S HERITAGE

At CMC Ltd, we restore classic Jaguars to universally acclaimed world-class standards.

The engineering and craftsmanship that lie beneath the beautiful coachwork make our cars better than new.

Whether you are looking to restore an historic vehicle or want a car that is upgraded for use in modern traffic on a daily basis, look no further than CMC.

Our cars are being driven throughout the world, so wherever you are we can build the car of your dreams.

This is why we have been chosen to restore some of the worlds most historic Jaguars, to name but a few.

9600HP The only surviving prototype and the worlds oldest E-Type Jaguar.

1VHP Chassis number 1 and first right hand drive, fixed head Coupé off the production line.

OKV1 First works racing D-Type which came second at Le Mans in 1954.

1600RW E-Type Roadster, Chassis number 4, Lofty's own car and the first one to be sold off the production line.

4868WK One of the 12 light-weight E-Types, universally known as the Lindner/Nocker car which is currently the subject of an incredible restoration.

Classic Motor Cars, Bridgnorth, England.
Tel: +44 (0) 1746 765804 Email: mail@classic-motor-cars.co.uk
www.classic-motor-cars.co.uk

Brussels. Home of the European Commission and a dirty word to many a red-blooded Englishman; particularly the kind of Englishman who likes to drive classic cars. Can't find traditional cellulose paint anymore? Blame Brussels. Fed up with speed cameras and road humps. Blame... er, well, blame your own government actually, but it's more satisfying to lay every kind of grievance at the doors of Johnny Foreigner. It's virtually our national sport, and one we're much better at playing than football.

But every day one man takes a little bit of Olde England into the very heart of Brussels, driving his Mk2 Jaguar 3.4 within a contemptuous stone's throw of the European Parliament's offices. Flying in the face of Continental convention – which is to drive expensive new cars, preferably those made in Germany – he uses his characterful old Jag every day. And he happens to be Belgian. »

Daily Express

Would you dare to use a 1960s Jaguar every day in one of Europe's busiest cities? Meet the man who traded the chance to drive a new BMW for the British classic Words: Mark Dixon Photography: Matthew Howell

If you're a regular *Octane* reader, dig out your old copy of issue 32 and you'll find in the *Letters* pages a missive from one Gilles Vink, the aforementioned Brussels native who has forsaken a modern company car so that he could run a classic Jaguar instead. As Gilles explained in his letter, he worked out that over a period of years it would be as cost effective to buy and maintain a really nice Mk2 as it would be to lease a BMW turbodiesel.

Gilles doesn't treat his old Jag like a concours queen, either. He drives it like any other company car user would have driven a Mk2 back in the '60s – and that means hard. Following Gilles as he speared along the outside lane of an autoroute at 85-90mph, leaving tinny modern hatchbacks rocking in his slipstream, was an uplifting experience. There's nothing like seeing an old car being driven quickly to stir the blood.

Later, I ride shotgun with Gilles as he surfs the traffic tide flowing out of Brussels, dicing with Golf GTIs and BMW 3-series. The Jaguar's high-speed stability is very impressive, and Gilles proves it by taking both hands off the wheel at an

'Gilles doesn't treat his old Jag like a concours queen. He drives it lik e any other company car user would have driven a Mk2 back in the '60s – and that means hard'

Far left and left
Gilles Vink looks and sounds more English than the English; rear seat belts testify to Jag's role as family transport.

indicated 160kph. The Jaguar's straight-six is turning over at a lazy 2000rpm; my heart is revving rather faster, but the car just laps it up and as for Gilles, nothing seems to ruffle the laid-back character of this surrogate Englishman.

But let's get real. 'Hard everyday use' and '1960s Jaguar' are not two phrases that sit comfortably together 40 years on. Surely Gilles must have been visited by the Prince of Darkness – as Americans drily refer to Lucas electrics – by now?

'Touch wood, we haven't broken down yet,' claims Gilles (who speaks better English than most of the English; a useful asset in his day job as secretary-general of a lobbying firm). 'I've done 30,000km without a hitch so far. The key is regular maintenance. It's very, very important to have the car serviced every 5000km. Otherwise all I do is put oil in it and clean it. It uses about a litre of 20/50 every 1000km, so I always carry a can in the boot.'

Just as significant is that before Gilles took delivery of the Mk2 it was comprehensively gone through by Belgian specialist Bernard Marreyt, who also sourced the car. Having the Jaguar thoroughly overhauled and restored where necessary pushed the purchase price up from £17,000 to nearer £30,000, but the pay-off has been in the total reliability that Gilles has enjoyed ever since. Three-and-a-half years of trouble-free motoring is something that many new-car owners might envy.

It's still early days in the classic-versus-modern equation yet, however. Gilles reckons he'll have to keep his Jaguar for ten years to break even on the running costs of a leased BMW, and the chances of the Jag needing no major work in that time are slim indeed. The upside, of course, is that if he keeps the Mk2 up to scratch he'll come out on the far side with a valuable asset. To improve the odds – and because his insurance policy restricts him to 10,000km per year – the Jaguar is garaged from November to March; Belgian roads are salted just as aggressively as their counterparts in Britain.

One factor that Gilles hasn't included in his calculations is the Jaguar's fuel consumption. It drinks Super Unleaded at a rate of roughly 18 litres per 100km of city driving, 12 litres per 100km on the open road: that's about 15.5mpg and 23.5mpg, respectively, so the extra-urban figure is actually not too far adrift of what you'd expect from a modern luxury model.

Gilles' Jaguar may be a 3.4 rather than the more coveted 3.8 but that makes no odds; the classic rags usually bang on about the 3.8 having more torque but compared with modern, high-revving screamers the 3.4 still pulls like a train from just about any speed. 'That's why the Jaguar is so good in town,' says Gilles. 'You can just trickle along in third gear in traffic. The Moss gearbox is a bit heavy to manipulate but you get used to it.' ▶▶

Jaguar Mk2 3.4
SPECIFICATIONS

Built
1959-1967

Engine
3442cc in-line six, dohc,
twin SU HD6 carburettors

Max power
210bhp @ 5500rpm

Transmission
Four-speed manual,
optional overdrive,
rear-wheel drive

Brakes
Discs all round

Weight
1486kg (3726lb)

Value
Cost £1842 new in 1959
Value now £10,000-25,000

'Three-and-a-half years of trouble-free
motoring is something that many new-car
owners might envy'

'Imagine a pride of Mk2 Jaguars prowling the concrete-and-glass alleys of Brussels, bringing a touch of edgy rebellion to the very seat of bureaucracy'

Both car and driver keep their cool in Brussels jams, too: the Jaguar has been fitted with a re-cored radiator, Kenlowe electric fan and alternator, while Gilles reckons that driving an old motor has a positive effect on his own attitude – 'it calms you down and makes you more careful,' he explains. 'People are usually very enthusiastic when they see the car: often they'll come over for a chat when I'm parked up.'

(Our photographer, Matt, can vouch for the Jaguar's effectiveness as a pulling tool: sitting behind the Mk2 in the editorial BMW Z4M, feeling pretty comfortable at the wheel of a £45-grand roadster with the top down, he was chastened to see that a party of pretty female students waiting on the pavement gave their undivided attention to Gilles and his Jaguar, while totally ignoring the cool – and younger – guy in the sports car.)

It's not all wine and roses when you drive a Mk2 every day, however. 'Long trips are more fun for the driver than they are for the passengers,' admits Gilles. 'This summer, when the outside temperature reached 38 degrees, it got incredibly hot inside. I'm seriously thinking about having air conditioning installed. But the car is otherwise perfectly suited for long journeys. We go down to the South of France a lot for holidays, which can add up to more than 3000km of driving, and the rest of the time it's used every other weekend for jaunts to the seaside or into the Ardennes. My wife Chantal thought I was crazy to buy the car but now she loves it. She finds German cars very good but, well, rather boring.'

Wouldn't a 1960s Mercedes have provided just as much style with a greater guarantee of reliability, though?

'I did consider a Merc and even thought about an old Peugeot,' admits Gilles, 'but the Peugeot wasn't classy enough and I don't care much for '60s Mercedes, while the 1950s models are too expensive. And, of course, I'm a self-confessed Anglophile. My house is full of English furniture and I used to own an old Morgan 4/4. I drove that car all over Europe.'

Ah, so Gilles has an authentically masochistic streak, too. How very English...

That particular character trait hasn't been required for his time with the Jaguar so far. If he has any regrets, it's simply that the car's history is a complete blank. It was bought as a solid and original left-hooker by Bernard Marreyt but its previous life since 1964 is unknown.

According to Gilles, though, it will soon have some sibling companionship on the streets of Brussels. 'A friend of mine has just bought a Mk2 as his daily driver, and so has the boss of TNT in Belgium. They seem to be catching on.'

Imagine a pride of Mk2 Jaguars prowling the concrete-and-glass alleys of downtown Brussels, bringing a touch of edgy rebellion and individuality to the very seat of bureaucracy. It's enough to bring a tear to the eye of any red-blooded Englishman. Or Belgian. △

» Bernard Marreyt: +32 2 582 59 28, www.marreyt-classics.com

Above
Thorough preparation means that Gilles' Mk2 has no trouble keeping its cool in city traffic.

Tyres and Wheels for an XK Jaguar

As can be seen from the photograph below, even though the tyre options for your car all claim to be the same size they are obviously all very different. Which one you choose depends on the use you are going to give the car, from gentle touring to road rallies, racing to shows on Sundays......................

From left to right we have:
The Michelin Pilote X: with a very high speed rating (W), period appearance and correct diameter, the Pilote X is probably the best tyre available for the sporting driver!

The Vredestein: Popular among owners as Vredestein sponsor the XK race series! A suitable cheap option.

The Michelin X: With the benefit of being the first ever radial tyre in the world the Michelin X has the shape of a crossply and will keep your steering as light as a crossply while having the grip of a radial. At roughly the same price as the Vredestein the Michelin X is the best value period option.

The Avon Turbosteel: Prior to the inception of the Michelin Pilote X this was the best performing radial option, however it will lower your car slightly and may give heavy steering due to its wide footprint. Good value for the sporty driver!

The Avon Turbospeed: Possibly the best crossply tyre to fit to an XK with a more than suitable speed rating (H). A crossply tyre will give very light steering and a smooth comfortable ride, however by the very nature of its construction it will suffer from wandering on uneven roads.

The Pirelli Cinturato: The worlds first textile braced radial tyre (launched in 1951) is available once again. The Cinturato set new standards in tyre design in the fifties and is a fantastic option for the XK owner of today.

BORRANI WHEELS

The iconic Borrani wheel with its polished aluminium rim can now be supplied to fit all types of XK Jaguar, with varying offsets and widths available for race or road use. In period this was the ultimate upgrade for any car and as you can see they add the ultimate finishing touch to your pride and joy!

For more information regarding tyres or wheels please contact the boys at Longstone tyres on 01302 711 123 or visit www.longstonetyres.co.uk .

RUOTE BORRANI MILANO

Longstone CLASSIC TYRES

BORRANI WHEELS & CINTURATO TYRES--THE BEST PAWS FOR YOUR PUSSYCAT!

Pleasure rides

So you fancy an attractive classic to use on a regular basis? These sleeper
Jaguars – Series 2 E-type and XK140 – are the lesser-appreciated iterations
of supposedly more desirable models. Both offer greater driving pleasure

Words: Robert Coucher **Photography:** Ian Dawson

'The E-type Jaguar is simply the best sports car of the '60s. It is supremely fast and effortlessly comfortable. It handles superbly and is an absolute pleasure to drive. It remains one of the most beautiful cars ever conceived and, when you factor in the price, nothing else comes remotely close.'

So says the owner of this 1969 E-type Series 2. You would expect him to have a positive view about his Jaguar but the man has a wide canvas of motoring experience to draw upon. His classic car collection includes a superb Bizzarrini Strada, an immaculate Aston Martin DB4 Series 1, a concours Ferraro Lusso and a sharp TVR Grantura. From this impressive selection, all of which are 'on the button', the car Hugh James chooses to drive regularly is his E-type Series 2.

And that's the reason this get-together came about. We wanted to look at attractve classic cars that make for decent daily drivers. I suppose I should own up about the XK140 Fixed Head Coupé you see here, right now: it's mine. The plan was to end this piece with the flourish, 'I liked the XK so much, I bought it!' But regular readers will recognise MNJ 812 from the last two issues so I won't be disingenuous. I have recently spent months looking at purchasing an affordable and usable British sports car. The venerable E-type was on the short-list and I did drive a couple of lovely examples, but I ended up choosing an XK. Hugh James, on the ▶▶

Above
Editor Coucher
and E-type owner
Hugh James plot a
suitable Jaguar
test route.

other hand, chose the E-type Jaguar. So let's see where we agree to differ...

'I bought my first E-type in the early '60s when I was just 19 years old,' says Hugh. 'It was an old dog, having been the demonstrator for four garages, regularly crashed and patched up along the way. I paid £900 for the E and loved it. This 1969 Series 2 is my sixth E-type and is by far the best one I have owned. The early cars did not handle, they had poor brakes, they overheated and were generally underdeveloped. Over the years Jaguar really sorted the cars out, addressing the problems that were thrown up mostly by the American buyers who did not suffer the shoddy engineering quietly.'

Both of these Jaguars are the Cinderellas of their particular ranges. E-type aficionados wax lyrical about the early 3.8-litre flat-floor models with their outside bonnet catches. Well, yes, fine, as a study of purity of form. But an early Series 1 E-type, with all its inherent faults, is not a great driver. The later 4.2-litre series 1 E-types are much improved and very desirable, but the less elegant Series 2s, though rendered slightly ungainly by larger lights and bumpers (trust me, girls won't notice the difference), are in reality the best driver's cars. Especially when you factor into the equation that good examples command less than a third of the value of the earlier models.

In a similar way, the XK120 is the pure XK that everyone raves about. Certainly the 120, in Roadster or FHC form, has the most sublime shape, but is also the least practical XK, with its lousy

Burman recirculating ball steering, lack of effective engine cooling and just about enough room in the cabin for the diminutive Norman Dewis in his thin-soled loafers! The later 140, with more interior space, improved cooling and decent rack-and-pinion steering, had been effectively developed by the factory.

Jaguar continued to evolve the XK with the launch of the XK150 in 1957, a larger, heavier and more refined grand tourer. It did the same with the E-type Series 3 V12 in 1971.

So this XK140 and Series 2 E-type are similar in that they are both mid-model cars and have suffered in perceived value because of that. The good news is that they both benefit from Jaguar's ongoing engineering improvements, making them well sorted for the modern world. The better news is that they have not become the fatter and lazier versions that followed.

Looking more closely at Hugh James' E-type, restored some ten years ago, it is apparent that this is an immaculate car which can hardly be described as a mere daily driver. The XK, in comparison, while fully restored in 1991, is in rude good health but somewhat more patinated.

'The trouble with all E-types is that they rust,' says Hugh. 'The central monocoque tub rots in all the usual places like the floor and sills and the bulkhead. The heavy engine is bolted to the tub via an intricate spaceframe and this has to be rust-free to maintain torsional stiffness. In addition, the beautifully curved E-type bodywork is delicate, especially the huge bonnet. I can remember stories of drivers being decapitated when the bonnet

'The less elegant Series 2 E-types, though rendered slightly ungainly by larger lights and bumpers, are in reality the best driver's cars'

Above right
Engines are basically similar but the XK140 feels more vintage than the sophisticated E-type.

flew off because the hinges had rusted out. I urge all E-type buyers to have their cars very carefully inspected because they are very fast but also fragile. If the body structure is weakened in any area, they can be dangerous,' stresses Hugh.

In his quest for the near-perfect daily driver Hugh sourced his Series 2 from Santa Barbara, California. The Jaguar had had one careful owner from new, who drove it to the golf course and generally looked after it very well. This chap had also replaced the US-spec twin Stromberg carburettors with correct triple SUs to get the power back up to the claimed 265bhp from 246bhp.

Hugh shipped the E-tye back to his workshop and stripped it completely. As expected, the car was largely rust-free. A nut-and-bolt restoration included a change to right-hand drive and the fitment of a taller 2.7:1 differential. The engine was rebuilt to British specification and the maroon paintwork with tan hide was changed to British Racing Green and suede green interior. James left the side indicator lights in place for safety and added electronic ignition for instant starting in cold weather.

For ease of ownership and general driving, this Series 2 E-type is the best iteration. By 1969 the car's handling had been sorted out, and overheating banished by a larger bonnet opening which allows a staggering 68% more airflow, a water pump with 25% more capacity and sealed cooling system with twin electric fans. Effective Girling brakes replaced the early-spec Dunlops and the electrics are charged by a socking great alternator.

With a quick squint at the map, Hugh James points out a

favourite route through the South Downs and we head off in his E-type. Climbing into the coupé, the door aperture is small but the later seats are marvellously comfortable. Rear space is ample for weekend luggage through the large rear door. The interior is immaculate but does show signs of Jaguar's notorious penny-pinching. The dash is no way as attractive as the earlier models' and rather too much plastic is evident.

The engine fires at the twist of the ignition key, which replaced the charismatic starter button of old. First gear in the deft all-synchro 'box is high of ratio but the torquey engine has no problem with that. Within the first ten yards the steering is a revelation. Incredibly light and responsive, even though the car rolls on modern 205 tyres fitted to painted wires that are half an inch wider than standard. Through the Sussex lanes, the E-type is superb. It is hard to believe this is a classic of the '60s. The car is conducted via your fingertips, the clutch action is soft, the brakes are powerful, the ride pliant yet well-controlled. The E-type is quiet and refined and very, very fast. With the long gearing it whooshes along with intent: push the long-travel accelerator down to the carpet and it really gets up and goes, while the long bonnet can be aimed with precision thanks to the totally rebuilt and carefully set-up suspension.

From the driver's seat this is one of the most impressive E-types I have driven. And that's the irony. The Series 2 has been the unloved E-type for years while it is actually the best one to drive. Hugh James' example is in perfect condition and has cost

1969 E-type Series 2 FHC
SPECIFICATIONS

Engine
4235cc straight six, double overhead cams, triple SU carbs

Power
265bhp @ 5400rpm

Transmission
Four-speed manual, rear-wheel drive

Suspension
Front: independent via torsion bars and wishbones, anti-roll bar, telescopic dampers.
Rear: independent via lower wishbones with semi-axles as upper arms, four coil springs, telescopic dampers

Brakes
Discs all round

Performance
0-60mph 7.6sec
Top speed: 140mph

Weight
1250kg (2750lb)

Value
Cost new £2250.
Value now £8000,£15000 (unrestored); this example £30,000+

>>

Below
Equally at home in the country and The Smoke.

'The old fashioned design offers up more crossed-arm slides and general sideways demeanour at lower speeds than the E-type'

1955 XK140 SE FHC

SPECIFICATIONS

Engine
3442cc straight six, double overhead cams, twin 2in SU carburettors

Power
210bhp @ 5750rpm

Transmission
Four-speed manual with overdrive, rear-wheel drive

Suspension
Front: independent via torsion bars and wishbones, anti-roll bar, telescopic dampers. Rear: live axle, semi-elliptic leaf springs, telescopic dampers.

Brakes
Discs at front with servo (modification), rear drums

Performance
0-60mph 10sec
Top speed: 130mph

Weight
1409kg (3100lb)

Value
Cost new £1830.
Value now £18000,£34000 (unrestored); this example £32,000

him a good deal more than the market value. But that's irrelevant because he restored this E-type to use.

Climbing into the XK140 after the 'back to the future' E-type, you realise it really is a car of the 1950s. The interior, with its veneered dashboard and sprinkling of instruments and dusky aroma of patinated leather, is like an antique shop on wheels.

Being of more simple and robust separate chassis and body construction, the XK is a much simpler and more rugged car. The chassis is as strong as can be and is more easily restored than the E's complex tub and spaceframes. The vintage era continues with the XK and that can be good news...

The 140 fires with a flick of the key and a stab of the starter button. Nice. But from the off, goodness, the steering is heavy. As soon as you are rolling, it lightens up, freeing necessary muscle to swap cogs in the heavy Moss gearbox and to depress the clutch. The XK's smaller 3.4-litre engine produces a claimed 210bhp in this Special Equipment model, with its C-type cylinder head, and it needs to be revved more than the E's motor.

Through the lanes the XK is a different proposition to the E-type. It is more physically demanding of the driver, weighing some 3100lb versus the E-type's 2750lb. The feeling is vintage whereas the E feels amazingly modern. But I am a sucker for the XKs old charm. The lusty straight-six is smooth, with loads of torque, yet it is eager to rev thanks to larger-than-standard two-inch SUs. This XK has been subtly improved for everyday use and it shows. The aluminium radiator and large electric fan keep it cool, the BroadSport front disc brake conversion provides superbly powerful anchors, while the solid-mounted steering rack and thicker anti-roll bar render it responsive and planted. With its solid rear axle and wearing high-performance Blockley

crossply tyres all round, the old XK can be chucked about in the most rewarding manner.

The XK is no way as fast as the E through the Sussex lanes and the handling is distinctly old school slide 'n' oversteer as opposed to safe understeer. But, although it has a seprarate ladder chassis, the XK's ride is comfortable and it will hustle along the country lanes with unabashed enthusiasm. The old-fashioned design offers up more crossed-arm slides and general sideways demeanour at lower speeds than the more effective E-type, but the fun is attainable well within speed limits. The Moss 'box requires much more thought, with slow and deliberate upshifts and throttle blips on the downchanges. But getting the shifts right is very satisfying. Once out of the country lanes and other boring motorways, a flick of the overdrive switch morphs the XK into a remarkably effective long-legged mile-eater.

I offer Hugh James the driving seat but he declines. 'I like XKs and owned a 150 for a while. But I prefer the E-type, which is faster and much more modern.' He's absolutely right and the E is just the car for him.

For me, living in central London where the yummy mummies like to crunch-park their 4x4s, a fragile E-type would be a nightmare. The much tougher, big-bumpered, simpler XK is just the car I want to use in The Smoke, burbling down the Kings Road to the local deli, as well as on longer, faster drives through the lanes of Goodwood or Silverstone circuits. Because it is of more robust construction than the delicate E-type, I feel happier with a slightly patinated XK.

Hugh James is correct in his assertion: a Series 2 E-type is certainly the best '60s classic car to use as a regular driver. But I am happy with an alternative: the very '50s XK140.

THE E-TYPE, which was revealed to the public at Geneva in March 1961, was the kind of showstopper they don't make any more. It had everything: obvious descendance from the D-type whose glorious shape had added English allure to Le Mans-winning capability and a pedigree that supplied the shiny twin-cam engine and the disc brakes on all four wheels.

The E-type embodied all the technology but wore a body which subtly stretched the curves of its predecessor to create an ultimate phallus on wheels; that and three carburettors, three windscreen wipers and three-figure top speed. But although I didn't appreciate it at the time, almost of greater significance was that the E-type was not only real, it was available. No rarefied concept car to show what the company could do if it didn't have to compete and still make a profit, this showstopper was everyday usable using proven running gear from a volume manufacturer and offering all the necessary creature comforts.

And yet... it could be bought by anyone for about £2000. When a Cobra cost £2500 and a Ferrari nigh on double that, the Jaguar offered astonishing performance for a lot less money. There wasn't a schoolboy who didn't aspire to one.

A decade and a half would pass before this schoolboy fulfilled that particular dream and there were inevitably some revelations in store. Some of these were simply that cars of the 1960s didn't last as well as they do now and MoT failure when the tester's screwdriver found cornflakes where once was monocoque, was commonplace among the half dozen or so that passed through my hands. That and the smell of rotting carpets soaked by the water cascading into the evocative cockpit, the appetite for clutch plates, oil leaks, graunching subframe mounts, rattling exhausts, the crunchy synchro and whining first gear of the 3.8s, are all details I remember only too well.

I remember too the yellow glimmer of the headlights, the glow worm best that a Lucas sealed beam could then provide, refracted to uselessness by the crazed glass of the headlight fairings; this and the feeble brakes. No matter what you tried to make it better, the pedal always felt like a sponge and treading on it at three figure speeds only dipped that long nose by a few degrees then ≫

New for old

When a great design is tweaked with modern parts, is the result a better drive or a loss of period appeal? We compare an original Series 1 with a re-engineered Eagle E-type to find out

Words: Mark Hales Photography: Paul Harmer

U 888D

'A Jaguar engineer pointed out that none of the production cars was ever capable of 150mph, any more than the engine produced the claimed 265bhp'

faded to nothing by the time the speed reduced to legal proportions.

On the other hand, the E-type was one of the very few which really could send the needle way past 100mph with ease. When today's average 1.6-litre hatch will almost cruise at that rate, you forget what a white-knuckle event it was in 1975. I still frightened myself far too often in pursuit of the claimed 150mph. A retired Jaguar engineer pointed out that none of the production cars was ever capable of 150mph, any more than the engine produced the claimed 265bhp. But, for me it hardly mattered because in 1975, the six-cylinder E-type still had one supreme attribute: they were plentiful and could be had for a few hundred pounds – I bought a reasonably sound flat-floor 3.8 with a glassfibre bonnet for £250. The same car 15 years down the road, and you still couldn't go faster for the money.

I've driven a few race E-types in the meantime but until recently, hadn't sampled another road version until I caught up with the 1966 4.2 litre example on sale at Eagle E-type's Sussex emporium down near Uckfield. This was a rare item indeed in that it was almost

completely original apart from renewal of its Golden Sand paintwork. A good test for the memory banks then. Also interesting would be a chance to try one of Eagle's modified models. There is a huge range of options available but Eagle proprietor Henry Pearman insists that his obsessive intention has been to keep the true spirit of the original while attending to the weak spots. We would see.

The basis of an E-type, which would remain constant throughout its existence, is a monocoque tub, similar to the D-type's and similarly stiffened by its big sills. A subframe of square tubes is bolted to the front and mounts a long tall engine, which fills a long wide bonnet. Double wishbone front suspension is sprung by torsion bars which feed the loads back to the central tub rather than the front frame, while at the rear, the D's beam axle had been replaced by an independent set up featuring a subframe which mounted a central Salisbury differential with inboard disc brakes, a large bottom wishbone and a driveshaft that doubled as a top link. This (the radius rods at the back and the steering rack at the front) was mounted with rubber bushes, in line with Jaguar's

stated aim of refinement throughout the range. Grace, Pace, Space was the company motto.

There is no doubt that by 1966, the 4.2-litre E-type had registered some improvements over the original. The 'flat floor' of legend soon gained a recess to accommodate the heels of normal sized feet and the outside catches for the curvaceous bonnet had moved to the A-posts. The brakes had been improved (gone was the vacuum-operated set of bellows which added mechanical pressure to the pedal), the engine had grown by 400cc (a longer stroke gave it more torque although there was no claim of extra power) and the grating Moss gearbox with its huge long-throw shift had been replaced by a four-speed Jaguar item with synchromesh on first (extremely rare) and a shift action that felt slick for 1966. Some things, though, hadn't changed...

There was the wraparound screen with its nonexistent surround, and the skinny wire wheels which might just have worn radials (but probably had a set of crossply Dunlops) and which sit well inside the car's track to add to the priapic ambiance, the steeply upswept rump with the ❯❯

'The big six is up and running including ticking from the tappets and signature hiss from the triple Skinner's Union carburettors'

twin exhausts curving in symmetry to show the bulbs of twin motorcycle-style chromed silencers – additions because there wasn't room underneath for full size ones. The tiny, steeply curved doors, which never, ever shut first time unless you roll the window down and spread a hand outside, open to reveal the curving leather-clad sills with their internal bulkheads – features borrowed from the D-type to help stiffen the tub.

The spongy seat is old armchair comfortable (until you need some support when cornering) but ramps far enough back to stretch the legs almost flat. Ahead, those huge twin dials with their long needles sit to the right of the hinge-forward instrument panel with its line of smaller but still bold gauges above the row of identical switches with flat plastic blades. Then there's the lawnmower choke lever emblazoned with the instructions cold/hot/run, the useless chromed handbrake laying flat along the fading red leather of the transmission tunnel and the thin wood-clad rim of the wheel with the big knurled plastic collar that twists to allow adjustment for reach – another rarity. It is so memorable because

it was so distinctive even at the time. Only Jaguars looked like Jaguars.

There's the signature ring and clatter of the starter, no more than a couple of turns before the big six is up and running, complete with ticking from the tappets and signature hiss from the triple Skinner's Union variable-choke carburettors. Prod the long, pendant accelerator and the engine rocks the car while a gruff flatulence accompanies from behind. That makes the whole thing feel alive and it's hard not to keep doing it while you warm up the engine. Then the deliberately heavy gearknob adds inertia to overcome the synchros (and keeps the linkage quiet) before you hear the signature clonk and click as the wire wheels settle on the drive splines while the drive takes up. First gear moans gently as you ease away then before you have gone barely half a mile you sense the springy feel of the wheel, which together with the thin rim is another E-type characteristic. Like the Ferrari gearshift, it's a detail, which so defines the car that it deserves a bit of consideration.

It's hard to promote a spongy rack as a feature so perhaps it's better described as

being like a rudder on a boat or aeroplane. You apply pressure and it applies pressure back, which fades as the car answers the command, a slight delay which in this case means the messages coming back to your fingertips arrive about the same time as those reaching the seat. Together, they create an involving experience that you won't encounter in many cars made after 1980. Part of it is due to the Jaguar's lack of power steering and squashy rubber rack mounts (lift the bonnet and you can see the whole thing move away from your steering input) and these are usually one of the first things that go in the bin when updating the car. But when it was designed, the E-type would have worn a set of tall crossplies and, unless you have ever driven on them, it's hard to imagine how sharp they make the steering and how much kickback they transmit to the wheel. Jaguar designers would have wanted to soften this (and reduce the rattles it shows up), so rubber mounting the rack was a pragmatic solution.

Modern engineers use power steering to filter out any kickback and resort to all manner of geometric tricks to make radials point the car but they will often introduce »

Above
Just as it came out of the factory, albeit on radials not crossplies, and superb with it.

'The E-type would have worn a set of tall crossplies and unless you have ever driven on them it's hard to imagine how sharp they make the steering'

Left
Armchair comfort, huge twin dials, hinge-forward instrument panel, bold switches, wood-clad wheelrim and useless handbrake.

'The red sector is between five and six, but by 3500 or 4000rpm the punch has all but faded and you might as well snick that short-throw shift towards the next gear'

a twisting blade to the column, just to soften the front end's initial response and stop the car frightening non-enthusiast drivers. Whether Jaguar engineers created the E-type's steering feel by accident or design then is hard to say, but for me it is something to be savoured. Even if the crossplies have been replaced on this car by period Michelin radials, there's still enough of that gentle tugging against a reassuring bit of lock and enough kick over ruts and ridges to make the car feel deliciously tactile.

It's quick too, but not perhaps in the way you'd expect. Pearman reckons his is particularly sharp but he's right when he says the real muscle is in the mid-range. The red sector is between five and six, but by 4000rpm the punch has all but faded and you might as well snick that short-throw shift towards the next gear. From third to fourth will have you deep into camera profit zone and here the Jaguar does begin to feel less composed. The air is by then lifting that long bonnet and there's a touch of vagueness, especially

over crests where you also begin to notice the rubber mountings at the rear. It's not so much that the car suddenly falls apart at high speed, rather that it becomes less tolerant of sloppy handling.

It's the consistency of balance, though, which together with the smooth muscular engine and the talkative steering makes the car such a pleasure to drive. A bit of reassuring push on the way in, followed by a slight touch of tail-out oversteer right on the corner's exit is just as it should be and the only real thing to watch is savage control input, especially at lower speeds – like backing off suddenly in a roundabout. The rear end lifts, the rubber mounts for the subframe and trailing arms are less effective in tension than compression, the rear end loses its prescribed geometry and combined with a weight shift towards the front, slings the tail. It's easy to avoid and an E-type in original condition is still a wonderful thing to thread along the road. Nearly 40 years on, it's still a practical means of transport. Although the team at Jaguar may not have realised it, what they

created was already some way ahead of its time. In which case, how would Eagle set about improving this without spoiling this latterday-innocent tactile charm?

On offer was one of the company's better-than-new examples which had covered some 21,000 miles. Looking immaculate, it is hard to imagine that most of these miles had been racked up on long and hard historic rallies. While you might suspect the car had been rebuilt, there's not much to indicate it had been modified. Obvious giveaways are the subtly wider wheels and slightly lower set to the suspension, but other than that you'd have to lift the bonnet to see much more.

You wouldn't suspect either that four years ago, a worn out donor car was dismantled to its minutest parts and the body remade using new original pattern steel wherever possible. Extra gussets were installed where cracks are known to appear in the frames, drainage and sealing for doors and panels was improved, more efficient radiator and fans installed and

Jaguar E-type
SPECIFICATIONS

Engine
4235cc in-line six. Double overhead cams, two valves per cylinder. Three 2" choke SU carburettors.

Power
265bhp @ 5500rpm

Torque
283lb ft @ 4000rpm

Transmission
Four-speed all-synchromesh manual gearbox, limited-slip differential

Suspension
Front: double wishbones, longitudinal torsion bars, telescopic dampers. Rear: double wishbones, two coil spring damper units per side

Brakes
Discs front and rear

Weight
2750lb (1247kg)

Performance
0-60mph 6.5 secs, top speed 150mph (claimed)

Cost/value
£1830 (roadster), £1954 (coupé); value now £20-60,000 according to condition

»

Right
Changes to the Eagle E-type are not easy to spot: the smaller diameter, thicker steering wheel is one, though.

'The engine is much more powerful than the original; both in pull from down low but while the father begins to feel breathless by 4000, the son is still pulling hard beyond 5000'

Eagle E-type
SPECIFICATIONS

Engine
4235cc in-line six. Double overhead cams, two valves per cylinder. Three 2" choke SU carburettors.

Power
288bhp @ 5650rpm

Torque
287lb ft @ 4100rpm

Transmission
Five-speed all-synchromesh manual gearbox, limited-slip differential

Suspension
Front: double wishbones, longitudinal torsion bars, telescopic dampers. Rear: double wishbones, two coil spring damper units per side

Brakes
Eagle specifieds AP disc brakes

Weight
2750lb (1247kg)

Performance
0-60mph 5 secs, top speed 160mph (estimated)

Cost/value
Cost of completely rebuilt car plus modifications: around £125,000 depending on specification

so on – all the logical kind of things Jaguar might have done had they continued to make the model.

This owner had opted for an uprated engine (280bhp, still with the three SU carburettors but with mapped ignition), the five-speed gearbox which Eagle has developed in-house, bigger brakes and the lower, stiffer suspension set up.

There's no difference in the way the engine starts, but once warm it picks up more quickly. It doesn't rock the car, which is more stiffly sprung. Once on the move, you notice the steering is more direct, while the gearshift feels as nice and slick as the original.

After a mile or two the car changes. The engine is more powerful than the original but unobtrusively so; both will pull from way down low but while the father begins to feel breathless by four thousand, the son is still pulling beyond five. That encourages you to use a lower set of intermediate ratios and shuttle between third and fourth to nip past something, then slot an overdriven fifth to cruise. It's a much more modern style of progress.

Meanwhile, the chassis doesn't float like the original. This is much more modern and sharper in its responses. Part is due to the 6½in rims and good Pirelli radials, but the lower suspension and revised camber help to point the car with authority, after which the stiffer torsion bars prop it up and stop the front leaning, then the firmer dampers keep it pinned until the corner is done. Meanwhile, the lack of rubber bushing ensures that every bump and ribbet in the road sends a clear message to a smaller diameter, thicker wheelrim. There's a great deal more grip through the corner although the steering is heavier, but complete confidence in the front and the absence of the boat-on-a-swell sensation, makes for a car which does everything with firmer purpose.

Ease beyond the legal limit and you see it's superbly stable, partly because the suspension is tighter but also because the subtle lip added beneath that sharky snout helps keep out the air from underneath so banishing lift. And when the time comes to haul it back to

suburban speeds, the brakes prove to be authoritative: nice and firm at the pedal and with plenty of bite, which doesn't fade away like the original's. It's another vital part of the up-to-date driving experience.

The Eagle is a seriously competent high-performance machine. This example has been set up to compete at the sharp end of historic rallies so some of the original E-type's softness has been dialled out. At normal speed the Eagle jiggles over bumps like a modern Porsche and the front end follows white lines which the original doesn't. But that's the compromise you expect for fast road work.

There is something about being transported back to 1966 that requires you to maintain a 1966 pace of life. For those who want more, there is definitely something about blasting a car that looks as if it was made in 1966 through an Alpine pass at the pace of a modern GT. You'll be safe in the knowledge that this Eagle E-type will make fewer demands on your car control and won't run out of brakes. △

Science Class

'The windscreen was fairly vertical, so we pushed
the base of the screen right to the rear of the bonnet
line and the angle was then quite different'

Right
Fuel-injected engine developed by Klat and Watson gave 348bhp – slightly more than Jaguar managed.

'Klat had modified the cams within the fuel injection system with soft solder to change their profiles; by smelling the exhaust he got the mixture right'

Jaguar low-drag E-type

SPECIFICATIONS

Engine
All-alloy 3781cc 6-cylinder twin-overhead cam XK engine with Lucas mechanical fuel injection

Power
340bhp at 6500rpm (est)

Torque
350 lb ft (est)

Transmission
Jaguar 4-speed close-ratio all-synchro 'box

Suspension
Independent front suspension, upper and lower wishbones, torsion bar springs.
Fully independent rear incorporating, on each side, a lower transverse tubular link, radius arms and twin coil springs per side

Brakes
Dunlop disc brakes. Jaguar MkIX calipers. Special Dunlop aluminium piston blocks

Performance
0-100mph 12 secs. Top speed 170mph (depends on gearing). Standing 1/4 mile 12.8 secs

Value
£1,000,000-plus

In fact, in the paddock, Klat had modified the cams within the PI system with soft solder to change their profiles. By smelling the exhaust, he got the mixture right and cured the problem.

At Le Mans that year, Lumsden and Sargent were lying 14th after four hours and headed, in the GT class, by just two of the four Cobras and two of the four GTOs. The gallant British privateers gained another couple of places before having to retire with a failed gearbox.

This was the car's last international outing. Lumsden continued to race in the UK for a year and then the car passed through a number of hands before ending up in the States. Several years ago, it was bought by Sir Anthony Bamford and recently it was acquired by Lord Cowdray, joining the ex-Protheroe Low Drag Coupé CUT 7, which he also owns.

Cowdray campaigns CUT 7 on serious European events, such as the Tour Auto, and intends to use the Lumsden/Sargent car for these and to race it at invitation events such as the Goodwood Revival.

'A couple of the tours I do are back-to-back,' explains Cowdray, 'and if I have a bit of a problem with one then I've got a back-up car. I thought, why get something different? This is what I like.'

At the time Cowdray had not been able to drive his new purchase in anger – but his co-driver Rupert Chevely had.

'It is different to CUT 7. In the wet CUT 7 probably wouldn't be much slower but in the dry this car is much more rigid. It's a real racing car whereas CUT 7 doesn't have that same feel.'

This very special car benefited from the far-sighted approach of Peter Lumsden and Peter Sargent, and the ground-breaking input of Samir Klat. He was one of the first of a new breed who brought a more scientific engineering attitude to motor racing and 49 FXN was the beneficiary. Technically it is a very important machine but that's not the only reason it's so special.

Peter Sargent sums it up. 'I think it's the most beautiful E-type anywhere,' he says simply.

» Many thanks to Goodwood Motor Circuit, www.goodwood.co.uk. Thanks also to Lord Cowdray, Chris Keith-Lucas and Christopher Darwin – see www.gwtr.co.uk for details of his track days for older cars.

THE EXTRA E-TYPE

This V12 E-type is made from 100 percent genuine factory parts – but Jaguar didn't put them together, an enthusiast did, 31 years after factory production ended

Words: Nigel Thorley **Photography:** John Colley

The Jaguar E-type was the epitome of the British sports car, an icon of the 1960s that is still instantly recognisable today. It enjoyed a 13-year production run, during which 72,529 were sold – or could it now be 72,530?

Ray Parrott, a member of the Jaguar Enthusiasts Club and a Jaguar fanatic, knows all about E-types. He has five of them: a 3.8-litre Roadster, a Series 2 fixed-head Coupé, a replica Lightweight and now two V12 Roadsters. An avid Jaguar devotee from an early age, he's owned 25 models in 17 years but he isn't completely obsessive – he now has a Sunbeam Tiger, BMW 850 Alpina and a rally DB6, to complement the everyday Jaguar XKR and XJ6.

Ray is a self-taught engineer and has developed a significant number of skills in every aspect of vehicle restoration over the years. Now that he has set himself up with all the equipment and facilities needed to do most of the work on his cars, all his E-types get the 'Parrott touch' and have been adapted and improved for today's driving conditions. They are always kept in pristine condition and in regular use.

Ray's passion for what he terms 'the ultimate classic car' was further fuelled about two years ago when he was contacted by Mike Wilkinson of M&C Wilkinson Jaguar Spares, a Yorkshire-based Jaguar parts business of which Ray was a regular customer. Through his many contacts, Mike Wilkinson had been able to acquire a cache of original E-type parts. They turned out to be highly significant.

Below
Series 3 E-type is one of the few roadsters that arguably looks better wearing its hardtop – especially when painted black.

Back in 1974, when the final E-type left the Browns Lane assembly line, all the remaining parts were sold off to one gentleman who kept them in storage with the hope of using them for his own needs. He had several lorry loads of parts, all new and in their original packaging, which included significant items such as a complete Roadster bodyshell, an unused V12 engine and gearbox, a rear axle and all those little fixtures and fittings that go to make up a complete car. Eventually, due to age, the gentleman concerned sold the lot to Mike Wilkinson, who immediately thought of Ray because of his enthusiasm for all things E-type. What better person to benefit from some of these rare finds?

Discussions followed and it became clear after viewing a hastily compiled list of all the parts that it just might be possible to create a new E-type from them. Ray and Mike made a detailed appraisal during Ray's numerous visits to Mike's premises in Yorkshire.

The amazing thing was that, although some parts were inevitably duplicated, there was sufficient of most things to actually build a complete Series 3 Roadster. Apart from the bodyshell, which had only suffered a few minor dents and surface rust, there were several made-up assemblies ready for installation, like the complete instrument panel with wiring and the radiator with all its connections, electric fans and cowls. These assemblies had been made up at Jaguar for despatch to the assembly line, and were ready to fit to a car. »

'RAY PARROTT KNOWS ALL ABOUT E-TYPES. HE HAS FIVE OF THEM. HE'S OWNED 25 JAGUARS IN 17 YEARS – BUT HE ISN'T COMPLETELY OBSESSIVE'

'IT BECAME CLEAR AFTER VIEWING
A HASTILY COMPILED LIST OF ALL THE
PARTS THAT IT JUST MIGHT BE POSSIBLE TO
CONSTRUCT A NEW E-TYPE FROM THEM'

THE PROJECT

Do-it-yourself E-type
Ray Parrott found he had 95 percent
of the parts he needed – and some
he didn't, such as 1974 tins of oil.

One man's workshop
Over the years, Ray has built up an
impressive workshop to repair and
modify his classic Jaguars.

Back to black
E-type shell was painted white when
uncovered, but was resprayed black
to match other 'last of line' V12s.

The test run
Ray's meticulous assembly of all-
original parts resulted in an E-type
that drives literally like a new car.

> 'THE HERITAGE VOLUNTEERS
> ~ ARE THE ONLY PEOPLE
> WHO REMEMBER HOW
> THE XJ13 WENT TOGETHER
> ORIGINALLY. THERE'S NO
> SHOP MANUAL FOR THIS CAR'

the wall has been bricked up?' he's saying. 'That's where the exhausts used to come out. You can imagine the noise.'

Inside the run-down building of cheap red brick, you can see how the space was once divided into sections. Each one was an engine test cell, and no more than a few paces away all kinds of competition cars would be built. Gary can almost see the ghosts, and one of them looks like the Jaguar XJ13.

Experimental Jaguar 13, built in 1966 and first run in 1967, was meant to be the sports-racer to take on GT40s and Ferrari P4s. The mid-engined, V12-powered, 502bhp XJ13 would take up the racing-green baton where the D-type left off a decade earlier, and bring glory back to Britain. That never happened, not least because the FIA changed the prototype rules for 1968 and the XJ13's engine was considerably bigger than the new three-litre limit. All that effort, all that hope and expense, for nothing, except that it did result in one of the most beautiful racing cars ever built.

Maybe that unlucky number was the reason. Maybe an XJ14 would have won Le Mans and history would have been different. Who can tell?

THE PAST IS still the present. Next door to the *Marie Celeste*-like emissions lab is where Jaguar's Heritage cars live and are maintained when they're not on display.

Gary has just helped to dismantle that most mysterious and valuable of all the old Jags, the one that I am going to help resurrect. The XJ13 is being dismembered that it may live again, and the old guard is back. They're Heritage volunteers now, and they're the only people who remember exactly how the XJ13 went together originally. There's no workshop manual for this one-off car. It's all in their heads.

But why do it now? The history of the XJ13 is the stuff of Jaguar legend, and ill fortune has been the recurrent theme. After its racing plans were kyboshed, the XJ13 went into hiding until the production version of Jaguar's V12, of which

the XJ13's unit was the precursor, was about to be launched in the E-type and the XJ12 saloon. So in 1971 the XJ13 was dusted off and taken to MIRA, the Motor Industry Research Association's banked test track near Hinckley, for some filming.

Veteran test driver Norman Dewis was doing the driving, and near the end of the day he went for a final rapid run on the banking. The authorised version has it that the right-hand rear wheel collapsed, instantly pitching the Jaguar down the banking and into the infield, where it dug in, flipped end-over-end twice, rolled twice and finally stopped the right way up, a quick-thinking, miraculously undamaged and fortunately compact Dewis cowering under the dashboard. Strangely, though, there are photographs showing the wrecked XJ sitting with all four wheels seemingly intact. What really happened has gone fuzzy in the mist of history...

In 1973, the XJ13 was comprehensively rebuilt with nearly every panel re-made and replaced. It made occasional public appearances and at one event its engine was terminally over-revved. The other surviving engine was pressed into service but one of its pistons had been welded, which inhibited maximum-effort use. And so the XJ13 continued in its low-key way, until two years ago when two wheels fell off a high kerb in Copenhagen during unloading. The kerb hit the sump, gouging the steel sump pan, cracking the aluminium casting above it and breaking a stud. That was that, then. No more running, and the XJ13 was relegated to static display only. **»**

'My task today is to help with the final reassembly.
The engine and gearbox have been reunited with the tub and my jobs
include getting the gear linkage to work properly'

Right
XJ13 is wheeled into daylight for the first time since its rebuild, prior to ritual badge fixing, below.

'WE'VE BEEN waiting to get our hands on it for the last two years,' says Richard Mason, chief Heritage spannerman. I'm at Browns Lane, it's the end of March, and before me is half an XJ13. It terminates shortly after the cockpit, and the rear suspension, ZF transmission and subframe are sitting as a unit some distance away. The missing structural element is the engine, vital to the rear end's integrity and now over at Jaguar's Whitley design and engineering centre.

The dismembered XJ13 looks tidy and pleasingly patinated, but the paint is dull and scuffed and there's a general air of tiredness. The big task for the recommissioning is to bring the engine back to race-ready health, even though the XJ is hardly likely to be raced. It just needs to live at speed once again, to recall those heady days when David Hobbs and the XJ13 set a new UK circuit lap record of 161.6mph at the tricky MIRA track with its three flipped-up banked corners. The second-biggest task is to repair and refinish the body.

Otherwise it's just a thorough clean and check of everything else. Just. Oh, and some new tyres would be good. And it all has to be ready for a parade at Le Mans that June.

Three weeks later, Richard and I meet again to catch up on progress. We're off to Chesman Engineering in Coventry, where the XJ13's heads have been lightly skimmed and the ports cleaned up. Starting and stopping the engine over the

> 'I PEEL OFF FROM ITS BACKING A BRAND-NEW STICK-ON JAGUAR BADGE, CONFIRM THE CENTRE LINE, THEN ATTACH ADHESIVE TO METAL. THE XJ13 IS FINISHED'

years, without giving it time to warm up, has caused corrosion from condensation and the head gaskets have been weeping. Chesman will also machine some new camshaft bearings.

The heads are quite unlike later production V12 heads, most obviously because they have twin instead of single camshafts and the inlet ports sit between the cams, as they do on a Lamborghini V12. There are still two valves per cylinder but the combustion chamber is hemispherical in typical race-engine (and XK-engine) fashion.

Next stop Whitley and the engine development department, where the heads are delivered to the eagerly waiting Graham Hughes and Paul Harris. The rest of the engine is laid out on benches, apart from the block which is mounted on a stand next to the other XJ13 engine. That one, long presumed vanished but eventually found, has a chunk missing from a head and a very battered cam lobe, the result of that over-revving. It will

donate its steel 'sump' – actually merely a bottom cover plate because this is a dry-sump engine – to the rebuilt engine, and the Whitley boys will weld and re-machine the aluminium casting above it that had the crack and the broken stud.

Both engines' builds were recorded when new on detailed data sheets. Which engine was used during Hobbs' 1967 record run and Dewis's crash isn't known, but the engine being rebuilt now is definitely the better basis for a resurrected XJ13. Its con-rods are beautifully polished, for example, and everything seems machined a little more lovingly.

Time now to look more deeply at what makes this Claude Baily-designed engine what it is. Jaguar made seven prototype four-cam V12s (this one is number seven), one of which was used in a MkX test mule, but just the two XJ13 engines used gear drive for the camshafts – four straight-cut gears per bank, the first in each geartrain driven ➤➤

'Feel that V12 sing as it hasn't sung in years; try to imagine what it would have been like to race the XJ13 at Le Mans, had rules not killed the dream'

JAGUAR XJ13

SPECIFICATIONS

Engine
4994cc all-alloy V12, quad-ohc, two valves per cylinder, Lucas fuel injection, dry sump

Power
502bhp @ 7600rpm

Torque
386lb ft @ 6300rpm

Transmission
ZF five-speed manual transaxle, four-wheel drive

Suspension
Front: double wishbones, coil springs, anti-roll bar. Rear: double wishbones using driveshaft as upper lateral link, coil springs, anti-roll bar

Brakes
Ventilated discs front and rear

Weight
1125kg (2478lb)

Performance
175mph on gearing as tested

Right and facing page
Simister sets off on a cautious tour of the Browns Lane access roads, before a proper high-speed run at MIRA.

by chain from the crankshaft, mesh adjusted by moving an eccentric idler shaft. Also gear-driven is the scavenge pump in the sump; it and the pressure pump have a massive six gallons of oil to pump between them.

The block is similar to those of later production V12s apart from its smaller bore (87mm instead of 90mm). The stroke is the same short 70mm, resulting in a 4994cc capacity. Lucas mechanical injection squirts fuel straight into the intake trumpets, outboard of the throttle butterflies in typical racing practice. The distributor uses Lucas Opus electronic ignition and has the biggest cap I've ever seen.

Surprisingly, the aluminium castings exposed to the outside air have been painted in aluminium paint. It looks garish, but I'm told it quickly tones down once the engine gets hot – and that's how the engine was finished originally. As for gaskets, potentially a problem in a near-unique engine, Federal Mogul (which nowadays owns the Payen gasket name) has offered to make new major gaskets using the original dies that have miraculously been found. Paul and Graham will cut out the minor gaskets themselves.

Now, it's off to the Coventry Boring and Metalling Company with all 12 pistons. This fantastically useful machine shop already has the crankshaft, whose crankpins have been machined by 20 thou' to take new big-end bearings. CBMC will machine the ring grooves in the pistons to take new, wider rings. And good news: X-ray analysis has shown that the repaired piston is perfectly fit for maximum-effort use and it won't be necessary to make a new one. (The pistons in the other engine are of a different 'grade' and so are fractionally different in size.)

MEANWHILE, the front half of the XJ13 and its rear body panels are at XK Engineering, a short distance north-east of Coventry. Prime mover Graham Hall once worked on Jaguar's E-type lines and subsequently branched out into XK and E-type restoration. Nowadays the bread and butter comes from building Range Rover Autobiography special editions, but Graham is thrilled to have the XJ13 in his emporium.

'We're painting it in two-pack because it's durable and keeps its gloss,' he's saying. 'We've matched the colour with a spectrometer.' The panels aren't all stripped to bare metal – it's difficult going round all the rivets and there's the danger of stripper residue damaging the paint in later years – but sound paint is flatted back and re-primed. 'Yes, even around all those louvres...'

The last part to get its coats of dark green is the main rear body section, in the spray booth as we talk. The other parts, newly resplendent in their dark gloss, look fantastic.

IT'S EARLY JUNE and all the pieces are back at Browns Lane. The engine has gone together perfectly, with valves re-lapped and everything else found to be in excellent condition. AP Racing has rebuilt the twin-plate Borg & Beck clutch, the gearbox has been cleaned and flushed out and its oil pump – actually a standard SU electric fuel pump – has been brought back to life.

What else? Brake and clutch hydraulics stripped and cleaned, all seals re-usable. All rubber bushes found serviceable, all joints greased as needed. All oil and water pipes – they run through the cockpit – removed and flushed through, then refitted with new hoses. Sill end plates removed to inspect the fuel tanks – just the right-hand one is used now. Injector pump and alternator drive belts replaced. Pump flushed and bled, alternator and starter checked and cleaned. Wiring checked all over. A thorough recommissioning, in other words.

My task today is to help with the final reassembly. The engine and rear suspension have

been reunited with the tub and my jobs are to bleed the clutch, to get the gear linkage to work properly, to fit the covers over the differential and the exhaust manifolds and to wire in a rev-limiter. Then in with a new pair of batteries, wired in parallel for the normal 12 volts but ample amps.

And now, easy does it, it's on with that curvaceous, fragile and unwieldy rear body section. Mind the new paint, engage the pegs, lock the side sections to the sills with wire rods like the shaft in a piano lid's hinge. The side louvre panels go on next – they guard the engine's air supply – and we're done. Except for one thing. I peel off from its backing a brand new stick-on Jaguar badge for the nose, confirm the centre line, move the badge back and forth until we achieve aesthetic consensus, then attach adhesive to metal. The XJ13 is finished.

WHEN I WAS LOOKING to buy my house, I saw in a bedroom a grey-painted scale model of a familiar shape; it was the XJ13 wind-tunnel model, because the owners of the house were related to aerodynamicist Malcolm Sayer. I never thought then that I would drive the real thing, but that's what is about to happen...

Richard Mason has warmed it up, checked that everything is working as it should. Now it's my turn to trundle the XJ13 up and down the Browns Lane access roads. Just it and me, now, in real time, past made present once again.

I climb over the bare aluminium sill, pull the featherweight door shut, settle into the minimalist bucket seat behind a woodrim steering wheel and one of two Abbey Panels plaques (the company both built the body and rebuilt it in 1973). The cabin has been left as it was, four decades-worth of patinated functionality, and it's cosy in here. Pretty hot, in fact: a pair of oil pipes run above two water pipes right next to what passes for a passenger seat, and they're radiating a lot of surplus heat energy.

Ignition on, by toggle switch. Fuel pump on, ditto, accompanied by a loud whirr. Push the ignition switch further down against a spring, hear the constant-note churning of a hefty starter against 12 hefty compressions, and 502bhp of impatient V12 erupts into busy, gear-whirring, cam-chattering life. The exhausts are loud and sound angry but the V12 is ticking over as if plucked straight from a production car.

> 'THE CABIN HAS BEEN LEFT AS IT WAS, FOUR DECADES-WORTH OF PATINATED FUNCTIONALITY, AND IT'S COSY IN HERE. PRETTY HOT, IN FACT'

Above left

V12 is one of seven prototype four-cam engines and one of only two built to XJ13 spec, with gear-driven cams.

Above
Malcolm Sayer's aerodynamic shape is still gorgeous, 40 years on.

'THE XJ13'S EAGERNESS IS INFECTIOUS. THE HARD-EDGED BELLOW IS INTOXICATING AS I PASS 5000RPM WITH THE ACCELERATOR PRESSED DOWN AS HARD AS I DARE'

I've heard past stories of a heavy clutch and a cantankerous gearshift, but the clutch rebuild has fixed everything. It must have been a clutch-drag problem before, because now the tiny, right-hand gear lever finds gears easily as long as you don't move it out of sequence. And you nearly always have to select second before you can have first; it's a deliberate lock-out system.

Good grief, this is a torquey engine. It's still tight and we shouldn't venture beyond 4000rpm, but the smallest throttle-squirt hurls the XJ13 forward. The Experimental Jaguar lives again.

IT DIDN'T MAKE the Le Mans 24 Hours parade. The Heritage people ran out of time. But the XJ13 did make the Le Mans Classic three weeks later, after a 67-mile shakedown run at MIRA which uncovered one oil leak and a balance problem with the new Dunlop tyres. At Le Mans it ran faultlessly and fast.

And now we're at MIRA again, for a proper drive in an unfettered space. Now run-in, although

Richard asks that I don't go over 5500rpm (peak power arrives at 7600), the XJ13 is fully and finally the racing car reincarnated. The new paintwork even has smoke-marks around the exhaust pipes.

First, some gentle runs on the banking where disaster struck in 1971. It doesn't like small throttle openings, hunting and fretting impatiently, but further pressure unleashes huge energy and I back off immediately.

But after Richard has taken me for a rapid blast around the banked track, breaking his self-imposed rev limit because the engine is running so well and sending the most fabulous sound waves searing across Warwickshire, I get another go. This time it's on the Dunlop handling circuit in the infield, and there's a distinct impression that it's all right for me to exercise the XJ a little.

Can this be real? I'm in this unique racing car, for which Jaguar was once offered £7.5m and which has just had an expensive restoration so it can be used and enjoyed in the future. If I do something daft there won't be a future? But

the XJ13's eagerness is infectious. Its breadth of torque is breathtaking, the hard-edged bellow from intake trumpets and four lots of three-into-one exhausts is intoxicating as I pass 5000rpm with the accelerator pressed as hard as I dare.

Snick-up, blip-snick-down, aim for a corner, feel the light nose bite on those surprisingly squidgy Dunlops (they run at under 20psi), feel the instant turn-in and tail-loading typical of a mid-engined car designed for handling-literate drivers. I just know that a burst of power now would bring on a delicious drift, but there's too much at stake here and many eyes are watching.

So back on the straight, feel that V12 sing, try to imagine what it would have been like to race the XJ13 at Le Mans. What would it have looked like in race trim? Would it have sprouted spoilers and scoops, sullying the shape so it could stay on the road at 200mph? We'll never know. But I've just driven it further, faster and for longer than any other motoring writer in history. And gentlemen, it's been a privilege. △

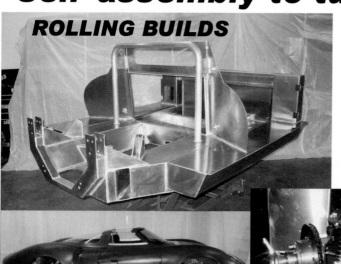

There's still a stigma attached to Jaguar's 200mph supercar but is that fair? **John Simister**, who was in on the XJ220 from the early days, finds that clever mods and a solid market are transforming its fortunes

Photography: John Colley

People can be very cruel towards fallen idols. There's glee to be gained from hubris, even when the pre-fall status was not gained by self-aggrandisement.

Hurrah! we all cheered, when Jaguar revealed its XJ220 supercar. Wow! we all exclaimed, as deposits were placed and late-'80s fortunes were poised to be made as the putative fastest car in the world became the must-have investment. Ha! we cried, knowingly, when the car-greed bubble burst just as the production XJ220 was ready to go to its first customers. Naughty Jaguar. Of course the buyers would want their deposits back: the XJ220 they were to receive wasn't what they ordered.

What they were fobbed-off with, as they saw it, was short of six cylinders, two driven wheels and eight inches of wheelbase. Never mind that it was more powerful than the car they thought they had bought, that it still had the pedigree of a Group C-derived engine, that with its shortened chassis it actually looked *better*. »

146

XJ220

THE SUPERCAR THAT CAME IN FROM THE COLD

'With a fraction of the budget and resources available to Porsche and Ferrari, Britain had produced the supercar to top all supercars'

Jaguar, in the eyes of a public always baying for the blood of a self-destructing British motor industry, had fouled up again.

Had it? Decades on from the production XJ220's début, with dust and values settled, air cleared and reality biting, the truth seems a little different. Forget the hype, forget the howling, look at the car. It's a marvel, and the fact that it exists at all is similarly marvellous. It is imperfect, too, but today there are ways of remedying most of the imperfections, as today's guru of all things 220, Don Law, will shortly reveal. Yes, Jaguar's sensationally curvy XJ220 has finally come in from the cold.

IT WAS 1988, in the spring. I was sitting next to Jaguar's then chief engineer, Jim Randle, at dinner in Juan-les-Pins. Jaguar was launching the XJS convertible, but I knew of something much more interesting than the XJS. I worked at *Motor* magazine at the time, and I'd got wind of something called the Saturday Club.

Motor's photographer had been recording the Club's activities on film but was sworn to secrecy. Other in-office references had been similarly guarded, but this much I knew: something big and supercar-shaped was going to appear at the 1988 British Motor Show. Jim Randle, however, would not be pressed. 'Wait and see,' was all he would say.

A CARMAKER is supposed to keep a parts and service back-up alive for its cars for at least ten years after production ends. For Jaguar, with all its big-company systems, doing this for the XJ220 was going to be a headache. The XJ220 had already, in 1993, had a Le Mans outing; five years later Don Law ran that Martini-liveried race car in the AMOC Intermarque championship, driven with great success by Win Percy. Helped by this experience, he found himself looking after ever more road cars.

'Jaguar had a ramp for the XJ220,' Don says, 'but they wanted to pass responsibility on. They couldn't do it officially until the ten years was up, but when customers started asking for modifications – brakes, driving position, the way the doors opened – Jaguar couldn't do that. So they said, "Go to Don." '

It's a strange position. Don Law Racing isn't an official Jaguar agent so Jaguar can't officially recommend Don's operation. But his company can supply parts that Jaguar cannot, including enough body panels to satisfy XJ220 ownership for years to come, and it carries out not just upgrades but running modifications, learned over years of XJ220 maintenance, to ensure reliability.

Currently there are about 100 cars on Don's books, including cars from mainland Europe and beyond which are sent to him for work. The two-year service (£4456 plus VAT) is vital. It includes replacing the twin-plate clutch, which copes badly with low-speed manoeuvring and has been known to fly apart if suddenly abused on a little-used car. Don had to get a gearbox casing re-cast to fix the aftermath of one such episode. »

'And the upgrades? Better brake servos, better discs and pads, modified calipers, an alternative master cylinder and a ducting system. Then there are changes to the driving seat and to the door hinges'

Top, left and right
XJ220C racer used carbonfibre body panels; 1988 prototype now at Browns Lane museum.

Left
Race car interior carries original digital display; tweaked V6 produces around 620bhp.

The service's other crucial component is replacing the cambelts and checking the valve timing, which will usually have moved thanks to strange vibratory forces between the pulleys and the camshafts, locked together only by being a taper fit. Don does a mod to prevent this, without which valve-to-piston contact is a permanent worry. This involves removing the engine, but that's easy because it sits on a subframe which drops out underneath.

Then there's the big one every six years, which involves replacing the fuel tank for £3500 plus VAT (running an XJ220 was never going to be cheap even if, in relative terms, the £130,000 you'll now pay for a good, regularly used one is surprising value). This is foam-filled, and contains a collector pot plus two lift pumps and internal filters, the whole assembly fed into the XJ220's structure via holes. Old tanks can leak into the honeycomb structure, damaging the epoxy, so replacement is important.

Oh, and should you come across an XJ220 which has done nothing more than delivery mileage and has lain dormant ever since, don't get too excited. It will need £20,000-worth of recommissioning before you can use it, including all the hydraulics, all the valve springs, many of the gaskets and the full belts/clutch/tank treatment. Tyres too.

And the upgrades? Better brake servos (there are two of them), better discs and pads (technology has moved on since 1991, and the brakes were under-specified then), modified calipers, an alternative master cylinder and a ducting system. Going for the fully ducted XJ220S type of system is expensive, though, and you'd have to lose those lovely 17in front, 18in rear wheels. Then there are changes to the driving seat so tall drivers

JAGUAR XJ220
SPECIFICATIONS

Engine
3498cc, 90-degree V6, aluminium block and heads, four overhead cams driven by gears and belts, four valves per cylinder, two turbochargers

Power
542bhp @ 7200rpm

Torque
475lb ft @ 4500rpm

Transmission
Five-speed manual, viscous limited-slip differential, rear-wheel drive

Suspension
Front and rear: double wishbones, coil springs, anti-roll bar, telescopic dampers

Brakes
AP Racing ventilated and cross-drilled discs all round, two servos

Performance
Maximum speed 211mph
0-60mph 3.6sec

Value
£100,000-150,000

can get their legs in and not have their eyes staring at the header rail, and to the door hinges so the doors can open wider (access as standard is highly awkward).

That's the practical stuff. Don Law can also reproduce the planned 220S niceties, with changes to the engine management, the valves and the pistons, plus the straight-through exhaust system which adds power and drowns out the engine's bag-of-bolts clatter at low speed (it's derived from a race engine, remember). Don also offers recalibrated dampers and new springs to sharpen the handling and cure the pitching, and even a mod to enable a suitcase to be stashed in the boot.

FINE. BUT IN THE END, is the XJ220 actually *any good as a supercar*? At speed, yes. Around corners, guardedly yes, as long as you're circumspect in the wet. The acid test of usability, though, is how it copes with traffic jams and traffic calming, rigours to try any supercar's patience.

I drove the JDHT's example from the Houses of Parliament to Buckingham Palace as part of the Queen's Birthday celebrations, crawling sometimes at just 10mph behind a police escort. Slightly acrid clutch aside, it was as good as gold, with a surprisingly docile engine for all its gnashing and uneven 90-degree thrum. Earlier that day, though, the Embankment was near-deserted and, well, I just had to, didn't I? Wake those turbos and by God, it's quick...

Welcome to the real world, XJ220.

» Thanks to Don Law, +44 (0)1782 413875, www.donlawracing.com.

Crown wheel and pinion
Jaguar XJ6 and ‚E' type
17/52 or 19 / 49

£670 / £700

available again

Fueltank for XJ S1, S2, S3
L/H or R/H, mild steel

£184

Weber carburettors, complete kits with inlet manifold and linkage

V12

WEBER

Getrag 5 speed gearbox
'E' type S3	£2467.50
XK120/140/150	£2232.50
'E' type S1 & S2	£2232.50
Mark II	£2232.50

Available of the shelf!

Wheel arch set for Jaguar XJ6/XJ12 S2/S3

chromed stainless steel, installation either with clips or screws.

set of four £66

Hardtop 'E' type S1 and S2
GFK, white

£530

Manual choke conversion
SU carburettor	£126
Zenith-Stromberg	£69

40 IDF	Jaguar 'E' type series III, XJ12, XJ - V12	£2,299
45 DCOE	Jaguar 'E' type 3.8 and 4.2	£1,485
45 DCOE	Austin Healey BN4 late, BN6 to BJ8	£1,500
45 DCOE	MGA, MGB	£424
40 DCOE	Sprite / Midget: 1275	£539
40 DCOE	Midget 1500	£756
40 or 45 DCOE	Mini	£420
4 barrel down-draught	Range Rover and Land Rover: all V8 3.5	£860
34 ICH	Land Rover: Series IIA + III - all 4 cyl.	£109
32/34 DMTL	Land Rover Defender	£205
45 DCOE	TR3 late, TR3A, TR3B, TR4, TR4A	£1,079
40 DCOE	TR250, TR6	£1,500
45 DCOE	Spitfire 1500	£539
40 DCOE	Spitfire 1500	£756

Crankshaft harmonic balancer
for Jaguar 6 cyl.

£214

Mitsuba fuel pump

positive or negative earth, 12 V

The one and only. for all carburettor engines

£106

Alloy Radiator with high efficiency core

'E' type
S1 4.2
S2 4.2

£970

On plug coil
X300 - XJ6 XJR all models 1995 - 1997, XJS 4.0 from VIN 194775

£57

Composite cylinder head gaskets
3.4/3.8/4.2	£100
3.8 Full race	£110
3.8 extra thick 1.8 mm	£100

That's not a distributor!

This is a complete ignition system
- Spark balancing
- Stronger spark
- Simple installation
- Maintenance free

select one of 16 advanced curves

4 - cylinder	£200
6 - cylinder	£200
8 - cylinder	£404
12 - cylinder	£658

(Exclusive from SC parts)

Ask for a free information leaflet!
or call 01293 847 203

Brake master cylinder
'E' type S1 4.2, S2, S3, 420
As stock lasts **£184**

Brake master cylinder
MKII, DV8, XK150	£122
XK120, XK140	£244
XJS S1,S2 LHD	£343
XJ6 S2	£343
XJS, XJ	£176
XJ40	£101
S-Type new	£100

Clutch master cylinder
MKII , DV8	£143
Jaguar XJS early	£249
XJS late	£106
XJ40 early	£49
XJ40 late	£76
'X' type	£760
'S' type 3L	£100

Chromed wire wheels

from **£187**

All wire wheels listed:
www.SCparts.co.uk
Free UK delivery for all sets of 4 wheels ordered with this advert

Overall
adjustable wrist due to double buttons, buttons made of soft plastic, covered zip avoids scratches on car paint, with belt and deep pockets. Overall of the 30's to the 50's. According to the overall of the famous Bugatti pilot, Louis Giron, who won 18 Grand Prix.

£88
sizes:
S, M, L, XL

Leather jackets

Heinz Bauer Manufakt stands for handmade, functionally designed high quality fashion.

OC o.Cabrio ORIGINAL CABRIO

To Jaguar enthusiasts, the words 'Browns Lane' and 'MIRA' are shorthand for two icons that are inextricably linked with the post-war history of Jaguar. From this combination three great sports cars emerged – the XK120, the E-type and, more recently, the XK8. After 50 years of producing the most famous Jaguars, Browns Lane is about to cease car production but MIRA, where every Jaguar has been tested, continues to play a valuable role.

The history of the Motor Industry Research Association (MIRA) goes back to 1946 and Jaguar moved to Browns Lane over a period straddling 1951/52. Previously, Jaguar had a rather more modest factory at Swallow Road in the Holbrook district of Coventry, to which they had moved when they made the brave but crucial trek south from Blackpool, where it had all begun, in 1928.

Until the MIRA facility became available, testing had been a much more haphazard business, involving the use of local roads and the odd Continental foray – the XK120's first test outside factory grounds was a run up the nearby Keresley Road. The rapidly developing facilities at MIRA allowed Jaguar to raise its game considerably and the two would work in parallel to create the sports cars, the volume small saloons, the prestigious large saloons and even the C- and D-type racers. All could be labelled: 'Developed at MIRA, built at Browns Lane.' »

Testing times

As Jaguar production comes to an end in Coventry, *Octane* takes three
generations on a nostalgic trip from Browns Lane to the MIRA test facility

Words: Philip Porter   **Photography:** Matthew Howell   **Archive photos:** MIRA

'Norman Dewis, Jaguar's chief tester from 1952 until 1976, was one of a
number of engineers who decided what facilities were needed at MIRA'

Jaguar is most famous for its sports
cars. The sales of saloon cars were, of
course, considerably greater and crucial
to the prosperity of the company, but it
was these sports cars that added the
excitement, the zest, to the whole range
and to the Jaguar name.

The three generations of sports cars
represented on our pilgrimage from
Browns Lane to MIRA are very different
indeed. If you were searching for just one
word to quickly sum up the differences,
that word would probably be 'weight'.
They successively felt lighter and lighter
to drive.

As is well-known, the XK120 almost
happened by accident. Hastily created to
stir up some publicity and as a means of
trying out the new twin-overhead-cam
engine on long-suffering enthusiast
customers, it just blew everybody's socks
off. Demand was overwhelming. Jaguar
had a problem because it was already
outgrowing its factory and, when the
engine was launched in the Mark VII
saloon, the pressure on space was to be
all too intense.

The XK120 was without a doubt the pre-
eminent sports car of its day, and, although
it now feels quite a heavy car, it still has
highly respectable performance. It is a car
that demands driver involvement if it is to
be driven quickly, and, to owners, that's
what gives it character. The steering is a
little heavy and lacking in feel. The brakes,
unless uprated, are pretty feeble and the
gearbox is slow. These judgements,
however, are being made more than 50
years after the car burst upon the dour
pre-war motoring scene. At the time, the
XK120 was a revelation.

What makes the 120 so good today?
Probably most outstanding is its reliability,
coupled with excellent performance; and,

of course, the classic good looks that
captivated people so in the 1950s and still
do in this more cynical age. The 120 is an
old sports car that can be used. It can
potter down to the shops or be driven
thousands of miles on rallies. That brilliant
engine is still the heart of a really great
sports car.

The same is true of that star of the '60s,
the sensational E-type. Again, the car set
new standards when launched in 1961.
Again, one can, in hindsight, criticise the
brakes and the gearbox on the original
cars but they did not take the shine off the
exceptional package.

The difference is that over a decade
Jaguar's standards had jumped and the
steering was now superb, the ride and
roadholding positively sophisticated and
the performance leagues ahead of
anything but a few ludicrously expensive
esoterics. For that reason, the E-type also
makes a very practical classic car because,
like its forebear, the 'E' can be used for
tootling or for rapid long-distance
motoring in style.

Climbing out of a 120 and into an ➤➤

'Finding period locations at Browns Lane isn't easy: major investment in the 1990s means it's now a thoroughly modern car factory'

'Before the war, all Coventry's roads were made of cobble stones and after the Blitz they were shipped to MIRA and used for the Belgian pavé'

Left
Crash-testing an E-type; historic raised banking is still in daily use.

Above and right: Building the banking used for the action shots in this feature; MIRA opening was, appropriately, by a Jaguar MkVII saloon.

E-type you would think there was more than a decade between them. Their characters are totally different, which is how it should be. Both have their own flavour. The E-type feels much more modern, much lighter, with livelier performance, precise steering, greater roadholding powers and just more sophistication all round.

Both XK120 and E-type were at the pinnacle of sports design in their respective eras, but what about the modern XK8? We are jumping two generations here so it's not surprising that the XK8 is a very different animal. It is not pure sports car; it is a grand tourer. The convertible version even has a power-operated hood.

Times have moved on. Customers' requirements and aspirations are very different from what they were 40 or 50 years ago, and the modern XKs have done a fine job for Jaguar. They are also undoubtedly classics of the future. As their predecessors did in their time, they will no doubt plummet in value when the replacement is launched next year, and will endure a period in the doldrums before better examples start to be sought and revered. Perhaps now is the time to

start hunting out exceptional Jaguar XK8s and XKRs.

Of the cars we drove on our sentimental journey, the XK120 was bought by David Nursey about 30 years ago. It was a bargain at £600, as it was actually worth nearer £800 at the time... David is often Clerk of the Course at Shelsley Walsh and the car always looks stunning, parked in an old hay barn right by the start-line at race meetings.

The E-type was bought by me in 1977. It is the oldest in existence and was used for publicity, including the infamous 150mph road test in Autocar, and a mad dash to Geneva for the press launch. In 2000 the car, which had become pretty sad and been off the road for 25 years, was transformed by an amazingly dedicated conservation restoration by Classic Motor Cars of Bridgnorth. The car originally had a blueprinted engine to achieve the magic 150mph top speed and that wonderful level of performance has been lovingly and faithfully recreated.

The XK8 was provided by Coventry-based Jaguar specialist, Chris Forbes of CF Motors. It is a 1997 example which is for sale at £13,000. To say the XK8 is light years ahead of the classic sports cars is to

be unfair to the older cars. When the XK8s and XKRs were launched, they put Jaguar back at the top of its niche: a niche holding relatively few competitors, of which the Mercedes SL was by far the most obvious.

Early XK8s are now relatively affordable but, as Chris explains, you have to be very careful about what you are buying. Find a good one and they are very rewarding cars, offering terrific value for money. Like most things in life, the more you pay, the better the car. Earlier examples suffered from engine problems with the piston bores, though a number of these have had replacement engines or major rectification work.

Browns Lane was the obvious place for our three classics to rendezvous, although finding a location that looked 'period' to suit the older cars isn't as easy as it was a few years ago. Major investment in the 1990s and a corporate update since the Ford takeover means that Browns Lane today is a thoroughly modern car factory, right down to the obligatory heritage centre that any prestige marque worth its salt now boasts. But the Browns Lane story started when the XK120 was in its infancy, and company founder William

Lyons had to go through some pretty tortuous negotiations to move his business up another gear.

After WWII had ended, Britain needed to rebuild its economy and earn crucial foreign currency. The emphasis was totally on export business; Jaguar led that overseas charge and set a brilliant example with its success, particularly, in America with its Mark V and XK120.

This healthy situation meant increased production and that translated into a need for an expanded factory. This was not easy at Swallow Road. On the one side the site was bordered by the Dunlop factory and on the other by open fields. Lyons applied for planning permission to expand the site by 50 percent and was turned down.

It seems that the authorities, which were still exerting a wartime level of control over trade and industry, wanted

Dunlop to expand on its existing site and Jaguar to sell them its own factory. So Lyons began a rather tortuous dialogue with various officials at the Ministry of Supply about acquiring a wartime 'shadow' factory that had been occupied by Daimler during hostilities. It was situated at Browns Lane, on the outskirts of Coventry in an area called Allesley.

Over the next months Lyons would show himself to be a shrewd, tough negotiator. Initially, the Ministry wanted an annual rent of £75,000. Lyons was not impressed and looked at other sites in Scotland, Wales and Northern Ireland. But the export effort desperately needed Jaguar and, by shrewd bargaining and some brinkmanship, Lyons finally agreed a rent of £30,000 per annum for the first five years and the sale of his current factory to Dunlop for £450,000.

So Lyons had a deal that brought two

massive benefits to his company. He now had a one million square foot factory (nearly twice the size of Foleshill and one of the largest in Coventry) and some very useful capital to invest in new models, such as the forthcoming small saloon range. A few years later, long after the move to Browns Lane had been successfully completed, he re-opened negotiations with the Ministry of Supply and finally bought the site outright for £1.25m in early 1959.

At about the time that Jaguar was moving shop from Swallow Lane to Browns Lane, a wartime airfield at Lindley, near Nuneaton, was being transformed into the MIRA research and testing facility. In the early 1950s it had already been used unofficially for testing for a while, as the perennially young Norman Dewis – Jaguar's chief tester from 1952 until 1976, who was then with Lea Francis – explains. »

'The XK120 and E-type were at the pinnacle of sports design in their eras but the XK8 is not a pure sports car; it is a grand tourer'

'The facilities at MIRA allowed Jaguar to raise its game considerably and the two worked in parallel to create the sports cars, saloons and even the racers'

Above

Long bonnets are still a feature but Jaguar's sports cars have become much more sybaritic to meet the expectations of today's buyers.

'We used to go up Higham Lane and there was a big steel gate which we could open sufficiently to get a car through. We would then use the old runways for basic test work. It was just a disused aerodrome with grass growing on it.

'The MIRA was then based at Brentford in London but they decided they wanted to build up their facilities and become more connected with the motor industry in the Midlands. They chose Lindley as being a good central point and "Ossie" Dolby was put in charge of the track. He even made his office up in the old control tower.'

Dewis was one of a group of test engineers who formed a committee to decide what facilities were ideally needed for vehicle development. 'One of the first things created was the Belgian pavé, for testing for structural weaknesses. Dolby went out to Belgium and actually measured the size of the cobbles and the depth of the gaps between them. The pavé was then constructed exactly as it

was in Belgium! Before the war, all Coventry's roads were made of cobble stones and after the Blitz Coventry didn't know what to do with them, so they were shipped to Lindley and used for the Belgian pavé.'

One of the other major facilities was the triangular high-speed track with seriously banked corners. Lyons played a hand in this important development. He was a member of the National Advisory Council (NAC), and the minutes of a meeting held in October 1951 report that: 'Mr Lyons urged that since the need for the high-speed track was generally accepted, the sooner it came into operation the better.'

This high-speed track was to be used by most of the manufacturers, day in, day out. Norman Dewis spent a large part of his life at MIRA and, towards the end of 1960, one of the cars he drove regularly to develop the E-type was the one in this feature, 9600 HP. The XK8 was also extensively tested at MIRA and I recall,

when I was writing a book about the model, being taken by one of the testers over some unbelievably vicious curbs that would be mounted at 40mph – all in the interests of preparing vehicles for whatever a customer might throw at them out there in the motoring world.

Today MIRA is continuing the work it pioneered back in the early 1950s, when the 'export or die' dictum meant that British cars had to be capable of dealing with the worst kinds of roads found in the world's remotest areas.

And Browns Lane will remain Jaguar's spiritual home, even though production of cars is being moved to Birmingham. They can take the cars out of Coventry, but they'll never take Coventry out of the cars. At least, that's what Jaguar enthusiasts hope.

» Thanks to David Nursey for the use of the XK120 and Chris Forbes for the XK8; Ken McConomy at Jaguar; and Neil Bradley and Richard Adams at MIRA.

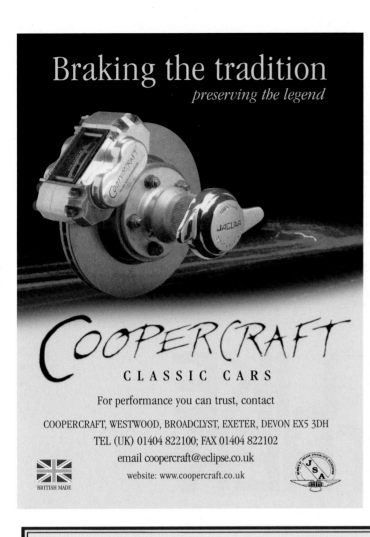

Jaguar wins
the world's two
toughest races:
Daytona and
Le Mans.

A DAY LIKE NO OTHER

Some thought the glory days of Peter Whitehead's
1951 win for Jaguar, and the four victories that
followed, would never be repeated. But in 1988
Jaguar proved them wrong...
Words: David Lillywhite

Were you there in 1988 when Jaguar returned to the Le Mans winners' podium, 31 years after the company's last win there? If you were, then there's no need to describe the ecstatic reaction of the crowd, the waving of the flags, the general air of relief that a British team really could deliver at Le Mans all over again.

Le Mans has always been popular with the British, but by the mid-1980s attendance was falling and major manufacturers seemed to have lost interest. Porsche had been left to dominate but, in the background, Jaguar had been building up to Le Mans for several years in a bid to increase its worldwide credibility. Curiously, it had all started in America when Bob Tullius, of Group 44 Racing, decided to build his fifth competition Jaguar.

This new Group 44 car, to be named the XJR-5, would be a far cry from XJRs one to four – an E-type, followed by three XJ-S racers, all with V12 engines.

Group 44's XJR-5 also used a V12, but was a pure race car, rather than being based on a road car. Although on the heavy side, two XJR-5s competed at Le Mans in 1984 and 1985. In 1984 both retired at around the 14 hours point. But in 1985, although one XJR-5 retired after nine hours, the other survived to finish 13th. Suddenly the motoring press and the British public began to take more interest in Le Mans.

Above
Group 44's Bob Tullius.

Top left
The Group 44 team (here with an XJR-7 in 1987) was always immaculate in white.

Top right
1990 Le Mans winning XJR-12 was evolved from the '88 Jaguars.

Group 44's efforts had been supported by Jaguar Cars North America. But in the UK, Jaguar Cars engaged Tom Walkinshaw's TWR to oversee its Group C racing efforts. TWR had achieved great success with Rover, Ford, Mazda and BMW, before getting involved with Jaguar in 1982 (with a successful adaptation of the XJ-S for the European Touring Car Championship).

There was immediate rivalry between the two Jaguar-supported siblings; to make matters worse, Walkinshaw commandeered the XJR moniker for TWR's new carbon-fibre monocoque, V12-powered racer, named the XJR-6. In 1985, just a few months after Group 44's 13th place at Le Mans, TWR entered the XJR-6 into its first race. It wore Silk Cut purple and white livery in place of traditional British Racing Green.

The TWR XJR-6's first full season, 1986, was a success on the whole, but not at Le Mans. Three cars were entered: one ran out of fuel, one retired with a broken driveshaft and the last suffered damage when a tyre blew. Porsche won once again.

Bob Tullius was still fighting, too. TWR might have used his XJR tag, but it didn't mean that Group 44 couldn't use it too. Jumping in ahead of TWR, Tullius named his next car the XJR-7, and raced it 28 times between 1985 and 1988, although never at Le Mans. But it wasn't long before he lost Jaguar's backing.

Group 44 had planned an XJR-8 (it was built and has appeared

'THE LEADING XJR-9 REGULARLY SWAPPED THE LEAD WITH THE THREE FACTORY PORSCHES – THE LEAD WAS NEVER MORE THAN A LAP'

occasionally since). Instead, Walkinshaw's next car was named the XJR-8, an evolution of the XJR-6. Three were taken to Le Mans by TWR, which prompted *Autocar* to preview the event with the headline 'Jaguar's three-car team looks set to triumph at Le Mans on Sunday'.

So it was that the 1987 Le Mans crowd was swelled by thousands of British, many visiting the circuit for the first time. It looked like the race would be a straight battle between the Silk Cut XJR-6 Jaguars and the Rothmans Porsche 962Cs but thanks to gearbox breakage, a blown tyre-caused accident and valve spring failure, all three Jaguars retired. Porsche won again.

In 1988 the Jaguar/TWR returned, backed by a massive British crowd. Mercedes was entered for the race but withdrew just before the start after a 220mph tyre blow-out on the Mulsanne straight in practice.

Porsche was looking for its eighth win but TWR wasn't going to make things easy. It took five cars, all XJR-9s (updated versions of the XJR-8), which travelled in two articulated transporters, accompanied by three truckloads of spares, 14 drivers, 75 full-time staff, 21 volunteers, with a plane on hand to fly in spares from TWR's Oxfordshire base. There were a further 80 staff for catering, another plane to ferry around VIP guests and a dedicated Dunlop tyre engineer with 2500 tyres.

Above
Tom Walkinshaw of TWR took over where Group 44 had been forced to leave off.

Top
Le Mans 1988 and three XJR-9s take Le Mans by storm, finishing first, fourth and sixteenth.

When the 1988 race began, the cars set off at unusually high speeds, eventually breaking speed and distance records for Le Mans. The leading XJR-9 regularly swapped the lead with the three factory Porsches, in a race so close that the lead was never more than a lap – by the end of the race, all 3313 miles of it, the XJR-9 of Jan Lammers, Johnny Dumfries and Andy Wallace won by just two minutes and 36 seconds, with Porsche second and third and another XJR-9 in fourth. The last of the three surviving XJR-9s was 16th overall.

The crowd went mad. This was the first Jaguar Le Mans win since Flockhart and Bueb's famous 1957 victory in a D-type. On a worldwide scale, the good feeling and publicity generated by the win confirmed to other manufacturers that Le Mans was still a race worth working for.

What happened next? Well, for 1989 the XJR-9s reappeared at Le Mans, but managed only a fourth and an eighth position. For short circuit racing, Jaguar switched to new cars, powered by turbocharged V6s (starting with the XJR-10) but the V12 was developed into the XJR-12, specifically for endurance racing.

The policy paid off, and the XJR-12 took first and second places at the 1990 Le Mans and second and third in 1991. Jaguar returned only once more to Le Mans, this time competing in the GT class (and winning) with three XJ220Cs.

KW03 SWV

The tell tale flashing blue lights bounced off the Palmer Jaguar's wing mirrors as I pulled over. Two police officers stomped into my peripheral vision and asked me to remove my helmet. 'Right, there are two reasons why we've stopped you Sir,' said one. 'The first is that it's a bloody nice car. And the second is that it's supposed to be green and white.'

In my defence, I launched into a tedious explanation of how this car is the only prototype and that the original track car was green and white to highlight its Jaguar engine. 'Oh,' he said, 'we were worried that it might have been stolen and resprayed.' Sounding faintly patronising, I pointed out that had I nicked a £51,500 sports car, I would not be crawling through the centre of Bedford on a Monday lunchtime wearing a helmet emblazoned with my name. To my relief, they started to grin. 'So mate,' said my new-found friend, 'what'll she do?'

Everyone, it seems, is curious about the JP1. Not since I gave a busty table dancer a lift in a Smart Crossblade have I been so flattered by such constant public attention.

The origins of the JP1 can be found in the Zeus racing car that won the

»

Words: Alistair Weaver **Words:** Charlie Magee

Available in track-only and road-legal forms, Palmersport's Jaguar JP1 could be hurtling round Donington Park in the morning, then trundling down a city centre high street in the afternoon...

HIGH STREET RACER

'THE JP1 IS NO FLYWEIGHT IN THE CATERHAM MOULD, BUT MODIFICATIONS TO THE V6 BY COSWORTH HAVE BOOSTED THE POWER OUTPUT TO 277BHP, AND THERE'S 230LB-FT OF TORQUE'

British Supersports championship in 2001. When ex-grand prix driver Jonathan Palmer needed a new toy for his burgeoning corporate entertainment business, he approached Zeus about developing a track car based around the 3-litre V6 engine found in the Jaguar X-type. The deal gave birth to the JP1 track car, which has been molested by corporate customers at Palmer's Bedford Autodrome since last spring.

Over the summer, Zeus was absorbed into the fast expanding Palmersport empire and the JP1 morphed into a commercially available road and track car. Two examples will be available – the track-only JP1 TS costs £38,500, while the road-legal JP1 RS you see here is priced at £51,500. Just ten examples will be built initially, but Palmer is not ruling out an extended production run if there's sufficient demand.

'We're not making any bold predictions,' he says, 'but there's no reason why we can't build more.' Palmer is adamant that 'we have no agenda to become a small volume manufacturer, but as always in business, you can't rule anything out'. One detects that there is an air of false modesty – JP is certainly not a man to dabble.

Palmer was personally involved in the development work. The self-confessed 'busy man' shared the driving duties with Le Mans racer Christian Vann, while ex-Zeus boss Peter Sneller took care of the engineering logistics.

The principal differences between the road and track car concern the ride height and tyre choice. To cope with 'traffic calming' bumps and other urban detritus, the RS is 35mm higher at the front and 45mm higher at the rear than the TS.

The addition of such fripperies as number plates, headlights and a speedometer has increased the road car's mass by 50kg to 700kg, which is split 42/58 front to rear. The JP1 is therefore no flyweight in the Caterham mould, but modifications to the V6 by Cosworth have boosted the power output to 277bhp, and there's 230lb-ft of torque. A power to weight ratio of 396bhp per tonne should be enough to appease even the most diehard of track day fans.

Palmer expects even the road-going JP1s to spend most of their time on circuits. My first taste of the car was on Autodrome's West Circuit. The car transition from track to road car has denied the JP1 a little of its beauty. The wheelarches are larger, which gives the front-end a slightly bulbous aspect and the headlights look a little clumsy. The dour silver and white paint job also did it few favours.

Getting in is race-car simple – step over the sill and onto the seat before sliding your legs into the footwell. It is surprisingly spacious, accommodating my 6ft 3in frame with ease, and the Kevlar seats prove extremely comfortable, once you've got used to a reclined driving position. With the four-point harness in place, the view ahead is almost pornographic. Rather than bother with a dashboard, Palmer has used a delicious quick-release Momo steering wheel, which incorporates a set of Stack instruments between ten-to-two and ten-past-one. It looks fabulous although it's frustrating that it can't display vehicle and engine speed simultaneously. The push button switches for the headlights and indicators, by contrast, are fiddly and awkward. Caterham-style toggle switches would

Above
Changes to the ride height – 35mm higher at the front and 45mm at the rear – help the JP1 cope better with urban living.

Left and right
The makers of the JP1 expect future owners will primarily use it as a track day weapon, with just the occasional foray down the local high street.

'THIS CAR IS BREATHTAKINGLY QUICK. WITH A USEFUL SPREAD OF TORQUE, THE ACTION BEGINS FROM AS LITTLE AS 3000RPM, WHEN THERE'S A RELENTLESS SURGE OF THRUST UNTIL YOU CHANGE UP AT 7000RPM'

Left and right
No need for a dash as the quick-release Momo wheel incorporates a set of Stack instruments; motor is the same as that used in a 3-litre Jaguar X-type, but it has been touched by Cosworth.

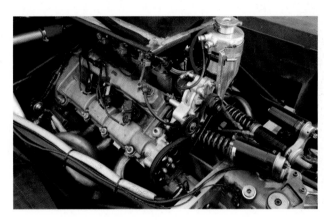

Above
The addition of road-going extras have added another 50kg in weight, although it has to be said the tax disc holder accounts for an extremely small part of this...

surely be a much more user-friendly solution.

To start the JP1 you twist a key, prod an ignition switch then the starter button. The loud engine note is accompanied by a rattle from the Hewland gearbox as the clutch bites. This six-speed unit is shared with the corporate entertainer and based on the unit found in contemporary Formula 3 cars.

Gears are selected sequentially by tugging on the metallic gear knob, with a dashboard display revealing the cog in use. Changing up is achieved without the aid of a clutch – an ignition cut system allows the next ratio to be selected simply by pulling firmly on the lever. Downshifts require a prod of the clutch and a blip of the throttle, but the whip crack response is accompanied by a satisfying mechanical clunk.

This car is breathtakingly quick. With a useful spread of torque, the action begins from as little as 3000rpm, when there's a relentless surge of thrust until the shift lights demand a change at 7000rpm. Palmer expects it to hit 60mph from rest in under four seconds and it's geared for 175mph.

The JP1 will top 60mph in first and reach 80mph in second. Given the car's lowly mass and plentiful torque, this is not a major problem but a set of sprint ratios would be more fun, particularly on the road. Palmer agrees but reckons the car already has the shortest first gear available for the gearbox. 'Apart from spending £150,000 redesigning the Hewland 'box, there's not a lot we can do,' he says.

It is also surprisingly user-friendly. Sensibly long throttle travel panders to those with a clumsy right foot and the turn-in is crisp. Even on the standard Yokohama AVS Sport road tyres,

the mechanical and aero grip levels are impressive, but the car's attitude is still pleasingly adjustable. Push the limits and the JP1 responds with mild and reassuring understeer, but this can be eliminated with a judicious right foot and glorious power slides can be provoked with relative ease.

The ride is nothing short of astonishing for such an extreme machine. Excellent damping and minor bump absorption rekindles memories of the seminal Lotus Elise. Only on very bumpy minor roads does the JP1 start to feel nervous.

It was also coping surprisingly well with the congested streets of Cambridge, until it broke down. Suddenly, a hundred tourist cameras were trained on me pushing the Le Mans replica. Dave Branston, the engineer who had accompanied us on the drive, identified a fuel vaporisation problem. After it had cooled down, the car ran faultlessly back to Bedford. Sneller admitted that they had tweaked the fan system before my arrival and is adamant that the problem is now fixed. Given that the car ran successfully in the mid-summer heat of Monza, we'll give him the benefit of the doubt.

It was dark for the return journey, and with the front wheelarches softly lit in the moonlight and the instruments glowing red before my eyes, I found myself imagining life on the Mulsanne Straight. The Palmer Jaguar isn't cheap, but it is a hugely accomplished road and track car. Even the Bedfordshire Constabulary can attest to that.

» Alistair Weaver, a Sir William Lyons Award winner, has written for most major modern motoring publications and UK newspapers.

Jaguar
Prototypes

1 SS Jaguar 100 Coupé

Apart from the production range of SS Jaguar models displayed on Stand 126 at Earls Court in 1938, there was a striking closed coupé of the familiar SS Jaguar 100 sports car. This Lyons-designed body was an interesting precursor of things to come and one can see hints of XK120 fixed-head and maybe a little Bugatti influence in the tightly furled cabin. The show car, which had the $3^1/_2$-litre engine, was priced at £595 and a $2^1/_2$-litre was listed (though never built) at £545. The unique prototype was fitted with an all-synchromesh gearbox.

The first owner, who received it as a 21st birthday present, found the car to be rather impractical and modifications had to be made to the interior to make it driveable. Apparently the doors dropped too and the red colouring on the steering wheel rubbed off on the driver's trousers! Such are prototypes...

2 XL

Little is known of the XL but it is undoubtedly the step between the pre-war SS100 sports cars and the sensational XK120 of 1948. Lyons liked to work with full-size mock-ups, and this styling exercise was built in 1946-47. It is certainly confusing that L comes after K in the alphabet but, in fact, the name of the production 120 was taken from the engine designation, which was XK.

3 Bubble-top C-type

Legendary aerodynamicist Malcolm Sayer designed the XK120C, or C-type as it came to be known unofficially, in 1950-51 and it famously won Le Mans in '51. During March the following year he drew a number of alternative body shapes, all variations on the theme, and this closed version was among them. Assuming drag of the 1951 C-type to be 100 percent, he calculated that drag for this configuration would be 84.5 percent. If you were to cut the roof off this design, you would be left with the head fairing behind the driver – just as it appeared on the D-type in 1954.

4/5 Light alloy car

The 'light alloy car' has to be one of the most significant Jaguar prototypes ever built. This car introduces the familiar elliptical mouth that is still a hallmark to this day. It is very much like the E-type but, built in 1953, was way ahead of its time and startlingly modern – one can see similarities with Alfa Romeo's fabulous Disco Volante (flying saucer) designs. The other significant aspect of this car is that it was Jaguar's first monocoque sports racer and was the link between the C-type and the D-type. It was variously named the C/D, the prototype D-type, XK120C Series II, XP11, XKC 054 and XKC 201 but, at the factory, was generally referred to simply as the 'light alloy car'.

6 Brontosaurus

The Brontosaurus served to prove that even styling genius William Lyons was human. It was a very curious machine that he had built, possibly with some record-breaking in mind, and it did very little other than hurtle around the factory perimeter with Lyons at the wheel. Its other purpose was probably as a 'wake-up' call to Jaguar's designers, whom Lyons, possibly with some justification, was always urging to hurry up and complete their designs. Lyons had his own small team of designers for creating prototypes and produced this to show things could be done quickly. The Bronco, as it became known, was not one of his better efforts.

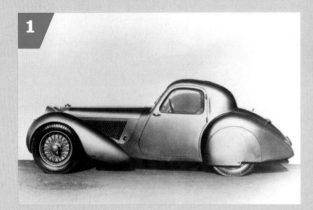

ORIGINAL BODY, DIFFERENT LOUVRES,
REAR SPATS, BUBBLE CANOPY

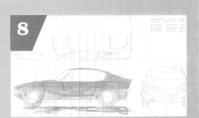

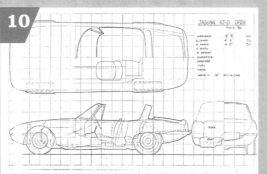

7 Shortened 2+2 E-type

For several years after the launch of the two-seater E-type in 1961, Lyons and Heynes had dithered over producing a larger, four-seater version. They had built longer examples, wider variations and changed their minds to such an extent that the Experimental Department built a mock-up with telescopic tubes so it could be widened or lengthened at will. Eventually, the 2+2 model appeared and in production form was simply a modified fixed-head coupé. However, the alternative thinking continued and there was a view at Jaguar that the E-type, particularly the 2+2, was too long for European markets. In May 1966 Sayer drew this shortened 2+2.

8 XJ 3-litre GT

Among the design and development of the sports cars and saloon cars, projects overlapped, converged or diverted. The XJ saloon, for example, started life as a large sporting GT. This mid-sixties design, which was based on the E-type, was described as a 'four-seater sports sedan'. It was seen as a supplement to the sports car range or a replacement for the small Mk2 saloons for which Jaguar disastrously never produced a successor. One can see the fashionable Kamm tail treatment and the beginnings of the XJ-S front wing and headlamp treatment.

9 XJ21 by Winterbottom

In the latter half of the 1960s, the ageing Jaguar management agonised over the E-type's successor and a plethora of designs was produced, at least on paper. The debate raged on and one contributor was a young designer by the name of Oliver Winterbottom, who would later work for TVR and Lotus. This design went as far as a quarter-scale clay model, with details such as aluminium wheels made in the Daimler toolroom.

10 XJ21 convertible

A number of XJ21 designs were done by Sayer in 1967/68 but one appeared to find favour and actually progressed quite far down the line, as one internal memo confirms. 'The bodies are styled and arrangements are being made with PSF [Pressed Steel Co] for the tooling.' Open and closed versions were drawn and both were 2+2s. However, someone got cold feet, or maybe it was a casualty of the fatal British Leyland debacle that had commenced in 1968. It was cancelled. Mistake!

11 XJ-S by Sayer

The XJ-S was something of an amalgam of thoughts by Lyons and Sayer, but it was actually Sayer who, in September 1968, proposed building a 'a 2+2 sports based on XJ4 parts'. (Confusingly, XJ4 was the internal name for the production XJ6 that would be launched that year.) 'The image sought after is of a low, wide, high-speed car at least as eye-catching as those the Italians will produce...' In arriving at the final shape, which was constrained by increasingly influential US federal safety regulations and, in particular, the belief that open cars would be outlawed, Sayer produced a sheaf of designs, including this one.

12 F-type

Another car shown at the Detroit motorshow in early 2000 that Jaguar should have produced.

The F-type concept oozed the sheer sculptural sensuous beauty of the 120 and E-type and would have been a particularly worthy successor. It would also have had a 'halo effect' on the whole range, giving Jaguar that sense of vibrant excitement again. In fairness, present and forthcoming regulations might have made the actual execution challengingly difficult. Jaguar directed its limited funds to the overdue introduction of diesel engines instead. Deposits were taken, though, and harm was done because Jaguar has always been famous for fabulous sports cars and needs such a models in order to survive.

Coventry climax

In the summer of 2005 car making came to an end at Jaguar's Browns Lane after more than 50 years. But there's more to the marque than a Coventry address

Words: Mark Dixon

Photography: Mark Dixon/Jaguar Daimler Heritage Trust

Look to your left as you make the final approach to Jaguar's car plant at Browns Lane, Coventry, and you might well see sheep grazing in the fields. They're a reminder that the Browns Lane factory is a comparatively recent addition to Coventry's rich industrial heritage: it wasn't built until 1939, which is why it's located on the fringes of suburbia rather than close to the city's red-brick Victorian heartland.

Nearly all the great Jaguar models, from XK120 onwards, were made at Browns Lane and, although Jaguar had other sites over the decades, Browns Lane was its headquarters for as long as most people can remember. All that changed in the summer of 2005, when Jaguar production was transferred from Browns Lane to Castle Bromwich, as part of previous owner Ford's plans for improved efficiency.

Above and left
Mk2 saloons being built in Browns Lane's main assembly hall in 1964; new XKs and XJs get the bright-light treatment during final inspection.

»

Above

Aerial view of Browns
Lane in 1995: circled is
the admin and reception
building, with the main
assembly hall – the WWII
shadow factory – running
front to back.

Browns Lane wasn't built as a car factory, although ironically
it was occupied during WW2 by one of Jaguar's later acquisitions,
Daimler. In the mid-1930s the Air Ministry – belatedly realising
that Hitler wasn't such a decent chap after all – drew up a plan
to involve several of Britain's big car makers in producing aircraft
components. The Ministry would stump up the capital for new
factories and pay the car companies to set up shop in them.

Daimler, Rover, Austin, Standard and The Rootes Group all
signed up to the scheme, by which it was intended that each
factory would monitor, or 'shadow', the others' progress to
co-ordinate production. The new plants were consequently
known as Shadow Factories, and Browns Lane was officially
Daimler Shadow Factory No 2. Until recently, traces of camouflage
paint could still be seen on some of the older buildings.

This first career as a wartime assembly plant explains why
Jaguar had the luxury of one of the longest continuous assembly
lines in Britain. The main assembly hall, also known as No 1
Factory, is where sports and saloon models are put together,
entering as painted bodyshells and exiting as fully functioning
cars. Its spaciousness is what attracted William Lyons when he
was seeking to expand Jaguar after the war.

Since 1928 Jaguar had occupied a site at Swallow Road,
Coventry – another wartime factory, a munitions plant dating
from WW1 – but the authorities refused Lyons permission to

develop it further after WW2. Fortunately, Lyons was on first-
name terms with the permanent secretary to the Ministry of
Supply, which controlled all those recently built shadow
factories, and he brokered a deal whereby Lyons could lease the
million-square-foot Browns Lane plant.

Transferring production from Swallow Road to Browns Lane
was a mammoth task. It took more than a year to complete the
move, using lorries commandeered from around the Midlands at
weekends, but it was done so efficiently that a machine
operative could leave work at Swallow Road on a Friday and
start on the same machine at Browns Lane on the Monday. On
November 28, 1952, Lyons was able to officially show off the
completed plant to his dealers and suppliers.

The 1950s were good years for Jaguar, as the company
launched a slew of new models, including saloons both large –
MkVII – and small (Mk1). But it so nearly all went disastrously
wrong on the night of February 12, 1957, when a fire that had
started in the woodworking shop spread to the main factory
building. By the time the fire brigade arrived, they were facing
an inferno not seen in Coventry since the Blitz.

More than 270 cars, most of them completed MkVIII and MkI
3.4 models awaiting despatch, were destroyed by the blaze.
Several XKSS sports racers, perhaps as many as nine that were
in the process of being converted from D-types, melted into

'By 1996 Jaguar was winning industry awards for quality, which will come as a shock to anyone who remembers the 1970s'

Above and left
The contented smile of a happy workforce; sewing seat trim on what looks like a pre-war Singer – Jaguar contracted out seat production in 1990s.

puddles of alloy as the fire obliterated a quarter of the factory. But the wartime spirit had not yet evaporated, and more than 130 companies offered assistance, including some of Jaguar's closest rivals. Limited production resumed 36 hours later and within six weeks it was back to normal . As it turned out, 1957 would be Jaguar's best-year yet for numbers of vehicles built.

In the following decade, Jaguar became Coventry's largest employer, thanks in part to the acquisition of Daimler. Both factories received some modernisation but the 1970s marked the beginning of a period of stagnation for Jaguar after it was subsumed into the vastly inefficient British Leyland empire. Sales improved again in the 1980s, but then boom turned to bust and Jaguar's future looked precarious again. In December 1990 the cavalry finally arrived in the shape of Ford.

At the time there was much teeth-gnashing about another prestige British manufacturer passing into foreign hands, especially since one of Ford's first actions was to cut the 12,000-strong workforce by one-third to improve efficiency. However, 15 years or ownership proved Ford to be a relatively benevolent parent. In 1993 a new £8.5m overhead-mounted assembly line was installed at Browns Lane and by 1996 Jaguar was winning industry awards for its manufacturing quality, which will come as quite a shock to anyone who remembers some of the cars that were produced under the Leyland regime in the mid-1970s.

Unfortunately, having the best product in the world is no good if you can't find enough buyers for them, and the strength of the pound hurt Jaguar sales badly. Even so, it was a severe shock when Ford announced in September 2004 that it was transferring car production from Browns Lane to Castle Bromwich in Birmingham and shedding more jobs in the process. The collapse of MG Rover helped put this news into perspective. Browns Lane will survive, albeit in a much reduced state, with the Jaguar Daimler Heritage Trust continuing to occupy the fine new building it moved into in 1998.

Obviously this was a difficult time for Jaguar, but when *Octane* toured the plant in April 2005 there was little sense of resentment in the air. The irreverent banter that characterises British car factories still competed with the whirr of power tools and the hum of forklift trucks, and despite the recent media intrusion, no-one objected to having their picture taken. Ironically, because many Jaguar workers have been with the company a long time, they're at an age where the prospect of early retirement starts to look quite attractive.

Jaguar enthusiasts shouldn't get too misty eyed about the move, either. Sir William Lyons wouldn't have hesitated to move from Browns Lane if it became economically necessary. Tradition is all very well but, as events at Longbridge proved, staying in business is more important. △

ORIGINAL KIN

With original C-type Jaguars commanding stratospheric prices, Robert Coucher takes the opportunity to drive an exacting replica of one of the most important Jaguars ever
Words: Robert Coucher **Photography:** Jason Furnari

The C-type Jaguar is one of the most evocative shapes to have emerged from the company's works at Browns Lane. No mean feat as Jaguar has long been famous for the attractive design of its curvaceous and feline bodywork. As well as being beautifully formed, the Jaguar C-type is an eminently successful racing machine having won Le Mans in 1951 and finished first, second and fourth in 1953. Beauty combined with race-winning prowess equals a very sought-after motor car.

The Racing Green C-type you see here is not an original. Just 53 originals were built, between 1951 and '54. Interestingly, 43 were sold to private owners and most are on the road today. The rare originals now command a price tag well north of £450,000. To be honest this is the difficult bit. This car, chassis number 71 0053 (yes, it's significant), is a reproduction. I was feeling slightly uncomfortable as we track-tested Duncan Hamilton's 1953 winner in the August 2003 issue. What can you say about a good copy when you've tested the original? Then I realised that, actually, there couldn't be any better reason to have a go.

As soon as the Racing Green C-type rolled out from its covered trailer I knew it was something special. Finished in the right sort of British Racing Green, this C looks particularly pared down and lean. The shape is spot on and the car's stance is just right. No modern rubber or other annoying 'subtle improvements' are evident. This car looks exactly as it should. More so, in fact, as this is a reproduction of the ultra-special 1953 Le Mans winning lightweight C-type. Price? Yours for £110,000 plus, depending on your exact specification. You should know that we insured the original for over £2 million in August 2003.

Colin Bowler and Peter Hugo of Racing Green Cars, who have brought this C-type down to the test track, are bubbling over. Certainly, they are in the business but their enthusiasm is genuine. In their opinion it is the finest reproduction they have ever come across. Built to special order, the Racing Green C-type is correct right down to the last rivet. Okay, if you feel you have been-there-and-done-that with rivets, the Jaguar is correct down to the original Lucas junction boxes and cotton braiding covering the wiring loom. This is beginning to look like an exercise in fanaticism, which is what you need if you want it to be as near original as possible. No point in having Ikea hinges fitted to your reproduction Chippendale cabinet, is there?

Racing Green offers three versions of the C-type: a production model that costs £85,000, fitted with twin SU carbs, drum brakes and a 140bhp motor. Next is this 1953 Le Mans model with disc brakes, triple Weber carbs and 205bhp at the rear wheels, which costs £110,000. The ultimate Lightweight model with lightened bodywork and 280bhp at the rear wheels costs £135,000.

My favourite C-type is that lovely old thing driven by Aubrey Finberg, which is as fast as you like, covered in scrutineering tags and scruffy and patinated. Aubrey flew past me at a race track on the Tour Auto some years ago and I still savour the image of the rather ratty old C roaring and sliding by, well over the ragged edge.

So what's getting the chaps from Racing Green Cars so excited? As mentioned, this C-type is a visual reproduction of a 1953 factory lightweight and at just 950kg, it is almost as light. The bodywork is hand-formed in 16-gauge aluminium, although you can specify the lighter and more dent prone 18-gauge. Lightness is further engineered in with an aluminium radiator and fuel tank, fabricated exhaust manifold… and you

'THE C-TYPE IS CORRECT RIGHT DOWN TO THE LAST RIVET. OKAY, IF YOU FEEL YOU'VE BEEN-THERE-AND-DONE-THAT WITH RIVETS, IT IS CORRECT DOWN TO THE ORIGINAL LUCAS JUNCTION BOXES AND COTTON BRAIDING COVERING THE WIRING LOOM'

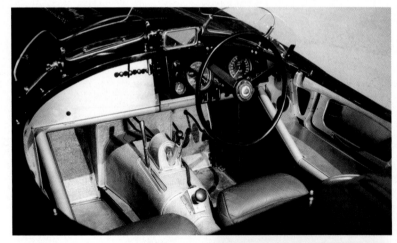

Clockwise from above
Hand-fabricated pedals, Smith instruments, flexy Bluemel steering wheel; no modern rubber nor annoying 'subtle improvements'; handmade aluminium rimmed 16in wire wheels.

can even specify a thinner gauge tube chassis.

The 3.4-litre engine is massaged, balanced and blueprinted with factory C-type modifications. Compression ratio is up to 9.0:1, and C-type cams are fitted with triple Weber 45 DCOE carburettors. With the Webers you get the lightweight inlet manifold, correct water rail, air box, manifold inner guard and bonnet scoop, all as per the 1953 works car. The sump and manifold are cast just as the original. Horsepower is rated at 205bhp, which is not that far off the 220bhp the 1953 cars were producing in race trim.

Naturally the car features the exact C-type front suspension set up: fully independent with adjustable torsion bars, anti-roll bar and Koni dampers. The rear suspension is correct solid rear axle with Panhard rod, adjustable torsion bars and dampers. The C-type rack-and-pinion steering is in place as is an original spec Bluemel steering wheel.

With the C-type safely out of its transporter, the fluids are checked and the engine is fired up with a crack of the exhausts. The Jaguar straight six may be old fashioned in design but it still has the power to grab your attention. This one, with its deep breathing Weber carbs and straight-through exhausts exiting on the near side, goes straight to the hairs on the back of your neck.

As the C-type is warmed through, you take in more of the detailed and beautifully finished craftsmanship. I feel my slightly sniffy attitude begin to wane as I walk around the growling feline form. It is small and low and the deep green paint slides over the bodywork, accentuating the rise and fall of the beautiful compound curves. Everything under the bonnet is a replication of the original C-type, including all the difficult and intricate fittings. This car has twin Joseph Lucas sports coils as per the racers. But one component it does without is the complicated and near useless Plessey brake pump, which never really worked that well in the original. Naturally if you want one fitted, Racing Green will be only too happy to oblige.

The cockpit is absolutely correct down to the hand-fabricated pedals. The transmission tunnel is covered in that silver painted heat-resistant matting and the dash houses all the correct Smith instruments. The original and flexy Bluemel steering wheel really is a lovely touch, as are the handmade aluminium rimmed 16in wire wheels and large alloy filler cap. Little details like the correct spring-loaded door hinges and the split chassis leg with its visible joint make all the difference.

This is incredible attention to detail. This C-type is not built in a pragmatic way to facilitate production. It is built with all the foibles and intricacies that were built into the original.

Chassis number 71 0053 started life as a Jaguar MkVII. The number is nice because it is a real Jaguar chassis number and, by happy coincidence, just 53 C-types were constructed. Also, many of the original C-type's mechanical components were lifted from the MkVII production line.

But enough of the looks and details. How does it feel on the road? With the engine warmed through the car is ready to roll. The dainty driver's door feels very light when opened and you need to hoist yourself over the wide sill and into the narrow, flat seat. Some complain that it is unsupportive but if you are 5ft 8in you sit low, wedged between the transmission tunnel and the spaceframe. The steering wheel is 1950s big but the clutch goes down with ease. Yes, it's a modern Borg & Beck diaphragm unit and much lighter than the original.

Pop the gearshift back into second then ease it forward into first, noting that this gearshift lever is shorter than the other C's, »

'THE C-TYPE IS SMALL AND LOW AND THE DEEP GREEN PAINT SLIDES OVER THE BODYWORK ACCENTUATING THE RISE AND FALL OF THE BEAUTIFUL COMPOUND CURVES'

although they all differ in some way. The Jaguar trundles off the mark helped by all that low-down torque oozing from the friendly engine. At first, going for second gear produces a recalcitrant response from the gearbox. This Moss 'box feels new and very stiff. But as the oil warms it does improve, as does my double-declutching technique. This C only has aero screens fitted but the wind buffeting is manageable. I would opt for the full Perspex screen, personally.

Getting acquainted with the C and beginning to relax into it, I notice how benign and unobtrusively fast it is. The steering is beautifully accurate and as the Dunlop racing tyres come up to temperature, the car begins to feel playful. You sit almost on the rear axle, so the Jaguar seems to swivel round your hips. With narrow tyres and firm but well-damped suspension, it initially leans into the corners but thereafter it just loves to drift, cornering on the throttle. Being so light and imbued with all that torque, the C is capable of lightning fast reactions but it always seems to retain a degree of languid ease.

Then, of course, there are those famous brakes, the real reason why the less powerful Jaguar trumped the Ferraris at Le Mans in the 1950s. The

C-type brakes are superbly powerful and confidence inspiring. The system replicates the 1953 Dunlop brakes with full six-piston calipers at the front and fours at the rear.

The C-type is now warm (although the water temperature needle always remains bang on centre gauge and oil pressure stays firm), so it's time for one last fling. Confidence and a bit more persuasion get the Moss box cooperating and the sticky Dunlop rubber (6in front, 6½in at the rear) is smearing effectively over the tarmac. Pushing the long-travel throttle pedal all the way really wakes the previously relaxed engine bringing on all of its 205bhp. It spins with real enthusiasm belying the long-stroke design. Into second, third and top the Jaguar begins to fly. Brake firmly, change down and it squirms a bit below your hips. Ease off the brakes, turn in and initially there's understeer, but get on the throttle early and power through the bend in a glorious old-fashioned, unreconstructed powerslide. The Jaguar is with you all the way, out the other side and, with the

hammer down, the exuberant slide opens out into a full blooded, flat-out drag down the straight.

With all these marvellous sensations rushing through your brain, fed through your fingertips, the balls of your feet and the seat of your pants, this C-type is an incredible experience and it certainly looks like the 1953 Le Mans winner. It is not as powerful or as firmly set up as the original car now is, which makes it much more usable on the road, but it does look the part and feels just like an original

C-type from the driver's seat.

The quandary is yours to ponder. This Racing Green C-type will always be a reproduction. But it is exquisitely crafted and provides all the right sensations. This beautiful example will save you at least £250,000 over the price of an original, road-going C-type. Only you can answer the question: 'what price originality?' △

» Thanks to Racing Green Cars which sells this C-type Jaguar on order: Station Road West, Ash Vale, Hampshire GU12 5QD, England. Tel: +44 (0)1252 544888. www.racinggreencars.com

'EASE OFF THE BRAKES, TURN IN AND INITIALLY THERE'S UNDERSTEER, BUT GET ON THE THROTTLE EARLY AND POWER THROUGH THE BEND IN A GLORIOUS OLD-FASHIONED POWERSLIDE'

Clockwise from above
Straight-through exhausts exit nearside; 3442cc straight six pumps out 205bhp, just 15bhp less than original in race trim; modern rubber doesn't get a look in – instead it's shod with original sticky Dunlops.

Modified Jaguar MkVII
SPECIFICATIONS

Engine
3781cc, six-cylinder,
twin overhead cam,
three twin-choke
Webers

Power
260bhp@5500rpm

Torque
270lb ft@3500rpm

Transmission
Four-speed manual

Suspension
Front: wishbones,
torsion bars and
hydraulic dampers.
Rear: semi-elliptic
leaf springs and
hydraulic dampers.

Brakes
Servo-assisted discs
Top Speed
125mph (est)

Value
£5,000

Neo-classic
Muscle

When the supercharged S-type R first appeared in 2003, it marked a
return to the supersaloon market, a sector Jaguar had abandoned with
the end of the Mk2. However, the opposition was considerably tougher
thanks to the arrival of the 400bhp-plus BMW M5 and, later, the Audi
RS6. We compare the original neo-classic saloon protagonists, and
throw an unlikely joker into the pack, the Lotus Carlton.

Words: David Vivian | Pictures: Andy Morgan

The Vauxhall Lotus Carlton can still hold its own against supersaloons ten years its junior. Only brash looks betray its age alongside the smoother Jaguar, Audi and BMW.

Surely the rush of heavy metal has never looked or sounded better than in the movie *Bullitt*. And I'm not talking about the Mustang GT390. Even with its ripped-off GT40 soundtrack and the benefit of Steve McQueen's tasty car control, the permanently smoke-wreathed, axle-tramping Ford took forever to dump that black and comparatively unwieldy Dodge Charger.

In real life it wasn't like that. The stunt team responsible for the celluloid duel admitted that the big cube combatants weren't evenly matched. Out of the crate, the bulky Dodge had too much for the 'Stang; the problem was getting the cars to stay in the same shot. Now tell me you weren't rooting for the Charger all along. Then you wore thick-framed Ray-Bans for a week, right?

If so, you're probably up for this. We're about to ignite a four-way, multi-cylinder fight between Jaguar's modern-day re-interpretation of the hot Mk2, the benchmark of all supersaloons, the revered E39 generation BMW M5; the multi-talented all-wheel drive Audi RS6; and the original 1990s loony-saloon, the Lotus Carlton. Oh, and we have Thruxton at our disposal…

This will, of course, be a blast. Heaps of weight, preposterous power. Which is a different proposition entirely to achieving speed by removing mass. Major metal wrapped around weapons-grade firepower requires alternative thinking. Might as well crank commitment up to max too, because there's little room for error once things get moving. Everything to do with sliding may seem to happen in slo-motion but the physics are just as inevitable and the values more spectacular.

You can't just jink or twitch your way out of a situation, either. Go with the flow, but only having already worked out which way the flow is going. No good focusing on your fingertips. We're talking big, pre-emptive inputs, liberal use of corrective lock and throttle travel; real, physical cockpit action. You have to loosen up, wipe the sweat from your palms, take control.

Then? Well, there's just something about lighting up rubber the size of real estate, seeing the scenery streak to liquid grey-green then pan from windscreen to side window, smoke simultaneously funnelling across the span of all three mirrors. The sensation of speed may not be as intense as in a tarmac-skimming sports car, but the feeling of momentum is vaguely awesome. Mighty forces are at work and you're at their fulcrum, and it honestly doesn't get much better if

'This car was too much to stomach for some people, and not just Porsche 911 pilots'

you like your action large. Which we do.

Little encouragement is needed to break loose at the rear with the traction-scavenging electronics switched off, the S-type R does its best to ape the BMW's balletic ballistics through the snaking Complex and will go just as smokily sideways but dissipates more speed in the endeavour. It also requires a little more work at the helm to keep the slide tidy; bumps the M5 doesn't seem to notice modulate the Jag's rear-end grip and unsettle the calm of the suspension. It sounds a little strained fully wrung-out too, sharply metallic supercharger whine souring the more mellifluous backbeat of its big, quad-cam V8.

But it's immediately apparent that, without doing any of this, the Audi RS6 (with 444bhp on tap) doesn't seem to slow down for Thruxton's corners. It has enormous all-drive grip, traction

and drive out of bends. It will even kick its tail wide at a businesslike angle if you lift out of its preferred steady understeer suddenly. From the outside it sounds like the super-concentrated American V8 of a Le Mans Corvette racer muffled by a 30-tog duvet. On the inside it's as quiet and comfortable as it possibly can be given the ambient scream of the tyres and violent transient shifts in g-force pressure against those sculpted Recaros. Astounding and anodyne at the same time.

The natural off-the-leash attitude of the BMW M5 (400bhp) is a kind of insouciant, fag-on oversteer McQueen himself would dig. Given sufficient incentive, it will scribe long, languid, 'it's-nothing-really' arcs with clouds curling off the rear arches all day long. It relaxes into a powerslide with a sigh. Nothing much seems to change. Steering weight and feel are just as good on

opposite lock. Stability and suspension control, too. All the driver has to do is balance the relative quantities of throttle and corrective steering. There isn't an optimum angle of drift as such. Shallow or deep, the M5 is cool with both – and anything in between. On the track, it was born to burn rubber.

But the most brutal sight of the morning is truly astonishing. Somehow larger. Somehow darker. Somehow broadside for an eternity. Different sound, too: lower, less distinct, more akin to a force of nature. That once feared presence is back – the Lotus Carlton.

We registering any public hysteria yet? Choppers been put on alert? Perhaps it's just as well the more recent guns in this gang – Jaguar S-type R, Audi RS6, BMW M5 – are down with the concealment angle. Soberly suited in true »

Reservoir Dogs style, they're careful to present a reassuringly benign face to the world compared with the LC. Muscular bulges have been smoothed and chamfered, unsubtle wings and chins left on designers' drawing boards.

The only common signifiers of their phenomenal performance are disc brakes that are nearly as big as those vast wheels which fill the wheelarches as snugly as knuckles in a duster, and calipers (eight-pot for the RS6) hanging behind the spokes like sides of beef. Step back and the look is superhero-trying-to-blend-in, especially the Audi

which somehow squeezes a set of 19x8.5in rims under its carefully inflated arches. The M5 and S-type R stuff barely less extravagant 18-inchers under their lightly flared wings and opt for fatter rims at the back: a race car-aping ten inches for the BMW, half an inch wider than the Jaguar's. All beautifully de-emphasised, of course, although the M5 – understated almost to the point of anonymity – only just manages to keep its enormous potential for supercar slaying on the safe side of discretion.

Back in the early 1990s, the Lotus Carlton knew

nothing of unerstatement, much less political correctness. The 176mph, 377bhp 'cause for public concern' was neither self-conscious nor apologetic. Quite the opposite, and it's easy to understand why. Between them, GM and Lotus had to perform a modern day miracle: turn the acme of humdrum family saloons, the Vauxhall Carlton, into something that could embarrass any supercar this side of a Ferrari F40 and all for considerably less money than a Porsche 911 Turbo.

Apart from the mind-boggling feat of actually summoning the necessary performance, the idea was to bury the original saloon's homespun image beneath a hugely suggestive muscle suit as pumped-up as today's equivalents are down-played. In the event the Carlton bit wasn't completely subsumed. Just enough of it remained to twist the knife into the egos of drivers of more conventional supercars humbled by its pulverising pace. This car was too much to stomach for some people, and not just Porsche 911 pilots. Questions about its right to exist were asked in Parliament. Sensitive souls wanted it banned.

Which makes it infamous, iconic and, quite possibly, legendary – a kind of McLaren F1 of tin tops. Its right to be here needn't be questioned. It earns its wild card both for being the bad-ass blueprint for the megasaloon genre and submitting

On track at Thruxton the RS6 is stonkingly fast (left). On the road, Jag can't shake off BMW, prompting thoughts that this cat may be a little off-colour. Carlton not as polished as other cars, especially handling-wise, but by golly it's a lot of fun.

a set of stats that haven't sagged with age, even though engine technology has ascended from the tree tops to the stratosphere in the intervening decade. You just wouldn't think a 24-valve 3.6-litre straight six developed from the 3-litre lump in the GSi 3000 (even one blown by two Garrett T25 turbos fed through a 'chargecooler') could pose any kind of threat to the state-of-the-art, superheated V8s deployed by the class of 2003. And with a quoted peak power output of 377bhp at 5200rpm, it's true that the Carlton is 23bhp shy of the 400bhp pumped out by the normally aspirated 5-litre M5 and supercharged 4.2-litre S-type R and a breezy 67bhp behind the 444bhp twin-turbo 4.2-litre Audi.

Game over, then? It's hardly begun. The Lotus Carlton's first ace is that it weighs 1685kg – beefy enough to qualify for the 'heavy metal' brigade, but significantly more svelte than the next lightest car, the 1720kg M5. The Jag piles another 80 kilos on top of that and the Audi is 40 heavier than that. It means that with a power/weight ratio of 231bhp/ton, the LC gives little away to the M5 (236bhp/ton) and pips the 226bhp/ton S-type R. Only the RS6 is out on its own with 245bhp/ton.

But not even the Audi can match the old-timer for raw twisting effort: 419lb ft at 4200rpm plays 413lb ft. All right, that's 413lb ft between 1950 and

5600rpm but the Carlton's torque curve looks about as peaky as Ayres Rock and benefits from mechanical six-speed drive to the rear wheels rather than via a torque converter to all four.

The only other car with a manual six-speed 'box, the M5, has a comparatively modest-looking 368lb ft at 3800rpm to play with. True, its ratios are somewhat snappier (the LC will pull 80mph in second and is geared to do 287mph in sixth – or 2250rpm at 100mph) but then, when it comes to

the torque/weight ratio our almost pristine LC (preserved by Vauxhall Heritage for perspective-focusing exercises just such as this) is way ahead of the modern game with 253lb ft/ton, followed by the Jaguar (230), Audi (228) and the BMW (218).

When John Barker took the Lotus Carlton to Millbrook for *Performance Car* in 1991, it recorded the following figures: 0-60mph in 4.8sec, 0-100mph in 10.6sec, a standing quarter of 13.2sec (at 114mph) and a top speed of 163mph round the

two-mile bowl, which would have equated to a surefire 170mph+ on the flat, possibly even that controversial 176mph claimed top speed. Too good for modern cars limited to 155mph, though there seems little doubt the S-type and M5 would be able to crack 170mph given the opportunity; and Audi reckoned the RS6 would be knocking on the door of 190mph. It also claimed the RS6 can blast to 60mph in 4.7sec.

At Thruxton, this German-registered car couldn't quite dip below five seconds, and was into the high 11s on the clock before it hit the ton. Even the best independent figures we've seen for the RS6 put it nearly a second off the pace of the Lotus Carlton at 100mph. Old metal rules in the sprint.

When we strap the kit to the Jaguar, it's even further adrift of its maker's claims – so perhaps there's something about the circuit. But it also fuels the subjective impression that this particular S-type R doesn't feel quite as ferocious as the example that took the scalp of the M5 the last occasion they met.

As we strike out for Exmoor, the suspicion is confirmed. This time out, the M5 has the legs of the Jaguar. Whenever they find themselves on a

straight long enough to exploit the difference, it's the German car that either sticks like glue or eases away. The Jaguar is sensationally swift – aided by its exquisitely responsive and smooth six-speed automatic gearbox – but it's the slowest car here. At least in a straight line.

Talking transmissions, the Lotus Carlton's is lifted from the Corvette ZR1 of the time and heavy duty in every sense – tough enough to cope with the prodigious torque but saddled with an imprecise, industrial weight gearchange and thigh-numbingly heavy clutch which occasionally whiffs of pad material but never actually seems to slip – a trait it shares with that original *Performance Car* test car. Fortunately it has one truly great gear: fourth will take you all the way from jogging pace to 143mph, dispatching 80-100mph in a staggering 3.8sec on the way. Even so, the M5's six-speed 'box (which has never won any awards for slickness) is a model of sweet-actioned acuity by comparison. It's a joy to stir it just to access the creamy warble and urgent upper-reach push of the 5-litre V8.

The Audi's Tiptronic automatic is good to use. Slotting the selector across to an alternative '+/-'

gate gives sequential access to the 'box via deft fore and aft nudges of the lever. Alternatively, you can thumb the paddles on the steering wheel. This is the best bet. Using just third and fourth and the engine's Galactic spread of torque is a phenomenally effective way to travel for what seems like just a handful of revs. The Sport slot on the main lever's gate is a waste of time. It delays up-shifts, thus wasting revs and petrol. Such is the pulling power of the Audi's partially Le Mans-derived lump, it's doubtful if it even needs kickdown.

'The M5 feels almost ridiculously nimble
and it's dynamite to hustle'

It's something of a precision-machined sledgehammer, the RS6. A build quality tour de force with flawlessly formed details and a lean beauty that makes the Jaguar and BMW look fussy and the LC almost impossibly macho. Devon, it has to be said, is a long way from its natural habitat. You sense it's aching for those long, straight, lightly trafficked strips of unrestricted autobahn. A place where the rumble from under the bonnet signals the onset of acceleration that almost sucks the moisture from your eyeballs. And all with no perceptible effort whatsoever.

Roads this twisty and bumpy aren't doing it any favours – the RS6 is no sportscar. It handles with immense security and has the best brakes of a fabulously well-endowed group. But it isn't agile enough to seem anything other than bulky, despite the massive cornering forces its gumball tyres are capable of generating. And its steering, while meatily weighted, is curiously inert. The harshness of its ride is a shock, too. Although fine with large amplitude bumps and dips, the suspension

Above: kill the traction control and the M5 can lap the track almost entirely sideways. Carlton (opp top) similarly adept at dispensing big grins. All these cars have storming engines (below, l-to-r): Audi's 444bhp twin-turbo V8 the brawniest; Jag V8 uses supercharger to get 400bhp; Carlton's 377bhp twin-turbo straight-six; BMW's 400bhp normally aspirated V8.

doesn't even try to soak up the single sharp inputs, ripples and ruts which occasionally jar through the cabin structure. Any luxury pretensions are swiftly blown.

In contrast, the M5 feels almost ridiculously ➤➤

Compare and contrast four very different interiors (clockwise from top left): GM wasn't very good at interiors in 1991, hence Carlton's cliff-like dashboard; M5 typically solid, clear BMW affair; Jag clubby and cosy; Audi exquisitely detailed and screwed together. It's the most spacious car here.

Go figure

The first acceleration run wasn't very good. The big saloon was only as quick to 60mph as a Ferrari Testarossa. The next one was just right – sidestepping the clutch at 2800rpm, feeling the rear Goodyears slip momentarily before the twin-turbo motor's fearsome 419lb ft of torque was converted wholly into forward motion. Nought to sixty? 4.8sec. 0-100? 10.6. This was January 1991 and I was figuring the Lotus Carlton for *Performance Car* magazine.

We knew the Carlton was going to be quick, but this surpassed our expectations. Its in-gear acceleration figures once the turbos spooled-up simply demolished the supercar opposition of the day. Over our benchmark 50-70mph in fifth it was more than half a second quicker than Lotus's own Esprit Turbo SE. From 80-100mph only the 455bhp Lamborghini Countach QV could keep up, though we were yet to figure the then-new Diablo. Of all the other cars on sale in early 1991, only the Ferrari F40 was quicker.

John Barker

nimble and, mostly thanks to its extraordinary body control, it's dynamite to hustle down a demanding road while staying remarkably comfortable. The Audi may be stronger but the BMW is both sharper and more supple. RS6 brawn is heavier but M5's is more enthusiastic. Its throttle responds more energetically to any given input and it revs harder at the top end. It needs to, of course. The only duff element is steering that's too light and rather feel-less. Hitting the Sport button adds the necessary amount of weight and feel but also sharpens the already sharp throttle response – which is a matter of taste. It would be better if the functions could be separated.

The Jaguar is softer, more compliant and benefits from a sympathetic pair of hands at the helm that can deftly administer small inputs to balance the car's attitude mid-bend. Its steering is beautifully weighted but meatier and more communicative than the BMW's, a quality put to good use by the terrific grip of the 18-inch Continental Sport

Contacts and the chassis' well judged cornering balance with its broad neutral phase. Body motions are closely controlled and contribute to the most cosseting ride of all. Mostly, though, this is the most flingable S-type by a margin.

Ultimately, the Lotus Carlton doesn't corner as quickly as the others. But it does have a chassis that can involve and satisfy broadly along the lines of the M5's and instill huge confidence in its driver. All right, it doesn't compete with the BMW's subtlety and finesse – though it beats the Audi – and body roll is quite pronounced when pressing on.

So was it worth the Lotus Carlton coming out of retirement for one final fight? The LC is still hard enough to put at least two of this year's pretenders in casualty. Even the RS6 which, on paper, carries a 67bhp advantage, is shaded. And outrageous grunt is the Audi's principal weapon. To say that the Lotus Carlton wreaked havoc among the young pretenders is being almost laughably kind to their bruised egos.

The fact that it came within a whisker of relegating the most powerful production saloon on the planet to last place is little short of astonishing. In the end, though, the RS6 (so fast,

so beautifully put together, so effective) just manages to rub out the ghost from the past. Point-to-point it's by far the quicker car – in fact, it's quickest of all – and as a pure object of desire it scores heavily. Fact is, though, the LC had it licked for outright pace and driver involvement. A sobering thought.

The Lotus Carlton simply savaged the S-type R for straight grunt but the Jaguar is such a beautifully poised and considered package it was never in any danger of being beaten by the old timer. On this occasion, though, it's shaded by the M5 – it wasn't quite good enough to topple the icon and become the new-age definitive supersaloon. The opening act of extremism at Thruxton and nagging doubt that our test car wasn't at the top of its form were enough to put the M5 back on top.

It isn't just because it seats four people in comfort. It isn't just because everything that contributes to driving pleasure – every last detail – has been meticulously developed and resolved. It's because if the bad guys had been chasing McQueen through the streets of San Francisco in an M5, they'd have given him a head start.

Just for the hell of it. △

As the Godfather of the neo-classic supersaloons, the Lotus Carlton is well within its rights to come back for a bit with the young pretenders. But we didn't expect this much blood.

	LOTUS CARLTON	AUDI RS6	JAGUAR S-TYPE R	BMW M5
Engine	In-line six cylinder	V8	V8	V8
Location	Front, longitudinal	Front, longitudinal	Front, longitudinal	Front, longitudinal
Displacement	3615cc	4172cc	4196cc	4941cc
Bore x stroke	95 x 85mm	84.5 x 93mm	86 x 90.3mm	89 x 94mm
Compression ratio	8.2:1	9.3:1	9.1:1	11:1
Cylinder block	Cast iron	Aluminium alloy	Aluminium alloy	Aluminium alloy
Cylinder head	Aluminium alloy, dohc, four valves per cylinder	Aluminium alloy, dohc per bank, five valves per cylinder	Aluminium alloy, dohc per bank, four valves per cylinder	Aluminium alloy, dohc per bank, four valves per cylinder
Fuel and ignition	Delco engine management, electronic multipoint fuel injection, twin turbo	Bosch electronic ignition and multipoint fuel injection, twin-turbo	Denso electronic engine management, multipoint fuel injection, supercharged	Bosch electronic engine management, multipoint fuel injection
Max power	377bhp @ 5200rpm	444bhp @ 5700rpm	400bhp @ 6100rpm	400bhp @ 6600rpm
Max torque	419lb ft @ 4200rpm	413lb ft @ 1950-5600rpm	408lb ft @ 3500rpm	369lb ft @ 3800rpm
Transmission	Six-speed manual, rear-wheel drive with LSD	Five-speed auto, Tiptronic, four-wheel drive, stability control	Six-speed auto, rear-wheel drive, stability control	Six-speed manual, rear-wheel drive, LSD, stability control
Front suspension	MacPherson struts, coil springs, lower wishbones, arb	Four link, coil springs anti-roll bar	Double unequal length wishbones, coil springs, arb	MacPherson struts, coil springs and anti-roll bar
Rear suspension	Semi-trailing arms, coil springs, lateral links, arb	Double wishbones, coil springs, anti-roll bar	Double wishbones, coil springs, anti-roll bar	Multi-link, coil springs, and anti-roll bar
Steering	Recirculating ball, power-assisted	Rack and pinion, power-assisted	Rack and pinion, power-assisted	Recirculating ball, power-assisted
Brakes	Vented discs front and rear, 330mm front, 300mm rear, ABS	Vented discs front and rear, 345mm front, 330mm rear, ABS	365mm vented discs front, 330mm discs rear, ABS	Vented discs front and rear, 345mm front, 328mm rear, ABS
Wheels	8.5 x 17in front, 9.5 x 17 rear	8.5 x 19in front, 8.5 x 19in rear	8 x 18in front, 9.5 x 18in rear	8 x 18in front, 9.5 x 18in rear
Tyres	235/45 ZR17 front, 265/40 ZR17 rear, Goodyear Eagle	255/35 ZR19 front, 255/35 ZR19 rear, Conti Sport Contact	245/40 ZR18 front, 275/35 ZR18 rear, Conti Sport Contact	245/40 ZR18 front, 275/35 ZR18 rear, Michelin Pilot Sport
Fuel tank capacity	16.5gal/75 litres	18gal/82 litres	15gal/69.5 litres	15.4gal/70 litres
Weight (kerb)	1658kg	1840kg	1800kg	1720kg
Power-to-weight	231bhp/ton	245bhp/ton	226bhp/ton	236bhp/ton
0-60mph	4.8sec	4.7sec (claimed)	5.3sec (claimed)	4.9sec
Max speed	176mph (claimed)	155mph (limited)	155mph (limited)	155mph (limited)
Price new	£48,000 (1991)	£57,700 (2003)	£47,400 (2003)	£52,000 (2003)
RATING	★★★★✓	★★★★✓	★★★★★	★★★★★

GT3

GTs are all about devouring long distances as well as satisfying the keen driver. We take three of the best 700 miles across France to storm a legendary hillclimb

Words: Richard Meaden **Pictures:** Gus Gregory

JAGUAR

'It really is a terrifically sexy shape, all teardrop curves and sleek aggression'

In an age when you can fly to Nice in a little over 90 minutes, and for £50, driving for nine hours and spending ten times as much for the privilege may seem more than a little anachronistic. But then there are few more glorious anachronisms than the modern GT. And few cars better encapsulate the romance of fast, long distance driving.

The epitome of our enthusiasm and fascination for sustaining big speeds over big mileages, they embody a blend of prestige, presence and performance that place them in motoring's major league. That they stop short of the exhibitionism and impracticality of a stratospherically priced supercar just seems to add extra strings to their bows.

Not that you should feel short-changed if your dreams 'only' stretch this far. The consummate Porsche 911 C4S, seductive Maserati 4200GT and newly revised Jaguar XKR are three of the finest modern exponents of the classic GT genre. To hold the keys to any one of these cars in your hand is to truly appreciate the meaning of the word wanderlust. Which is why rather than idly trotting out that empty cliché about one-hit forays to the Mediterranean, we are going to put mileage where our mouth is. Driving the length of France non-stop, we'll test their mile-munching capacity with a 700-mile autoroute schlep. Then, in a total change of pace, we'll plot a course for one of the greatest and most historic hillclimbs in the world

– the daunting, spectacular Mont Ventoux – to see how each cuts it as an out-and-out driver's car.

It's an intriguing, double-edged test of three very different cars. The all-wheel-drive, manual 911 is clear favourite to revel in the twists and turns of Ventoux's barren, volcanic slopes, but its focus on engrossing dynamics could prove wearing on the arrow-straight peage. The supercharged Jaguar's effortless pace and cosseting delivery is tailor-made for the autoroute but its bulk and supple set-up is likely to be rather less suitable for scratching to the 2000 metre summit of Ventoux. Dark horse here is the Maserati. We'd hoped to have a manual version, but in many respects this paddle-shift Cambiocorsa version should strike the ideal balance, combining easy motorway flexibility with brutal, normally-aspirated response and lightning-fast gearshifts on the maximum attack mountain ascent. Which car wears the yellow jersey for the return leg home is, frankly, anyone's guess.

That old GT romance is in short supply at the Meaden household at 2:30am on a Monday morning, when the strident tones of a Radio 4 newsreader blare insistently from the bedside

alarm. In almost a decade of working with photographer Gus Gregory, this is the most extreme example of 'Gus O'Clock' I have ever experienced. It's so early it hurts. But a 3am departure is what's required to get me from my sleepy Northamptonshire village to the Nikon-wielding nightwalker's Reigate lair, and then on to Folkstone for a 6.30am Eurotunnel train.

Despite the sleep deprivation I'm relishing the prospect of taking a large bite out of Europe in Jaguar's finest. Yesterday, Eddie Irvine raced to a fine third place at Monza, and although I've long been wondering why Ford persists in bankrolling Jaguar's disastrous, politics-riven F1 effort, the sight of a British driver, clad in British Racing Green up there with Ferrari is a genuinely stirring sight. As that surge of pride is still with me in the early hours of Monday morning, perhaps there's more to this F1 halo effect than marketing babble.

The XKR has long been a supremely effective, desirable machine, but thanks to the S-Type R, the XKR now benefits from the new saloon's larger, 4.2-litre, supercharged V8, along with a host of other detail changes, both to the hardware and cosmetics. Headline news is the power and torque »

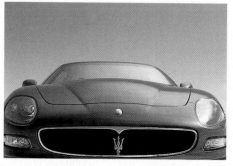

Jag XKR has always been a looker, but in new Racing Green paint with darkened Xenon lamp surrounds it's stunning, as is its ability to keep the brilliant 911 C4S in sight on tricky roads.

'The XKR storms out of bends with gobsmacking force'

increase, up from 370bhp and 387lb ft to 400bhp and 408lb ft, but there have also been tweaks to the CATS suspension and the steering assistance, and the fitment of some mighty Brembo discs and calipers. This car has all the 'R Performance' goodies, including stiffer springs, those incredible 20in 'Detroit' alloys and more supportive sports seats.

Visually the XKR has never looked better. It really is a terrifically sexy shape, all teardrop

Freshened XKR claims 900 changes, most obvious of which is superb 4.2-litre supercharged V8 from S-type R (below). Maser also has a V8 (below right) though naturally aspirated and rather more rev-happy than Jag's relaxed lump. Meaden at play in the Jag (below far right) amid acres of leathery woodiness. Porsche (opp page far right) much less opulent, but a remarkably good long-distance car nonetheless.

curves, muscular haunches and sleek aggression. Someone at Jaguar must be a mind reader, for those wheels, the Jaguar Racing Green paintwork, crimson leather, silver-grey wood and tactile all-leather 'R' steering wheel is my ideal combination.

Despite the obvious physical allure, driving an XKR never gives me an instant hit of excitement. Perhaps it's the auto 'box. More likely it's the nagging feeling that Jags are driven by people a generation older than me. Whatever, I'm an hour down the motorway before it dawns on me that I'm actually really enjoying the Jag, luxuriating in the instant, effortless response, glassy gearshifts and deliciously soothing ambience. It is utterly sublime.

A few hours later, and with Gus and his camera

gear stowed, the Jag's xenon headlights cast a cold, sharp beam of light across the unmistakable rumps of a yellow C4S and dark green Maserati waiting at the Eurotunnel ticket barriers. The contrast between the two is stark; the chic, aloofly aristocratic Italian and the brash, muscle-bound nightclub bouncer from Stuttgart. Where the slinky Jag fits in, only time will tell.

After 40 minutes of immersion in the muggy, stale fug of the Eurotunnel carriage it's a pleasure to emerge into fresh air and lightly trafficked roads. The sense of freedom you get on French autoroutes is incredible. No hassle, no jams, no selfish trucks blocking the middle lane, just fast, free-flowing, well-disciplined drivers making rapid

progress. The temptation to exploit the lack of traffic is huge, but past experience suggests Gendarmes are getting increasingly tetchy about Brits using their motorways as race tracks. Reluctantly we settle into a discreet 100mph cruise and watch with dismay as turbodiesel after turbodiesel leaves us in a turbulent wake of soot and carcinogens.

Pretty soon we make the first of many fuel stops. Predictably the smaller, lighter Porsche is the most frugal, managing a comfortable mid-20s average, although its small fuel tank means no great range advantage. The Jag and Maser are thirstier machines, managing similar and similarly depressing 20mpg averages. Only the Maser's

bigger tank gives it the legs on the XKR.

Swapping from the Jaguar into the Maserati shouldn't be much of a culture shock. Both have big capacity V8s, two pedals and a bias towards luxury. In fact with four full-size seats, compared with the Jag's laughable rear and the 911's no rear seats whatsoever, the 4200GT takes its GT role most seriously. But as soon as the Ferrari-developed 90-degree V8 fires into life it's obvious the Maserati is a flightier, more highly-strung machine than the laid-back Jag.

Cruising at a ton in the XKR equates to just over 2500rpm. In the 4200GT the tacho needle is pointing vertically at 4000rpm. Since it revs to 7500rpm this elevated cruising gate is relative,

but the engine is also more vocal and less well isolated, so you're constantly aware of the motor's work rate. The trade-off is almighty 6th gear acceleration, the like of which you'd have to slot fourth in the Porsche or kickdown in the XKR to match. It really does leap forward with shocking vigour, and although we never summoned the nerve to verify it, the 176mph top speed seems all too believable.

While there's no question the Maserati is the swiftest straight-line machine, questions are already being asked about its chassis. Expansion joints thump through the car like gunshots, and if encountered mid-corner the whole car skips and shimmies momentarily, where the Jag simply >>

input than the Jag or Maser but provides more stimulation whilst retaining some semblance of civility. It's not as comfortable to passenger in as the other two, but that's down to the optional sports seats. Swap them for more padded recliners and the C4S runs the more genteel GTs surprisingly close.

Poking some 6000 feet into the sky, Mont Ventoux is less than an hour from the autoroute. First used as a venue for a timed motor trial a century ago, the meandering mountain pass also plays host to a lung-bursting stage of the Tour de France cycle race. It's steeped in competition history, and is a special place for fans of pedal power and brake horsepower alike.

We approach the mountain from the south, passing through endless rows of vines heaving under the weight of plump, purple grapes. The road begins to head for the clouds miles before the actual start of the competitive hillclimb course, and our sense of anticipation and excitement increases with the gradient. Lurid graffiti smothers the road, evidence of last year's Tour, and as the vineyards give way to trees and rocky outcrops, the magnitude of the climb becomes apparent.

Lined with armco barriers, this looks more like the nadgety parts of the Nürburgring's Nordschleife than a mountain road. It's fast too, long straights spooling away before us, climbing at around 30 degrees and feeding into inviting, just-blind combinations of lefts and rights. The camber always seems to be with you, but as you begin to fall into a rhythm a nasty hairpin always seems to trip you up.

As predicted, the Porsche is in its element, howling its approval up the straights, tucking neatly into the turns and giving maximum reassurance when indecision afflicts your right foot. It provides so much information through the steering wheel and thinly padded seat that you know exactly how much grip remains untapped.

The Jag is working hard in the rear view mirror, creeping up to the 911's fat tail on the straights, dropping back a little when the braking zones loom. Acting as point man is always tougher than following, but I'm still impressed to see the XKR

steamrollers them into submission. Even the 911 copes more convincingly, despite dynamics honed for hooning rather than schmoozing. In fact it nearly matches the XKR's compliance, if not its unconstrained muscularity, as we discover when I swap to the Porsche for the final motorway stint

Three different approaches to exterior style (above from top): elegant Jag; aggressive Porsche; suave Maser. Interiors (below from left) contrast too: lavish XK includes special sports seats amongst R Performance goodies; 911 also has optional sports seats, adding to functional air; 4200GT beats them both for sheer style, and it's a full four-seater too.

before we turn off the autoroute at Orange and head for Mont Ventoux.

With every generation of the 911, purists bemoan the gradual softening of its character, but I reckon there's method in Stuttgart's madness. I'd love to attack Mont Ventoux in a 964RS, but the drive from Calais would require a box of Nurofen meltlets and emergency roadside chiropractic manipulation. Even fitted with quasi race seats and a throaty sports exhaust, the C4S is a comfortable long-distance partner. It demands more

'Through corners the 911 allows you to work beyond its limits'

doing so well. So too is its driver, John Hayman. 'The XK's evolved into a GT that can 'do' Europe and give its finest driving roads a right good bashing when it gets there. It storms out of bends with gobsmacking force and it also deals with the braking points brilliantly. Frankly, it carries ridiculous mid-corner speed for something of that size and weight.'

Just as we're beginning to really enjoy ourselves, blue flashing lights ahead call a halt to proceedings. A Gendarme is standing in the middle of the road, and as we cruise gently to a halt we are rather embarrassingly shrouded in our own brake smoke as the 911, Jag and Maser instantly barbecue their brake pads. Up ahead two of his colleagues are crouched by a stricken cyclist. No-one else is involved, but judging by the scarlet rivulets trickling from beneath the sheet things aren't good. 'Mort?' we ask. 'Mort,' the Gendarme replies. Gulp. Shaken, we continue past the scene of the accident, but our hearts aren't in a full-bore ascent so we decide instead to find a hotel for the night and raise a toast to the unfortunate cyclist.

Next morning we head out early and find the mountain deserted. I plump for the Jaguar. With oodles of power and torque, enormous reserves of grip and plenty of feel, it's easy to settle into a very rapid pace without trying very hard at all. You don't even have to palm the auto gear lever around the J-gate, although the extra engine braking does give the Brembos a helping hand if you do. It's when you want to try that bit harder the Jaguar's limitations are revealed. Exiting the tighter hairpins the gearbox is fractionally slow to react, then as it kicks down the 4.2-litre V8 unleashes rather more grunt than even the 20in rear Pirellis can cope with and the inside wheel spins up like a Catherine wheel.

It's this reluctance to be hustled that holds the XKR back through corners where the 911 allows you to work beyond its limits and still feel like you're in charted territory. The XKR feels much more at home through fast corners, perfectly balanced and delightfully, minutely adjustable. For such a hefty car it's miraculous, so much so that it's almost churlish to point out that the C4S still trumps it for involvement and poise. The brakes are also man enough to stop the Jag

repeatedly from serious speeds, although much like the steering, the pedal doesn't have the uncensored feel and firmness of the Porsche.

Ever since my early stint on the autoroute in the Maser I've been silently dreading putting it to the test on Mont Ventoux. You know within the first few yards whether a car is well sorted, and the 4200GT didn't feel at one with itself, even on the motorway. We're half way up the mountain now, and as I round one of the countless fresh air corners, the summit of Ventoux fills the windscreen. Crowned with a sinister space telescope and devoid of any vegetation, the rocky peak looks like part of a lunar landscape. Spooky isn't the word.

In the Maserati there's no time to gawp at the scenery. It really does go like the clappers, pulling hard to 5000rpm then searing on with renewed vigour to 7500rpm. Wringing out the 4200GT is a brutal process, each pull on the right-hand paddle hammering the next gear home with all the mechanical sympathy of a hardened hire car driver. It sends a shudder through the structure of the car and, even at more restrained speeds, emits a wince-inducing cog clatter that sounds like you've ❯❯

'Powering towards the exit you can feel the Maserati's tail load up'

run over a loose manhole cover. Maserati should try an M3 SMG for hints on how to do it properly.

Chassis-wise the 4200GT is an odd one. Crashy at low speed, the stiff ride never translates into confident body control, and the front and rear ends constantly fight with each other for your attention. Turn-in is rapid and grippy, but there's little feel to back it up, resulting in a tense, jumpy feel as you steer for the apex. Once powering towards the exit you can feel the tail load up, but the point at which the rear end begins to slide is masked, making the eventual breakaway swift

and unforgiving. And that's in the dry. Driving hard in the wet is like walking on eggshells.

Interestingly, given the luxury of driving repeatedly around the same corner for photography, it's possible to discover that the Maser regains some composure and balance when steered on the throttle, but I'd trade this for more feel and some progression before the onset of a slide. Likewise some added stability under braking would be welcome, as any steering input while braking heavily can seriously upset the chassis.

The outcome of this test was never going to be

black and white because by definition cars like this are more concerned with shades of grey. We'd expected the Maserati to play a numbers game, getting closer to the XKR's refinement and loping long-distance stride than the 911, then using its power and paddle-shift to push ahead of the Jaguar on the mountain roads. What we found was a car that displays a dismal lack of cohesion. A brittle ride and stressed high-speed cruising make heavy weather of the distance work, while snappy dynamics, a paucity of feedback and a frankly appalling transmission make the 4200GT Cambiocorsa a frustrating, intimidating experience on roads where it should be able and engrossing. There are fleeting moments of brilliance, and you begin to warm to the Maserati's flawed charms, but then the gearbox fumbles or the weather conditions deteriorate and you're reminded of what an ill-sorted, unhappy car the 4200GT is.

We knew the 911 would be king of the hill at Mont Ventoux, just as we expected the Jag to cream the autoroute. What we didn't expect was the 911's lesson in how a lack of opulence doesn't equate to a lack of long haul comfort, nor the Jaguar's pace and poise when chasing the Porsche's tail. My heart tells me I'd rather have the 911, if only for its out-and-out ability on give and take roads. But the XKR does such a magnificent job of shrugging off a solid day's driving and then raising its game at Mont Ventoux that my head insists it gets the nod. On this very special journey the XKR proved to be the consummate GT. △

On these French roads the Maserati (opp top) has occasional moments of inspiration whereas the 911 (opp bottom) is inspiring all the time. The climb to the 6000ft peak of Mont Ventoux is a real challenge for these cars, but this test isn't just about balls-out driving thrills. GTs have to be able to go the distance too.

	XKR-R	911 C4S	4200GT
Engine	V8	Flat six	V8
Location	Front, longitudinal	Rear, longitudinal	Front, longitudinal
Displacement	4196cc	3596cc	4244cc
Bore x stroke	86 x 90.3mm	96 x 82.8mm	92 x 80mm
Compression ratio	9.1:1	11.3:1	11.1:1
Cylinder block	Aluminium alloy	Aluminium alloy	Aluminium alloy
Cylinder head	Aluminium alloy, dohc per bank four valves per cylinder	Aluminium alloy, dohc per bank, four valves per cylinder	Aluminium alloy, dohc per bank, four valves per cylinder
Fuel and ignition	Denso electronic ignition and multipoint fuel injection, supercharger	Motronic electronic ignition and multipoint fuel injection	Bosch ME7.3.2 electronic ignition and multipoint fuel injection
Max power	400bhp @ 6100rpm	316bhp @ 6800rpm	390bhp @ 7000rpm
Max torque	408lb ft @ 3500rpm	273lb ft @ 4250rpm	333lb ft @ 4500rpm
Transmission	Six-speed auto, rear-wheel drive, stability control	Six-speed manual, four-wheel drive, stability control	Six-speed semi-manual, rear-wheel drive, traction control
Front suspension	Double wishbones, coil springs, anti roll bar	MacPherson struts, coil springs anti-roll bar	Double wishbones, coil springs, anti-roll bar
Rear suspension	Double wishbones, coil springs, anti-roll bar	Multi-link, coil springs, anti-roll bar	Double wishbones, coil springs, anti-roll bar
Steering	Rack and pinion, power-assisted	Rack and pinion, power-assisted	Rack and pinion, power-assisted
Brakes	Vented discs front and rear, 355mm front, 330mm rear, ABS	Vented discs front and rear, 330mm front, 330mm rear, ABS	Vented discs front and rear, 330mm front, 310mm rear, ABS
Wheels	?? x 20in front, ?? x 20in rear	8 x 18in front, 11 x 18in rear	8 x 18in front, 9.5 x 18in rear
Tyres	255/35 ZR20 fr, 285/30 ZR20 rr, Pirelli P Zero Asimetrico	225/40 ZR18 fr, 295/30 ZR18 rr, Pirelli P Zero Asimetrico	235/40 ZR18 fr, 265/35 ZR18 rr, Michelin Pilot Sports
Fuel tank capacity	16.5gal/75 litres	14gal/64 litres	19.4gal/88litres
Weight (kerb)	1735kg	1415kg	1680kg
Power-to-weight	234bhp/ton	226bhp/ton	236bhp/ton
0-60mph	5.2sec (claimed)	5.0sec (claimed)	4.9sec (claimed)
Max speed	155mph (limited)	177mph (claimed)	177mph (claimed)
Basic price	£56,700 (1993)	£62,260 (1993)	£68,000 (1993)
RATING	★★★★★	★★★★★	★★★

'JAGUAR MAKES MUCH OF THE XKR'S ACCESSIBILITY, MEANING NOT ONLY THE PRICE BUT ALSO THE EASE WITH WHICH YOU CAN EXPLOIT THE HANDLING'

'AN XK WITH THE VOLUME TURNED UP'

If the XKR is anything to go by the future for Jaguar should be assured, even in these days of economic chaos and Credit Crunch catastrophe...
Words: John Simister

Back in 2006 I drove the XJ13. Then a few months later the Jaguar XKR. All right, the hottest XK has a mere 416bhp to the XJ13's 502, and it weighs rather more despite its all-aluminium construction. But, believe me, the XKR still feels mighty quick.

Bombastically so? No. Relentless is a better word, a sensation that the torque will just keep on coming. If there's a flaw with the new XK it is that the engine's torque delivery is not great at low speeds. Also, the suspension can feel a mite floaty. The new R version is designed to lay such dynamic solecisms to rest.

'It's an XK with the volume turned up,' says Jaguar development supremo Mike Cross. Power is up by 116bhp and torque takes a similar lift to 413lb ft. The supercharger is the key, of course, but its insistent whine is the one part whose volume has not been turned up. It's much quieter now, but still present for those of us who like to hear machinery at work. And the exhaust, thanks to an Aston/Ferrari-like bypass valve, sounds fantastic.

You'd probably recognise an XKR by its mesh grille, skeletal wheels, four tailpipes and those bonnet vents. If not, the sound will identify the sub-species, a particularly crisp-edged interpretation of a V8 beat, best heard from the convertible version, in a tunnel.

This convertible is the first large open-top production car I've driven with responses almost as sharp as those of its solid-roof sibling. Such is the structure's stiffness that the open XKR runs the same firmed-up suspension as the coupé.

The XKR's adaptive dampers have a clever trick too: as you turn into a bend, the rear dampers stiffen an instant before the fronts to help point the tail. This, plus weightier steering with strong hints of genuine road feel (rare in a modern car), makes the XKR a delight to thread along a good twisting road. Its six-speed ZF automatic transmission helps here; already excellent in the XK, it gains a yet quicker shift time in manual mode for the XKR. Automatic mode is near-faultless, too. It is, in fact, the best torque-converter automatic in the world.

Jaguar makes much of the XKR's accessibility, meaning not only the price – at £67,495 for the coupé, it's a bargain next to rivals – but also the ease with which you can exploit the handling and remarkably cultured ride. It's a cracker. If Jaguar continues like this the future should be bright indeed. △

C A T L A P P I N G

We join Jaguar putting
the new XKR through
its paces at the
Nürburgring

Words: Chris Harris
Pictures: Mark Bramley

I have a long-held theory about the Nürburgring. It pertains to a gross untruth that has been perpetuated in the motor industry for some time now, namely that simply turning a wheel on the world's most hallowed asphalt is enough to improve any performance car; that a car is automatically better because it has been developed on the Nordschleife.

This is nonsense and has led me to deduce that the following is actually the case: for every model that has benefited from dynamic surgery at the Ring, there is another whose primary function as a road car has been spoilt by the place.

When Jaguar announced in 2003 that it was building a test centre at the Nürburgring to help develop all future models, I shuddered at the thought of the potential consequences. Of all the manufacturers whose core values might be crippled by extended Ring exposure, Jaguar was surely the most vulnerable. Even among its high-performance 'R' models, ride comfort has always been a prerequisite, yet if it's possible to isolate the one aspect of vehicle dynamics that supports my theory, it's that all too often a car is over-damped because it was optimised to cope with the treacherous compressions and bumps of the Nordschleife at

maximum lap speeds. With this approach, you often reach a confused conclusion: a car whose suspension is designed specifically for an environment most owners will rarely, if ever, experience. This is why the Astra VXR will lap the Ring with speed and composure to embarrass a Golf GTI, only to disintegrate into a shambles on a bumpy British B-road.

But in fairness to Jaguar, many new models have appeared since its decision to have a base at the circuit, and none has succumbed to the type of fidgety ride that plagues many of its German rivals. It points to a Jaguar development philosophy that has discovered how best to use the circuit for road-car applications, and when the invite came to see how the company had worked on the new XKR, it seemed like the perfect opportunity to prove, or perhaps disprove my theory.

Should my Lottery numbers roll in, I will buy the Jaguar Nürburgring Test Centre. In real-estate terms it is to car nuts what a penthouse apartment in St John's Wood is to cricket fans. The huge workshop, vast boardroom and endless supply of tyres are situated just yards from the 2km-long Dottinger Hohe straight. It is every DIY mechanic's dream. Six hydraulic ramps squeeze through a floor cleaner than most kitchen surfaces.

'The Jaguar Nürburgring Test Centre is every DIY mechanic's dream'

Left: XKR test mule gains access to the circuit via well-hidden 'Industry Pool' entrance.

This is Wolfgang Schuhbauer's office. In fact, this is a large chunk of his world. Wolfgang's job title is Vehicle Integrity Manager, which is PAG-speak for test engineer, meaning he reports to chief engineer Mike Cross. But he also runs the test centre and has been instrumental in shaping Jaguar's approach to the circuit. Given that I have one question to ask, and Wolfgang has devoted a good portion of his life to this place, he is the ideal arbiter.

So I ask him whether the Ring does ruin as many cars as it helps. 'What is most important is the correlation between the Ring and the different markets,' he replies. 'There is no other track in the world that can do this. You see, when we come to test a car like the XKR we have a programme to define all the vehicle characteristics, and then durability exercises to make sure they work properly.'

Hardly a one-word answer. Then comes the clever bit, and something I never knew about the Nordschleife. 'What is so amazing about this circuit, and I'm sure that the people who built it all those years ago had no idea they were doing it, is that it just happens to put the modern road car through the most perfect test parameters. Of course, we still carry out cold tests in Sweden, and Phoenix is our hot weather base, but the fact is that if the cooling system works on the long uphill section after Bergwerk, then our computer data shows that it will work in the Middle East.

'It's the same with the gearbox. We can run to 130 degrees C oil temperature, and here we're seeing about 120. With all our other data we know that if the transmission can sustain this then it will be okay in every market. Likewise, the downhill section to Breidscheid. The pads on the XKR work

up to around 650 degrees C without fading, and this is the temperature they are at Breidscheid, but it also happens to be identical to the temperatures we see on our Alpine test route. This is the perfect test environment.'

Just for the record, the component that has the hardest time is the differential. They haven't needed to fit an extra oil-cooler, but apparently it was a very close call.

Notice that not once has Wolfgang mentioned set-up. That's because for Jaguar the circuit is a test-bed for replicating the absolute extremes that a car might be put through, be it harsh suspension strikes or wheel-bearing loads. The way the car drives is determined on the road.

Wolfgang: 'One of the main reasons, apart from the circuit, that we have the test centre here is the autobahn nearby. We still do lots of high-speed ➤➤

LIFE IN THE INDUSTRY POOL

If Jaguar's Wolfgang Schuhbauer sometimes talks about the circuit in cool, empirical terms, it doesn't last for long. He has in his possession the most valuable key in all cardom, and just looking at it makes him babble with excitement. It opens two large steel doors, hidden from public view, called the Industry Pool entrance. Limitless free laps of the Ring (well, at the expense of your employer, at least)... What it must be like to have that key dangling from your fob!

The Industry Pool is a unique organisation, a cooperative formed from bitter rivals who wouldn't lend each other a teabag anywhere else. They all agree to certain terms and then rent the circuit together. Such is the value of the place that they don't mind parading their latest ideas right under the nose of the opposition – though much of this is down to a host of gentleman's agreements, such as no prolonged ogling and no peeking through side windows.

Naturally, there is an emphasis on safety. Over the past few years the use of crash helmets and roll-cages in prototypes has become far more common, although not compulsory. Of course, there are accidents, although there has never been a fatality on an Industry Pool day and most incidents aren't serious. Test-driving at the Ring is a deeply hazardous pastime, though. It's one thing using a production-ready 997 GT3 to its full potential, but it's something quite different to be involved in the evaluation of unproven mechanicals years before a car is due to go on sale.

Things are getting critical, though. Speeds are rising and most people expect some big shunts over the coming years. Walter Röhrl tripped over in a Carrera GT at Schwedenkreuz, the fastest corner on the circuit. If the great man himself can get it wrong, lesser beings are bound to follow suit.

Most of all, this is a controlled test environment. Sparky racing drivers are frowned upon – in fact a few have been banned – and everyone's behaviour is under scrutiny. Each manufacturer is trying to achieve different goals with their test time, remember, and that requires patience and common sense. Which can't be easy when you're testing an RS4 and next year's M3 appears in your mirror...

testing there, and the B-roads around the Eiffel are some of the most challenging in Germany. Most people would be amazed, but we do about 80 per cent of our damper tuning on the road.

'Aerodynamic tests are becoming even more important. Sometimes we just go out on the autobahn with ten different sets of small wings or underbody changes. We remove stuff and put new bits on the car, and the driver has no idea what's going on, he is just sent out to see the difference. Straight-ahead stability, lane-changes, body control – it's amazing how small aerodynamic changes can alter the body control of a car at speed. Sometimes you get out of the car and think that someone's changed a damper, but it's actually a small change on the rear wing. We do this in the wind tunnel then on the road, and only at the very end is it then checked on the circuit through lap-time.'

Ah, lap times. Wolfgang isn't a big fan of the pelvis-thrusting that goes on with one manufacturer boasting a time two seconds faster than that next: 'For Jaguar, lap-time isn't important. Yes, we want the car to be fast, but most importantly it should have clean steering, good wet grip and be comfortable. It should be easy to drive. The big problem with these lap times is that many manufacturers now use special "cup" tyres that make a huge difference to the lap time. The XKR uses a new Dunlop with excellent wet performance and comfort, and which will take ten laps without a significant change in performance. With this tyre the car will run somewhere around 8min 15sec, but with a cup tyre we can reduce that by 20sec.'

Excuses because the XKR just isn't that fast over a lap? Not at all. He takes some cajoling into talking lap times because even the XKR is no sports car, rather a GT in the British tradition. Its chassis and engine calibration were carried out mainly on the roads and circuit here, but also up on the Welsh

Test cars can pound the
Ring for up to nine hours
a day – when the new Jag
goes on sale later this year,
we'll know whether it was
all worth it

'The Ring is invaluable because it allows a car to be run through every eventuality'

Right: Harris straps himself in for a first taste of the new XKR. Bottom: matt black bonnet adds to the impression that this is a hard-worked car, and it is – it would head off to Nardo for high-speed testing a few days later

RIDING IN THE NEW XKR

Is it possible to tell anything from the passenger seat of a heavily soiled XKR test mule? Yes – that the decidedly non-production Schroth harnesses have a vicious appetite for male genitalia, and that something the size and mass of a lump hammer appears to be loose under the passenger seat.

There are less uncomfortable aspects. The car has excellent suspension travel and the auto transmission is impressive: upshifts are unfelt and it exacts revolution-perfect throttle-bursts to match crank and gear speed coming down the 'box. Also, the ride over the kerbs at Hatzenbach is the best I've ever experienced in a road car. But other than that, these passenger rides are a bit arbitrary, especially in something carrying 150kg of roll-cage and instrumentation, and missing much sound-deadening.

In fact, what I find more fascinating than the ride itself is the condition of the car. Gnarled test-hacks have the same swagger as a Le Mans winner: they seem so wonderfully pungent and used. It seems sad that quite soon such a worthy servant will be carted off to the crusher.

moors. That process has become more time-consuming, though, because of the active suspension system the car uses.

'With the XKR we need three comfort and sports settings, and then you have to get the switching between those modes right. But then when you have that working you have to make it work with the DSC – what is the suspension doing with DSC engaged, does it stay in a soft setting? And then what is the gearbox doing, should it shift down? This is all so complicated because you have to link all of these things together'

Once again, the Ring is invaluable because its 300-metre change in altitude and 17-degree maximum gradient allow a car to be run through every eventuality. In fact, the only aspect of the track that proves anomalous for testing is it's relatively high at 800m above sea level.

Tellingly, Jaguar has once again chosen not to fit a limited slip differential to one of its most powerful models, the official line being that unless it's electronically controlled it brings too much understeer. Perhaps this is the one single engineering decision that defines the Ring/road dichotomy: the XKR could benefit from a slippy diff over a fast lap, but it doesn't need it for street life so it doesn't have one fitted.

More than anything, though, I get the feeling that discipline is the key to Jaguar's work here. Young male car-types being paid to lap this place takes the child-in-a-confectioner's analogy to its most extreme representation, but Wolfgang comes over all engineer as he describes it: 'We're very disciplined because we need to carry out precise test procedures. For durability work I will sometimes spend the whole day from 8am to 5pm doing laps,

but in earlier stages of development we will go back to the workshop every two hours to give the car a thorough inspection. This is the discipline here: time on the track, inspection, and always then taking the car on the road.'

And I suppose that answers my question. I can't be sure of exact numbers, but before leaving for the airport we head for the viewing point at Brunchen and watch countless development mules battling through howling understeer. Many of them will have springs and dampers signed-off on the back of these gruesome sessions, and they will be poorer cars because of it. The same can't be said of the new XKR. △

HERITAGE, NOT RETRO

JAGUAR'S NEW XF IS PURE JAGUAR WITHOUT RESORTING TO PAST GLORIES

Ian Callum, a man with a love of hot rods and a healthy disregard for fossilised design, has the most difficult job in car design or the most exciting, dependent upon your view of life.

Jaguar, clearly, had to move into the future, preferably by acknowledging the present en route (a task performed by the XK). The current XJ saloon was a retro re-hash too far and buyers, though keen on the Jaguar characteristics of power, pace, refinement and sporting Britishness, were wondering if the ideas cupboard had become a little bare.

So Callum and his team had to make the replacement for the S-type, and potentially Jaguar's most important car, something ultra-modern and forward-looking which was still obviously a Jaguar, both in looks and in driving feel. Everyone was going to have an opinion, so the team just went ahead and created what they thought should set the new Jaguar template. And if you don't like it, how would you have done it differently?

The more you see the XF out on the road, preferably moving, the more the idea falls into place. The nose has its roots in the first XJ6 with the recessed, squared-off grille, the four round headlights (behind polycarbonate covers here), the fairings behind lights and grille and the central bonnet bulge. The shape of the rear side window has a slight echo of Mk2 but otherwise the design detailing has shades of the current XK: wings stretched out over wheels, vertical vents behind the front arches, a bright metal strip between horizontal tail lights, front and rear screens with XK-matching rakes.

Inside, the forward leap is yet more radical. There's wood, but it's used in reverse. Sections you would expect to be tree-clad are knurled aluminium (dashboard) or leather (doors), with the wood running along beneath the dash or sunk within the door recesses. There's plenty of it on the high central tunnel, too; the XF actually has the greatest wooden acreage a Jaguar has had for years, but also the most discreet.

And the gadgets... this car redefines surprise and delight. Open the door, sit down, see the start button pulsate in red. Press it, watch the round knob on the centre console, a knob like a BMW iDrive controller, rise up. This is the gear selector, rotated instead of lever-slotted. At the same time, four pieces of aluminium spin round to reveal the facia vents. The XF is coming alive.

If you're doing this at night, you will also see the various switch panels outlined in blue like the keypad of a modern mobile phone. If you want more light, gently touch the interior light lenses and the bulbs behind illuminate. There's a silver symbol like an RAF roundel on the wood above the glovebox; touch that and the lid opens. The wood itself looks best in a straight grain, but traditionalists can have burr walnut if they must. The tops of dash and doors are stitched leather.

The idea is to create an ambience of modern, high-tech Britishness, and the best of the available stereo systems builds on that. It's made by Bowers & Wilkins of Worthing, Sussex, and as well as sounding fantastic it also lets you operate your iPod via the main touch-screen.

There is no manual XF, so the centre console can be designed entirely around the transmission selector, the electric parking brake and three cupholders. Crucially, the ZF six-speed automatic's manual mode (operated by steering-wheel paddles) works quickly and definitely enough to feel like a proper, well-judged mechanical shift and thus holds your interest, and after starting off there's no torque-converter slippage. It even brings up engine revs for a smooth downshift.

Under the skin and the aluminium bonnet, the structure is developed from the S-type's with sufficient efficiency that, engine for engine, the XF is just 15kg heavier than the S-type despite being much more rigid. The suspension uses the XK's aluminium components but the springs, dampers and bushes are calibrated for a more cossetting ride. And, vitally, the XF does feel like a proper Jaguar, smooth and supple over bumps, fluid in curves, proportionally positive and responsive to steering inputs, with credible weighting and road feel.

You feel a part of the car when you drive it, not a mere operator: it's relaxed but ready to go, never sloppy, always confidence-inspiring. The base engines are two V6s, a 3.0-litre petrol and the impossibly refined 2.7-litre turbodiesel jointly developed by Peugeot-Citroën and Ford. The cars I tried on the early drive in Phoenix, Arizona, however, were the two 4.2-litre V8s.

The naturally aspirated 298bhp version makes a pleasing V8 woofle with a metallic edge and hauls the XF with enough vigour to give a good time. The halo car of the range, though, is the supercharged SV8 with 416bhp and a subdued but still audible supercharger whine when aroused. It's not intended to be a hard-edged XF 'R'-type car – that comes later, with a new 5.0-litre engine and around 500 BMW M5-rivalling bhp – and still rides well thanks to two-mode adaptive dampers and despite very low-profile tyres (35 front, 30 rear).

Pressing a chequered-flag button makes the auto 'box more responsive even than the sport mode, sharpens throttle response and loosens the traction and stability system's strictures. Select manual mode, and you'll see the selected gear number appear large on the display between the speedo and tacho, changing from white to amber as the rev limit approaches. The SV8 is a lot of fun when set to this state of maximum alertness, if a little less light on its feet than the naturally aspirated V8.

Both cars feel like good Jaguars should. I think they look the part, too, all of which makes them more covetable than any German rival. Now just watch Jaguar's average ownership age plummet. Whoever buys Jaguar, be it Tata or the Jac Nasser/Wolfgang Reitzle-fronted First Equity, will surely be delighted at their new portfolio.

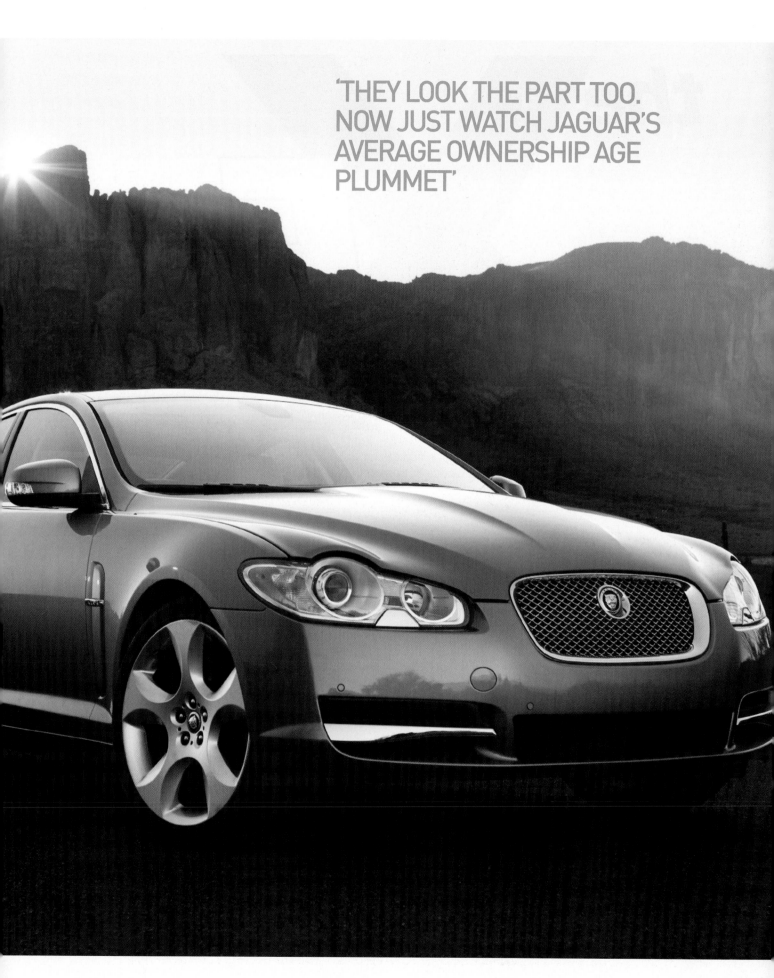

'THEY LOOK THE PART TOO.
NOW JUST WATCH JAGUAR'S
AVERAGE OWNERSHIP AGE
PLUMMET'

the XF factor

Jaguar's new XF SV8 isn't short of talent, but is it special enough to stop you buying a used Quattroporte for the same money? **Words:** Henry Catchpole **Pictures:** Gus Gregory

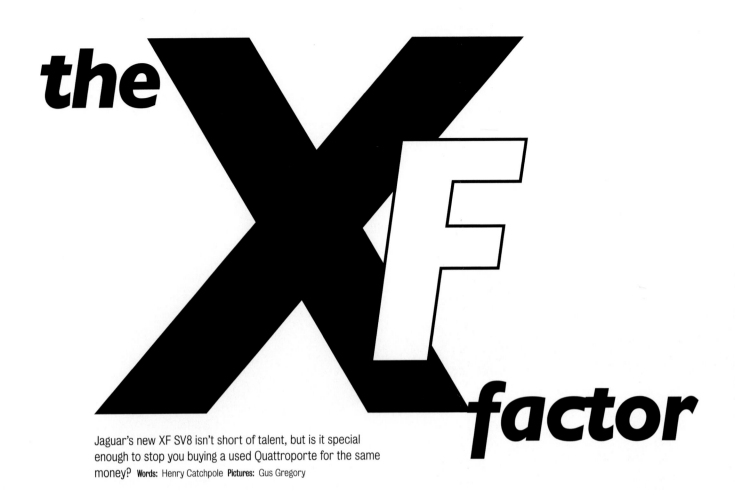

Some cars pass you by a bit when they're launched (there's a new Audi A-something saloon, you say? Are you sure? When did that happen?), but others ignite conversation from the moment you see the first sketches. They usually come from new companies, or ones with slightly iffy records, like Jaguar. The uncertainty means the possibilities for the new car are endless, and that means everyone has an opinion.

Take the Jaguar XF, a debate about which had been ping-ponging around the evo office for months. Desperate and ultimately futile attempt to breath some life into a terminally uncool marque, or brave new-wave icon that will seriously challenge the European competition and excite all who melt into its continuously surprising and delighting cabin?

Dep ed Jethro wasn't convinced. In fact he didn't think we should test it at all. Even associate ed Tomalin, a Jag fan to the core, wasn't sure about the lights or the 'gimmicks' (he's just coming round to the idea of automatic chokes and DVDs). Perhaps it was the incorrigible hope of youth that meant I was more susceptible to its potential? But that theory was blown out of the ecologically heated swimming pool by child-at-heart Metcalfe, who also thought it would be great.

So it's with enough curiosity to kill a big, leaping cat that John Barker and I approach the New Forest, where an XF is waiting for us. It's not just any XF either, it's the SV8. This isn't quite the ultimate XF, with a properly hot XF-R to come later, but it still has 410bhp – ten more than the old S-type R. It also has 413lb ft of torque – 30lb ft more than an M5 – and a 0-60mph time of 5.1sec, which is probably not what most people would expect if they saw it next to them at the traffic lights.

Certainly not if it was in tonally banal 'Vapour Grey', because despite its size (those are 20in alloys) the car that is waiting for us seems to be trying to camouflage itself with the surrounding heathland of the National Park. I've yet to see an XF in red or even racing green, but I can't help feeling that a brighter hue would help to make it look less like your father's car. Get past the colour, however, start to look at the lines as you walk round it and you'll find there are some really good ones. The rear three-quarters, for example, look distinctly Aston Vanquish in the way the windows meet the shoulders above the rear wheels. Gus Gregory seems keen too, and if a photographer as good as him likes it then it must be doing something right. What there's no doubt about is that the interior is a very good place to be. For some reason the insides of the doors are particularly cohesive and attractive, while the stripy wood looks modern, the touch screen (familiar from the XK) works well and the leather feels thick and well stitched.

And then the car begins waking up around you. First there's the pulsing start/stop button, which mimics a heartbeat with its red glow-glow-dim. Then there are the vents on the dash, which rotate in unison to reveal their slats. Finally, you notice the chunky cylindrical gear selector rising like a miniature podium from the centre console. It is, of course, all unnecessary, and to the sceptics amongst you it'll sound like so much naff electrical

gimmickry that will just go wrong one day, but when you're in the car it's genuinely pleasing and makes the XF feel a little bit special.

Press the pulser, turn the cylinder three clicks clockwise. The automatic handbrake releases and the Jaguar rolls smoothly away with the lightest of pressures on the accelerator. As soon as you're moving, the steering is instantly impressive. Almost all cars have a fraction of slack around the straight-ahead and need just the start of a turn before they'll weight-up properly, but not the XF, which always has a resistance and a reaction to your inputs, however small. It makes the SV8 easy to place accurately, which is just as well because the roads are narrow and the Jag is a big car. Although it's very well controlled you can feel the XF's weight, which gives it an air of luxury, a bit like a good piece of furniture.

The ZF gearbox is familiar from the XK and it remains simply the best auto you will find. It's smooth in D, almost uncanny in the way it intuitively changes down a gear in S (Sport), and is sublimely quick and responsive if you use the small paddles attached to the back of the steering wheel.

So far so good, but somewhere out there on this glorious February day is possibly the toughest test yet devised for the XF: for the same £55K, you could also have a year-old Maserati Quattroporte, a car with very similar vital statistics – 394bhp to the Jag's 410, an identical 5.1sec 0-60mph time – plus, »

'The rear three-quarters look distinctly Aston Vanquish'

Far left:
XF interior modern and intriguing. Note the air vents and gear selector in dormant state.

'I'm sure the XF can win over sceptics if they'll just get in it'

of course, looks to die for and one of the coolest brand images there is. Oh yes, and one of the best chassis in the class. If the XF can compete with the QP then Jaguar really does have a chance...

Even in a scrubby lay-by there are no bad angles on a Quattroporte. It is effortlessly gorgeous wherever you're standing. There's a delicacy to its lines that makes the 90kg lighter Jaguar sitting next to it look a bit hefty.

The Maserati's interior appears to have driven though a field of blue and cream cows before the centre console hit a tree, but the end result is somehow effortlessly classy. You sit noticeably lower in the driver's seat than in the Jaguar and it feels airier inside, although not quite as solid.

Twist the blue key, the starter spins for an Italian amount of time and then the Modenese V8 catches. Right paddle (long throw – the Jag's are more like switches) and we ease off down the road, the DuoSelect automated manual transmission dragging a little more clutch than you'd like. It only takes two hideously jerking changes in auto mode (the second only to make sure the first wasn't a mistake) for you to put the Maser in manual and leave it there forevermore.

The New Forest is blanketed in speed limits but the advantage of big saloons that have to ride as well as they handle is that you can slide slowly through the landscape, relaxed because the car isn't straining at a dynamic leash. Both Maserati and Jaguar have that calming aura that seems to instantly pacify their occupants, but when they do make a beeline for the horizon it's never less than exciting and impressive.

Tug down a couple of gears in the Maserati, throw open the throttle and it will cover ground quickly, accompanied by a great soundtrack. But getting into the SV8 afterwards it's shocking how much faster the Jaguar travels down the same road.

The engine is really thumping hard above 3000rpm, where you start to hear the supercharger shriek, but the combination of the blower and that gearbox means you can apply full throttle at any speed and be guaranteed an indecent amount of pace. The Maserati revs gloriously but it simply can't live with the Jaguar in a straight line.

Press the button with the chequered flag motif in the XF and everything tenses a little, except for DSC, which undoes a top button and loosens its collar. Heading towards corners there's that slightly unnervingly exciting feeling of nearly two tons travelling fast with momentum on its side, like an ever-enlarging snowball gathering pace as it rolls downhill. But the Jag's vented discs (355mm front, 326mm rear) are strong with a reassuringly firm pedal and rein-in speed with confidence.

Turn in and you'll find a fraction less resistance off-centre than the initial weight suggested, so you occasionally have to play with the steering a little rather than just making one movement through a turn. The XF's reserves of grip are huge and once into a corner the CATS (Computer Adaptive Technology Suspension) keeps the big car spookily taut so you can use the throttle freely to carve the rear of the car neatly round. On dry tarmac the tail moves but never feels like it will break free; on wet roads the XF is happy to oversteer and you can understand why you have to push the DSC button for some time to switch everything off (at which point it would be nice to have a limited-slip diff just to give you more control over how and when the tail cuts loose).

The Maser doesn't feel as alive as the Jaguar initially, mostly because the steering doesn't feel very enthusiastic after the XF's. The gearbox takes more concentration and, like the brakes, you tend to forward-plan more than you do in the Jag. But throwing it into a tightening complex of right-left-right turns, all is forgiven. Out of nowhere it instantly seems to shed half a ton, cornering absolutely flat through the direction changes, nose biting hard, tail balanced but alert and steering loaded with feel that makes the Jag seem a bit digital. Suddenly you can feel the Ferrari influence. And then the road straightens or a 30mph limit appears and it's gone again. You're back to wafting around, enjoying the landscape and avoiding ponies.

As I drive back to the office in the XF that evening, interior glowing blue like a swimming pool lit up at night, sliding round wet roundabouts, indicators tick-tocking like a grandfather clock, I'm sure that this new Jag can win over the sceptics – if they'll just get in it. At £54,900 the SV8 is a lot of money and of course most people will go for the £21K cheaper V6 diesel. But as I park up, press the stop button and watch the cylinder recede and the vents swivel shut, it doesn't feel absurd to have pitched it against the Maserati. The Quattroporte is seductive – it's better looking and it has the edge for driver satisfaction on a good bit of road, but the XF feels like the more complete package. In the Maser the chassis is magic and the other bits are trying not to let the side down; in the Jaguar the gearbox, brakes, engine and chassis are all a seamless match for each other, working in harmony. Debate over. Roll on the XF-R. △

	XF SV8	Q'PORTE
Engine	V8, supercharger	V8
Location	Front, longitudinal	Front-mid, longitudinal
Displacement	4196cc	4244cc
Bore x stroke	86.0 x 90.3mm	92.0 x 79.8mm
Cylinder block	Aluminium alloy	Aluminium alloy
Cylinder head	Aluminium alloy, dohc per bank, four valves per cylinder, variable valve timing	Aluminium alloy, dohc per bank, four valves per cylinder, variable valve timing
Fuel and ignition	Electronic engine management, multipoint fuel injection	Electronic engine management, multipoint fuel injection
Max power	410bhp @ 6250rpm	394bhp @ 7000rpm
Max torque	413lb ft @ 3500rpm	333lb ft @ 4500rpm
Transmission	Six-speed automatic gearbox, rear-wheel drive, traction control, DSC	DuoSelect six-speed automated manual, rear-wheel drive, stability control
Front suspension	Double wishbones, coil springs, CATS dampers, anti-roll bar	Double wishbones, coil springs, Skyhook dampers, anti-roll bar
Rear suspension	Double wishbones, coil springs, CATS dampers, anti-roll bar	Double wishbones, coil springs, Skyhook dampers, anti-roll bar
Brakes	Vented discs, 355mm front, 326mm rear, ABS, EBA, EBD, CBC	Vented discs, 330mm front, 316mm rear, ABS, EBD
Wheels	8.5 x 20in front, 9.5 x 20in rear, aluminium alloy	8.5 x 18in front, 10.5 x 18in rear, aluminium alloy
Tyres	255/35 ZR20 front, 285/30 ZR20 rear, Pirelli P Zero	245/45 ZR18 front, 285/45 ZR18 rear, Pirelli P Zero
Weight (kerb)	1842kg	1930kg
Power-to-weight	226bhp/ton	207bhp/ton
0-60mph	5.1sec (claimed)	5.1sec (claimed)
Max speed	155mph (limited)	171mph (claimed)
Basic price	£54,900	c£55,000 (second-hand '07 car)
On sale	Now	Now
RATING	★★★★⯨	★★★★⯨

Many thanks to Julian at Outwood Cars for supplying the Maserati for this feature. Their current stock can be viewed at www.outwoodcars.com

Right: Jag's supercharged V8 (right) feels more potent than the Maser's naturally aspirated engine – and there'll be more to come...

JDHT:
WHEN HISTORY MATTERS

The production lines at Browns Lane may have fallen silent, but there's plenty of history left to appreciate at the site – take, for example, the Jaguar Daimler Heritage Trust's unparalleled collection of historic cars...

Words: David Barzilay

For a Jaguar lover it's as close to nirvana as you're likely to get this side of Le Mans. Yet even before you enter the home of the Jaguar Daimler Heritage Trust (JDHT) collection, Browns Lane, Coventry there's something distinctly *Jaguar* about the place. Perhaps it's the art-deco frontage, the leaping cat over the doorway, the teasing view of the priceless cars within...

When the Browns Lane factory closed in 2005 many mourned the passing of a great car manufacturing complex. Once the birthplace of some of the world's most influential cars, Browns Lane is now eerily quiet. Yes, it remains the centre of Jaguar wood veneer production, but that's hardly the same. Further worries about the fate of the priceless JDHT collection of 160 cars were brought into focus by enthusiasts. In the climate of financial belt-tightening would there be a place for them?

»

'JDHT ALSO OVERSEES AN OUTSTANDING COLLECTION OF ARCHIVE MATERIAL, COMPRISING OF THOUSANDS OF DOCUMENTS'

'WE'VE ENJOYED HAVING THE LE MANS XJR STORY TOLD BY ONE OF ITS DEVELOPMENT DRIVERS '

Thankfully those concerns went unfounded. There was no way a company with such a rich heritage would ever allow that outcome, and as a result of continued investment the museum continues to go from strength to strength.

Walking through the glass double-doors is something all Jaguar aficionados should do – it's an amazing collection of cars and on any day you'll get great access to a fair proportion of it.

Formed in 1983, the JDHT was established as a registered educational charity by Jaguar Cars Limited and the British Motor Industry Heritage Trust (BMIHT), when they were both owned by BL. Its aim was to preserve the heritage of Jaguar Cars Limited and its predecessor companies: Swallow; SS; Jaguar; BSA; Daimler and Lanchester. The current building was built in 1998.

The Trust's major objective was to collect and preserve vehicles and artifacts that relate to the history, industrial development and social impact of Jaguar Cars. In fulfilling those aims, the museum has been a great success – the cars might be the highlight of any visit, but delve around the nooks and crannies and you'll find so much more. Like scale models, and research and development material? It's all there to see.

Unusually for a car museum, many of the exhibits at the Heritage Trust earn their living by taking part in charity and major motoring events around the world. If you're a follower of the Mille Miglia, you'll already be very familiar with the JDHT's competition cars.

JDHT also oversees an outstanding collection of archive material, comprising thousands of documents and around 50,000 photographs, which form a very special record of some of the Jaguar's history. Although you won't be able to delve through these treasures, it's available if you pre-book an appointment, or use the website to make an enquiry.

Above
Browns Lane in its heyday in the early 1960s, with E-types being built at record volumes to satisfy international demand. The collection is home to some of the most iconic cars built by Jaguar – the Stirling Moss D-type and an early E-type roadster..

The exhibition is open every day and a treat has to be the fact that you enter the museum through the famous Browns Lane Gate, which originally led to the factory. Once in the museum it's the openness of the place that surprises – the cars on display are given plenty of space. That means you can get nice and close and photography is not a problem.

On most days you choose to visit, there will be a member of the JDHT willing to take some time out to explain the history of the cars on display. And there's real enthusiasm and depth of knowledge too. There is little that beats having a car's story told by someone involved with it originally – we've visited and enjoyed having the Le Mans XJR story told by one of its development drivers.

Repeat visitors shouldn't be discouraged, either. The JDHT Team ensure that its inventory of vehicles is rotated so that there is always something new to see – they say that on any given day, you'll only experience 20% of what's in the collection.

As well as priceless gems such as the Le Mans C- and D-types and NUB120, there are some fascinating might-have-beens to ponder. The XJ40 estate and coupé, and XJ41 sportscar, are good examples of the good and bad cars that escaped production. Last of line classics are always a joy to see, too – the final E-type and XJS nicely complement each other.

The collection is growing all the time. In 2007 Jaguar gave the Trust the first new Jaguar XK off the line – CBO6 JAG, the last Jaguar S-type production vehicle and the Jaguar S-type diesel race car used in 2004 Nürburgring 24-hour race.

The museum runs monthly open days and has hosted many specialist groups including local school children and students. Entrance is free and for more information, visit the website, www.jdht.com or call the museum on +44 (0)24 7640 1289.

MILLE MIGLIA

SOME WORKS OUTING!

On the Mille Miglia with the Jaguar Daimler Heritage Trust team

When you're in your early twenties and taken on by Jaguar as a management trainee it's quite exciting. Walking past Jaguar's heritage in the shape of the company's long-nose D-type every morning gets the blood pumping and you wonder whether you might ever get to drive it.

Well, when the trainee becomes managing director, dreams can come true. This year Mike O'Driscoll got to drive the D-type in the Mille Miglia retrospective – but only under the watchful eye of Jaguar Daimler Heritage Trust curator Tony O'Keeffe and his dedicated team of support staff.

Tony is an old hand at the Mille Miglia (and was seriously injured in the 2005 Mille Miglia when the XKSS he was driving overturned) and what he says, goes. He decides who drives cars from the collection and how they should drive them, and nothing changed when Mike was in the hot seat.

How the whole event would work became apparent at one of Tony's famous briefings: 'It'll only last five minutes,' he said, but 48 minutes later O'Driscoll and the rest of the team knew exactly what was expected over the next two-and-a-half days. If you want to keep on the right side of O'Keeffe then keeping him up to speed on any Italian ice cream parlours that you find en route goes down well.

As usual, months of planning had been put into getting the JDHT cars ready for the 1000-mile event. Technicians Richard Mason and John Sawyer spend hours working on the cars to make sure that they are in top condition. However, this year was different and the pressure was on. Jaguar was sponsoring the event, the boss was driving in it, four cars instead of two were being fielded and Tony's aim was to make sure that as many Italians as possible saw the new Jaguar XFs that were being used by the back-up crews supporting each team.

Jaguar always sends the long-nose D-type and the C-type, but this year they were also fielding two XK120s: 'NUB 120', the famous ex-Ian Appleyard car which did so well in the rallies of the 1950s, and was to be driven by Max Noetzi and Stephen Voegeli from Jaguar Switzerland; and the fixed-head XK120 SE that had seen hardly any serious action since it took part in one of the most famous endurance records ever at the Montlhéry circuit near Paris in 1952. The car was only the second right-hand-drive version of the XK120 coupé. The idea was that Leslie Johnson was to drive it for seven days and seven nights at an average of over 100mph (161kph). Johnson's co-drivers in the attempt were Stirling Moss, Bert Hadley and Jack Fairman.

A spring broke on the fifth day and, although it was replaced and the run continued, no more records could be officially accepted. Nevertheless, Jaguar's goal was achieved. The car ➤➤

'O'Driscoll and Walker were clearly enjoying themselves on the roads across the Marche hills'

Above and right
Recordbreaking XK120 fhc; NUB 120 passes O'Keeffe and XF; Walker at the wheel in D-type.

averaged 100.31mph (161.43kph) for the seven days and nights, having covered 16,851 miles (27,120km). In addition, five new class records and four World Records were set for shorter distances, up to four days and 10,000 miles.

Since then the car has averaged between 60 and 100 miles a year. This year it behaved flawlessly, driven by CJ O'Donnell, Jaguar's global marketing director, with motoring journalist Ben Oliver as co-driver.

The morning after the briefing O'Driscoll found himself in the carpark at the Continental Hotel in Brescia being put through his paces by John Sawyer, who looks after the D-type all year round. Both he and his co-driver, journalist Howard Walker, passed with flying colours and Mike vowed to beat the rest of the Jaguar team on his first attempt. But old hands Tim Watson, vice president of communications and marketing for Jaguar North America, and journalist Mark Gillies, in the C-type, weren't concerned: they'd been here before, having taken part in several Milles.

The following day, during the display of all competing cars in Brescia, it was already getting competitive – even down to who was pushing cars faster to the final scrutineering. Then suddenly it was the start; O'Keeffe had given his final briefings and the Jags were on the road to Ferrara.

Everyone was in good spirits as the cars headed out of Brescia in the damp towards Verona, and O'Keeffe was like a mother hen checking up on his brood at every opportunity while running 20 minutes behind the rest of his team, to see everyone make it to the first night stop at Ferrara.

Friday is always great fun running down to Rome through San Marino and Assisi. The Jaguars were running well. We saw the C-type rushing up the dual carriageway into San Marino and waited for the cars to pass us on the other side of the hilltop principality.

They all flashed by, the D-type bringing up the rear, O'Driscoll and Walker clearly enjoying themselves as they negotiated the picturesque roads across the Marche hills that lead to Urbino. Then it was on to Assisi and the long slog to Rome, where the cars were welcomed by floodlit buildings and crowds of people. But just before that, and 60 miles outside the city, there was a cryptic text message. 'Agip Garage, two miles south of Terni. Stop. Stop.' There was no drama – just a couple of XFs parked up – and the D-type roared past running perfectly. Nothing seemed wrong; then O'Keefe and Sawyer were spotted sauntering from the garage clutching very large Cornettos…

By the time the support crews had checked the cars, prepared them for the next day and put them to bed it was after 3am, ready for the 6am start of the long slog that takes you from Rome to Siena, through Florence and back to Brescia. The C-type developed an ignition solenoid problem and the 'D' a fuel injection blip. But the crews quickly sorted both and nobody was forced to slow down.

Saturday came and went in a blur; the Jaguars were welcomed everywhere they went but all too soon it was over. By 3am the team had finally sat down to a late dinner. They still didn't know that Mike had beaten them all but when they did, the text messages came fast and furious. O'Keeffe was elated – and just a touch relieved. △

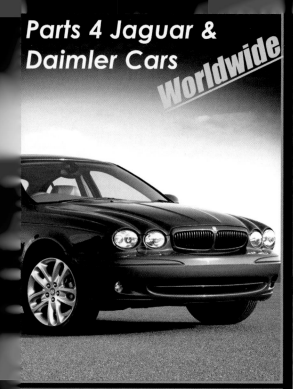

SIX-CYLINDER
Jaguar E-type

At least as beautiful as a contemporary Ferrari or
Aston, the E-type is still a relative bargain – but prices
for good cars are rising as more and more buyers
jump on the bandwagon

Words: Richard Dredge

'The relative
lack of
usability of
early cars
means it's
the 4.2-litre
editions that
everyone
wants'

Nine out of ten cool cats who
expressed a preference reckon this is
the most glamorous, sensual car of all
time. And is that any wonder? There
aren't enough superlatives in the
dictionary to do the E-type justice; if
grown men had car posters on their
bedroom walls, this Jag would grace
most of them. All those clichés about
setting the world alight are true; the
E-type really did rewrite the rulebook.

Besides having looks, pace, power,
engineering and heritage, the Jag also
offered an extra quality over its rivals –
relative affordability. While Aston Martin,
Ferrari, Porsche et al offered worthy
rivals, they were all much more costly.
That price differential has remained;
a superb E-type may be a valuable piece
of kit, but an equivalent DB4 or 250GT
will cost you rather more.

The mythology of the E-type started
early, thanks to an infamous road test in
The Autocar that (just) proved Jaguar's

claim of a 150mph top speed. In fact, the
car tested had almost certainly been
fitted with a specially prepared and
blueprinted engine, and a more realistic
top speed for production cars is round
about 140mph. That's still plenty fast
enough for most people, although hard-
chargers may want to consider a modern
five-speed gearbox conversion – oddly,
the E-type was never offered with
overdrive, unlike its XK predecessors.

Jaguar historian Philip Porter runs the
E-type Club. He owns several examples
of the breed himself, and comments:

'There is a massive spread of values
from £5000 up to £200,000 – or even
£1 million for a genuine Lightweight. At
the one extreme you can buy a 2+2
project car and at the other a superbly
restored, heavily upgraded Series
One roadster.

'Fixed-heads used to be around half
the price of roadsters but, quite rightly,
that gap has narrowed considerably in

the last year or two. Series One FHC
restoration project cars are still £9000-
12,000, while roadsters are in the
£10,000-17,000 bracket.

'Many factors influence values,
including structural integrity,
completeness, engine displacement
(unless a very early car, the 4.2s are
worth a shade more at present),
whether it's a 'matching numbers' car
and whether it's left- or right-hand drive.

'For a usable car that hasn't been fully
restored or upgraded, expect to pay
£20,000-28,000 for a coupé and
£26,000-33,000 for an open car. Really
excellent original or restored examples
start at £32,000 for coupés and £38,000
for roadsters. Some reputable dealers
charge considerably more – and with
good reason, as a proper professional
restoration costs at least £80,000 and
upgrades can add far more.'

Derek Hood runs JD Classics, one of
the UK's largest E-type specialists.

'Fixed-heads used to be half the price of roadsters but, quite rightly, that gap has narrowed considerably in the last year or two'

He, along with Henry Pearman of Eagle E-types, is responsible for some of the most exacting E-type restorations in the UK. The companies also offer a wide range of upgrades to make the cars more usable in modern conditions.

Says Hood: 'Early E-types always looked better than they drove, which is why buyers will pay a premium for cars that have been sympathetically upgraded. Improved braking, cooling and suspension systems are valued highly, as are five-speed gearboxes, fuel injection and discreet stereo or telephone installations.'

You might assume that it's the earliest E-types that are the most sought after, especially the flat-floor cars that were produced for just a year. This isn't the case though; the relative lack of usability of these early cars means it's the 4.2-litre editions that everyone wants, thanks to their better seats, nicer gearbox, stronger brakes and torquier engine.

Hood continues: 'We're now seeing the very best 4.2-litre Roadsters touching £200,000 but, to command such a price, the car will have had everything done, including a list of upgrades; a 3.8-litre car is worth around 15% less. It's no surprise that the best cars can attract such sums of money, as a properly executed full restoration can cost £160,000 and then there's the value of the project car to be taken into account.'

Engine

The XK powerplant that lives under the E-type's bonnet is renowned for its durability as long as it's looked after. Easily capable of giving 150,000 miles between rebuilds, the straight-six isn't especially stressed unless the car is regularly thrashed – and few owners use their E-types very hard.

Get the engine up to temperature before taking the car for a test drive; listen for any knocks or rattles as it gets warm. Do the usual checks for oil leaks as well as smoke from the exhaust; you can expect to see a few wisps when starting from cold but things should quickly settle. Once fully warm, look for at least 40psi on the oil pressure gauge, with the engine turning over at 3000rpm.

Allow the engine to tick over for a few minutes and make sure that the electric cooling fan cuts in; they often don't. If the needle on the temperature gauge just keeps climbing, the engine may well have overheated at some point – so make sure there's no evidence of the head gasket having blown, by looking for white 'mayonnaise' (the result of oil and water mixing) on the underside of the oil filler cap.

If the engine is smoking badly or it's very rattly, a complete rebuild is clearly on the cards – but don't get too hung up about this. You can rebuild an XK engine at home from around £2000, or pay £6000 or more to get it done professionally to a high quality.

Above
Even American safety regs – side repeater lights, uncowled headlights and wrap-around bumpers – couldn't ruin the E-type's sex appeal.

»

'Frankly, if all is well with the body, the car is unlikely to give any insurmountable problems elsewhere'

However, if you take the DIY route, be warned that the XK engine isn't as easy to revive as some other units. If the last engine you overhauled was a Ford Crossflow unit, expect the E-type to be more of a challenge.

Transmission

With a pretty much bullet-proof transmission, there's little to worry about where the E-type's drivetrain is concerned. It doesn't last forever though, so listen for clonks that signify worn universal joints or whining that betrays a worn differential. Fixing the former is straightforward; the latter is less easy to put right and rather more costly, with a replacement diff costing £750.

Gearboxes are also strong, but the recalcitrance of the Moss unit fitted to 3.8-litre cars is legendary. It's also noisier than the later unit, so don't expect a gearbox that's especially easy or pleasant to use, particularly when selecting first or reverse. If things are really noisy, expect to pay £900 for a rebuilt transmission, whether it's a Moss unit or a later one.

Suspension, steering and brakes

Ideally you should jack up each wheel and rock it diagonally to feel for wear in the bushes and bearings. Expect to feel some play at the rear wheels; if there isn't any, the bearings have been set too tight and will probably overheat and fail. There are bearings in the hub as well as the lower fulcrum; a little play in each of these can lead to what feels like an alarming amount of movement at the wheel, but it should be no more than an eighth of an inch or so.

At the front there shouldn't be nearly as much play in the wheels, although don't be surprised if you can detect a small amount. If it's bearing wear that's easy to sort, but it might be that the lower wishbone balljoints have worn. These act directly on the wishbone, which can be shimmed only so much before it has to be replaced at a little over £100 per side.

Remove the rear wheels and look at the axle cage mountings, which can perish or break. If you've already driven the car by this stage, and it feels rather lively at the back, it could be because the rear-wheel steering is coming into effect as a result of the wear. While you're under there, ensure there's no oil leaking from the diff onto the inboard rear brakes. Any signs of trouble and it's an axle-out job to put things right.

Bodywork, electrics and trim

Those glamorous looks can hide a

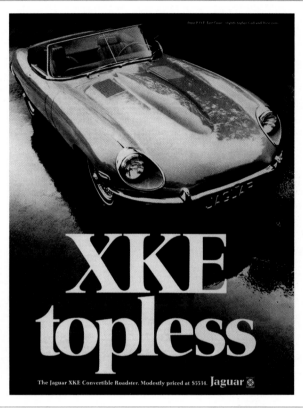

The Jaguar XKE Convertible Roadster. Modestly priced at $5534. Jaguar

XKE topless

multitude of sins, and it's easy to view potential purchases through rose-tinted eyewear. Don't let your heart drown out your head though; buying an overpriced dressed-up shed could leave you out of pocket to the tune of tens of thousands of pounds. Properly restoring an E-type is a hell of an undertaking, and many people get it wrong.

Frankly, if all's well in the body department, the car is unlikely to give any insurmountable problems elsewhere – but check all is what it seems.

If a car has been restored, poor bodywork repairs are one thing you'll possibly have to contend with. If the car hasn't been revived, E-types can rot just about anywhere, so check every square inch of metal – twice over. Lift the fuel filler flap and see what's lurking beneath: if it's a mess, other bits will have been missed as the car was clearly restored with no attention to detail.

Panel gaps should be tight and even, especially where the bonnet butts up against the bulkhead. With the bonnet accounting for nearly half the length of the car, it's tricky getting things to line up properly – which is why they often don't. Also check all the seams as well as the front valance, which frequently harbours rot.

Coupé tailgates rarely rust but boot lids do, along with door bottoms. In the case of the latter there should be a polythene sheet inside the door casing; it's usually missing. The door fills up with water as a result, and with the drain holes often blocked up, the water has nowhere to go.

Don't overlook the frame ahead of the front bulkhead, which supports the engine, steering and suspension. The tubes that make up this frame can crack as well as corrode, and it's not easy to check that all is well because it's rather overcrowded in there. If any work needs doing, everything ahead of the bulkhead will have to be removed for access.

Door locks can give problems so try locking, unlocking and opening each door from inside as well as out; don't underestimate the hassle you could have getting everything to work properly.

'We regularly spend 200-300 hours on this type of seemingly minor work on perfect-looking E-types whilst preparing them for our showrooms,' agrees Eagle's Henry Pearman.

Electrics give few problems, and there's nothing to worry about trim-wise because everything is available. It will soon get costly if everything needs doing though.

Jaguar E-type 3.8 Coupé
SPECIFICATIONS
Engine
3781cc straight six, twin overhead camshafts, 12 valves. Alloy head, cast-iron block. Three SU HD8 carburettors

Power
265bhp @ 5500rpm

Torque
260lb ft @ 4000rpm

Transmission
Four-speed manual, rear-wheel drive

Suspension
Front: independent via transverse wishbones, torsion bars and telescopic dampers, anti-roll bar. Rear: independent via lower transverse tubular links, twin coil springs each side, telescopic dampers

Brakes
Servo-assisted discs all round, in-board at rear

Weight
1202kg (2644lb)

Performance
0-60mph 7.1sec
Top speed 149mph

Value
Cost £2160 new
Value now £30,000-150,000

»Info

SPECIALISTS
» Butlin & Sons, www.butlinclassiccars.co.uk
» Classic Affairs, www.classicaffairs.co.uk
» Classic Autosports, www.classicautosports.com
» Classic Jaguar Racing, www.classic-jaguar-racing.co.uk
» Classic Motor Cars (sales, restoration), www.classic-motor-cars.co.uk
» Coopercraft (disc brake conversions), www.coopercraft.co.uk
» David Manners (parts), www.davidmanners.co.uk
» E-type Only (headlight covers, parts), www.e-type-only.com
» Eagle (sales, restoration, upgrades), www.eaglegb.com
» Jaguar Daimler Heritage Trust (heritage certificates), www.jdht.com
» JD Classics (sales, service, restoration), www.jdclassics.co.uk
» K&N Classic Cars, +44 (0)1243 574139
» Lane's Cars (sales), www.lanescars.co.uk
» Lynx Motors International (sales, restoration), www.lynxmotors.co.uk
» Martin Robey (parts), www.martinrobey.com
» Racing Green Cars (sales, upgrades), www.racinggreencars.com
» RM&J Smith, +44 (0)1270 820885, email rmj@rmjsmith.fsnet.co.uk
» RS Panels, www.rspanels.co.uk
» SC Parts, www.scparts.co.uk
» SNG Barratt (parts), www.sngbarratt.com
» Woodmanton Classics (sales), www.woodmantonclassics.co.uk

USA SPECIALISTS
» Classic Jaguars, Texas (parts, upgrades, restoration), www.classicjaguar.com
» Classic Showcase, California (sales, restoration), www.classicshowcase.com
» Doc's Jags/World of Jaguars, Arizona (sales, restoration), www.docsjags.com
» XKs Unlimited, California (parts, service, upgrades, restoration), www.xks.com

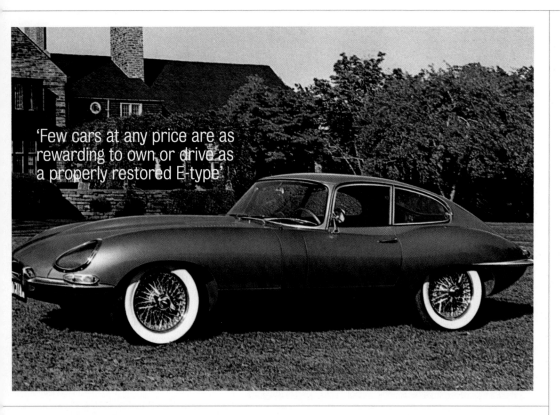

'Few cars at any price are as rewarding to own or drive as a properly restored E-type'

Above
Without doubt, the Series One fixed-head coupé is the cleanest-looking E-type of them all.

Conclusion

It's easy to overlook the differences between the various iterations of E-type, but you can't afford to do this because those differences are very significant. Put simply, if you get the wrong E-type for your needs you'll wonder what all the fuss is about.

Also, don't get taken in by the glamour of the roadster when the coupé is more affordable and every bit as good to drive – and better looking too in the eyes of many. However, bear in mind that with many coupés scrapped or converted to roadsters, fixed-heads are now rarer than open-topped examples – which is why their values are on the up.

If you're after an original right-hand-drive car, they're a lot rarer than you might think. Around 85% of E-type production was exported, which is why many right-hand drive E-types have been converted from left-hand drive at some point (this barely affects value though).

The bottom line is that you must ensure the car you buy is what it claims to be. Check the correct powerplant is fitted and that it's not a roadster which left the factory as a coupé (or ensure the price is much-reduced). The Jaguar Daimler Heritage Trust is invaluable in being able to provide you with details of

the car's original specification. However, you should also invest in a copy of Philip Porter's book *Original Jaguar E-type* (see panel, right), which will highlight any inconsistencies in the car's specification.

If the car does need any work, there's no need to fret about any problems with parts availability, because absolutely everything is available to revive an E-type, no matter how tired. The cost of all the parts and necessary labour is another matter, but a competent home mechanic can tackle just about any job.

We'll let Derek Hood wrap up: 'There's no such thing as a bargain where the E-type is concerned. We frequently encounter people who buy a car that's priced at £20,000 below what would be expected. Then the new owner starts delving and discovers that to get the car up to the standard they were expecting, the car needs £50,000 spent on it.

'Few cars at any price are as rewarding to own or drive as a properly restored E-type. And there's the rub: the car must be properly restored if any pleasure is to be derived from it – and there's a huge amount of enjoyment to be gained from E-type ownership.'

» **Thanks to Henry Pearman, Derek Hood and Philip Porter.**

»Info

CLUBS

» E-type Club. +44 (0)1584 781588, www.e-typeclub.com
» Jaguar Drivers' Club. +44 (0)1582 419332, http://jaguardriver.co.uk
» Jaguar Enthusiasts' Club. +44 (0)1179 698 186, www.jec.org.uk
» Jaguar Clubs of North America (umbrella organisation), www.jcna.com

BOOKS

» *E-type, End of an Era* by Chris Harvey. Haynes, ISBN 0 946609 16 0 (OOP)
» *Jaguar E-type (Great Cars)* by Nigel Thorley. Haynes, ISBN 0 1 85960 813 2
» *Jaguar E-Type, the Definitive History* by Philip Porter. Haynes, 0 85429 580 1
» *Jaguar E-Type, the Complete Story* by Jonathan Wood. Crowood, ISBN 0 1 86126 147 0
» *Jaguar E-Type 3.8 & 4.2-litre, Essential Buyer's Guide* by Peter Crespin. Veloce, ISBN 0 1 904788 85 8
» *Original Jaguar E-Type* by Philip Porter. Bay View, ISBN 1 870979 12 5

TIMELINE

» 1961: E-type launched at Geneva Motor Show in coupé and roadster guises, with 3.8-litre XK engine.
» 1962: Heelwells incorporated into front floors; earlier editions are known as 'flat-floor' cars.
» 1964: Engine now displaces 4.2 litres, while an all-synchromesh gearbox is fitted. There are also improvements to brakes, servo and seats.
» 1966: 2+2 E-type available, with longer wheelbase and higher roofline.
» 1967: Series 1¹/₂ model arrives, with headlamp fairings deleted and engine modified for US emissions regulations.
» 1968: Series 2 goes on sale, designed to meet US safety regs. Wrap-around bumpers, bigger sidelights (now below bumper) and different carburettors. However, brakes are improved and windscreen rake is increased on 2+2.

JAGUAR E-TYPE V12

1972-1975

The Series 3s may be the cheapest of the E-type range but they're also the smoothest and the best-engineered

Words: Richard Dredge   Photography: John Colley

Cars don't come more evocative than Jaguar's E-type, but steady rises in values over the past couple of years have taken the cars out of reach for many. However, while everyone clamours for the earlier six-cylinder models because of their greater design purity, the Series 3, or V12, is overlooked by many – despite being more usable thanks to its longer, wider bodyshell and far superior engineering.
If you've hankered after an E-type for ages and you're on a budget, the V12 is the car to go for. Don't be put off by the higher running costs: fuel consumption isn't an issue unless you plan to cover a significant mileage each year – yet maintenance costs can be high.
Low-mileage V12s abound, but check the history because clocked cars aren't rare. Similarly, restored examples are sometimes claimed to be original, but with so many truly cherished models out there, many run on a money-no-object basis, finding something worth buying really isn't difficult.

»

SPECIFICATIONS

ENGINE
5343cc all-alloy V12,
sohc per bank, 24 valves,
Four Zenith-Stromberg
carburettors

POWER
272bhp @ 5850rpm

TORQUE
304lb ft @ 5600rpm

TRANSMISSION
Four-speed manual or
three-speed auto

SUSPENSION
Front: independent via
wishbones, torsion bars,
telescopic dampers,
anti-roll bar. Rear:
independent via fixed-
length driveshafts, lower
transverse links, radius
arms, twin coil spring
and telescopic damper
units, anti-roll bar

BRAKES
Servo-assisted discs

WEIGHT
1527kg (3361lb)

PERFORMANCE
0-60mph 6.4sec
Top speed 146mph

VALUE
Cost £3387 new (1971)
Value £10,000-25,000

BODY

Look for poor panel fit, corrosion and kinked chassis tubes from low-speed knocks.
Bonnet misalignment occurs through the latter: because this section
is so huge, check for even panel gaps and make sure the bonnet isn't distorted.
Also ensure the car hasn't been jacked up where it shouldn't have been; the
radiator support is sometimes wrecked because of this, with the radiator potentially
pushed into the bonnet. All panels are available.

Most E-types have been restored, so ask who did the work and what was done,
and find out if there's a photo record. Be wary of cars that have had major home
restorations – without the proper jigs the bodyshell may have distorted. Lifting the
fuel filler flap may reveal bare metal and even rust, suggesting
a superficial restoration and likely problems.

Under the bonnet check for bulkhead corrosion, especially around the battery
tray. The scuttle sides contain box sections, which rot from the inside out. By the
time corrosion is visible outside, the inside is rotten, which means costly repairs.

The rear of the monocoque also rots, especially the B-posts and chassis
strengthening rails; sills are durable but check for filler. Get underneath and look
for corrosion around the rear radius arm and anti-roll bar mountings. Finish by
checking the double-skinned rear wings for rust, along with the wheelarch lips,
plus the top and bottom of each door.

Beware of ex-US cars changed to right-hand drive and plus 2+2s converted to
roadsters. Most conversions are fine, but values are lower. RHD chassis numbers
start IS.10001 (roadster) and IS.50001 (2+2); LHD cars are numbered IS.20001
(roadster) and IS.70001 (2+2).

Left
The 'ugly' E-type? Hardly! This roadster with optional hardtop is finished in the black used for 49 of the final 50 cars.

ENGINE

Properly maintained, the V12 covers 200,000 miles with ease. However, poor maintenance leads to overheating, so idle the engine for several minutes and watch the temperature gauge.

Harshness points to previous overheating; the long block and heads can distort through high temperatures. Because the block and heads are alloy, anti-freeze levels must be maintained. If they're not, internal corrosion will clog the cooling system.

Low oil pressure at idle isn't a problem but there should be at least 45lb (preferably 55lb) at 2500rpm. Oil leaks are common as the rear crankshaft seal tends to leak; once it has failed, a full rebuild is needed. A specialist charges £4000-plus, or you could do it yourself for £600.

The V12 has 20 rubber coolant hoses; check they're not perished because replacement can be involved and they need to be to correct specification – the coolant system runs at 15lb (earlier E-types are just 4lb) so the hoses have to be reinforced. A full set is £143.50.

Original rubber fuel lines will need replacing and the Zenith-Stromberg carbs go out of tune when their diaphragms perish. Rebuilt carbs are the best solution; there are four at £350 each. Incidentally, the V12 is happy to run on unleaded in standard form.

TRANSMISSION

Most V12s have a three-speed Borg Warner Model 12 automatic transmission, but the Jaguar four-speed manual is more sought after. They're both durable units, but the latter can suffer from weak synchromesh on second and third; check for difficulty selecting gears when the 'box is cold. If a revived manual 'box is needed, expect to pay £400 for an exchange unit. If ratio changes are jerky on the auto or there's any slipping, the unit needs a service, involving fresh fluid, filters and adjustment of the bands. If things are really bad an overhaul will be required; budget £1100 for a rebuilt 'box. Clutches, diffs and driveshafts are durable, but check for vibrations, clonks or whining.

STEERING & SUSPENSION

The rack-and-pinion steering is reliable, but wear in the column universal joints is normal. Replacement is easy and they're just £65 for the pair. If there are creaks from the rear suspension, it will be because the lower hub pivots have corroded; if not greased regularly they wear rapidly or seize. Don't be surprised if there's detectable play in the rear wheelbearings; if there's none at all they've been overtightened and will overheat as a result. At the front, be wary of too many shims between the wishbone and ball joint – two or three is okay but any more and there's a danger of the suspension collapsing. Fitting exchange wishbones is the easiest solution; it's a cheap and easy exercise.

TIMELINE

1971
E-type Series 3 introduced
1973
Twin exhausts replace four-branch system
1974
Fixed-head coupé discontinued
1974
Last 50 commemorative models built

SPECIALISTS

AJ Autocraft
www.ajautocraft.co.uk
Classic Jaguar Racing
www.classic-jaguar-racing.co.uk
Classic Motor Cars
www.classic-motor-cars.co.uk
David Marks
www.davidmarksgarages.co.uk
Eagle
www.eaglegb.com
Graham Whitehouse
(auto transmissions)
www.gwautos.com
**Jaguar Daimler
Heritage Trust**
www.jdht.com
JD Classics
www.jdclassics.co.uk
Lane's Cars
www.lanescars.co.uk
M&C Wilkinson
www.jaguar-spares-uk.co.uk
Martin Robey
www.martinrobey.com
Racing Green Cars
www.racinggreencars.com
SC Parts
www.scparts.co.uk
SNG Barratt
www.sngbarratt.com
Woodmanton Classics
www.woodmantonclassics.co.uk

CLUBS

E-type Club
www.e-typeclub.com
Jaguar Drivers Club
http://jaguardriver.co.uk
Jaguar Enthusiasts Club
www.jec.org.uk
Jaguar Clubs of North America
(umbrella organisation)
www.jcna.com

BOOKS

Jaguar E-type (Great Cars)
by Nigel Thorley. Haynes,
ISBN 0 1 85960 813 2
Jaguar E-type, the definitive history
by Philip Porter. Haynes, 0 85429 580 1
Jaguar E-type, the complete story
by Jonathan Wood. Crowood,
ISBN 0 1 86126 147 0
Original Jaguar E-type
by Philip Porter. Bay View,
ISBN 1 870979 12 5
E-type, end of an era
by Chris Harvey. Haynes,
ISBN 0 946609 16 0 (out of print)

Thanks to Gordon Yardley at
Woodmanton Classics

Left
Independent rear suspension, just visible here, will suffer if not greased properly.

BRAKES & WHEELS

The brakes should feel very strong, but imbalance isn't unusual – it's usually caused by oil on the in-board rear discs which has leaked from the differential. Fixing this is involved, as the diff' has to come out.Contrarily, the self-adjusting handbrake often seizes through lack of greasing; try to roll the car on a level surface and see if it quickly grinds to a halt. Steel disc wheels were standard but chromed wires are now more common – check for damaged spokes and worn splines, which get a hard time because of the V12's torque.

ELECTRICS & TRIM

Unrestored cars often have poor earths or brittle wiring – fix with emery paper (cheap) or a fresh loom (more expensive). The heater motor suffers from failed circuitry or seizure through lack of use, but access is easy as it's next to the battery under the bonnet. Check the radiator's thermostatic cooling fan cuts in, because failure can lead to major bills. Brightwork can be replaced: mazak door handles, tail-lamp housings etc tend to be pitted. A fresh mohair roadster roof is £700, add the same again for fitting.

'VALUES ARE GOING UP, IF RATHER STEADILY, AND THE CARS ARE SURPRISINGLY USABLE'

MARKET

High fuel prices and steep running costs have put many people off buying the V12 E-type, to the point where you can now get a usable 2+2 for £10,000 – but it won't be all that good under the shiny paint. Even the nicest 2+2s rarely fetch more than £25,000, while you can typically add around 50% to purchase an equivalent roadster. Transmissions don't generally affect values, but while buyers of fixedheads don't mind an auto, it's the stick shift that roadster fans usually want. Commemorative cars rarely surface for sale, and mint examples have been known to touch six figures.

CONCLUSION

Just 7990 roadsters and 7297 coupés were built, but survival rates are high and those that have lasted this far are generally cherished examples. With great specialist and club support, the Series 3 E-type makes huge sense on many levels: values are only going up, if rather steadily, and the cars are surprisingly usable, even on the longest journeys. Perhaps the only problem is the size and complexity of that V12. In fine fettle it makes the car, but if you get a bad one the costs will quickly add up. And, unlike the six-cylinder models, you're unlikely to get your money back.

BUYING GUIDE

JAGUAR DAIMLER XJ
1968-1992

Considered one of the best saloons in the world when new, the Jaguar and Daimler XJs are now something of a bargain. Choose wisely, and they can still be utterly rewarding

Words: Richard Dredge   Photographs: Magic Car Pics

CHEAP LUXURY is easy to find, but the value offered by Jaguar's XJ is spectacular. Five grand buys a mint XJ6 and a thousand more doubles the cylinder count; choose either and you'll have one of the most comfortable cars ever made.

Car of the Year in 1969, the XJ marked the start of a new era for Jaguar. Offered in three series with a choice of wheelbases, tra nsmissions and engines, your XJ could also be ordered in coupé form. Working out which to go for can be a challenge, but always buy on condition and treat the specification as secondary.

Jaguar and Daimler versions are worth the same, and which series you buy makes little difference. Condition is all, but coupés are worth slightly more than saloons. A worthy XJ6 is £2000-plus, £3500 bags a nice one, and £5000 gets you something really special. Add 20% for an XJ12 and the same again for a coupé. »

Right
Jaguar purists
consider the Series I
to be the most
desirable of all XJs.

SPECIFICATIONS
Jaguar XJ6
Series III 4.2
ENGINE
4235cc in-line six, DOHC,
12 valves. Alloy head,
cast-iron block. Lucas/
Bosch L-Jetronic injection
POWER
205bhp @ 5000rpm
TORQUE
236lb ft @ 3700rpm
TRANSMISSION
BW three-speed auto,
rear-wheel drive
SUSPENSION
Front: double wishbones,
coils and telescopic
dampers, anti-roll bar
Rear: lower wishbones
with fixed-length drive
shafts, coil springs and
telescopic dampers
BRAKES
Discs all round,
servo assisted
WEIGHT
1760kg
PERFORMANCE
0-60mph 10sec
Top speed 127mph
VALUE
Cost £14,609 new (1980)
Value now £2000-£5000

BODY

Because of inadequate rustproofing,
poor quality and low values, bodged XJs
abound. Few unrestored cars remain in
a good condition, while many renovations
aren't very well done, so be careful.

Rot areas include the bottoms of the
A-, B- and C-posts, the sills, rear arches
and valances. These areas, along with the
spare wheel well and the door bottoms, need checking. Less obvious are the
rear suspension radius arm mounts, the arms themselves, and the front and
rear screen surrounds, especially on the Series III. If there's any corrosion
around either screen, repair involves taking out the glass. Once removed, the
repairs aren't too difficult.

The bonnet hinge mounts also corrode, and can break altogether. The
bonnet can also rust, as can the bootlid, wings around the headlights, plus
the various jacking points; check these areas very carefully for filler by taking
a magnet with you.

The radiator support frame dissolves readily, which is an automatic MoT
failure; if left to fester, rust then eats into the front chassis structure. Repairs
are a big job on the XJ6 and even worse on the XJ12 because of poor access.
Your final port of call should be to check the front subframe, which can rot,
especially on Series IIIs and some Series IIs. Expect to pay upwards of £1700
for a specialist to supply and fit a used subframe.

'Few unrestored cars remain in good condition, while many renovations aren't very well done, so be careful'

ENGINE

Look for a service history, make sure the engine sounds right and ensure the oil is clean. A rebuild is needed at the first sign of wear; delay things and the bills will quickly mount.

The straight-six has an alloy head, so antifreeze must be maintained. Even a cared-for engine will need a fresh radiator every 5-10 years, at £220 plus fitting.

Expect oil pressure of 40psi when cruising – but senders and gauges can be unreliable. Smoking on the overrun or when the throttle is blipped points to hardened valve stem seals or worn guides, a £1500-plus fix. A greasy underside suggests a failed rear crankshaft oil seal, which requires an engine rebuild. Specialists charge £4000 for the full Monty, or you could do it yourself for upwards of £600 – but it's an involved job.

SU carbs suffer from worn automatic chokes. Rebuilt units are £416, an electric system is £300, or a manual conversion is £85.

The V12 is costly to rebuild, so ensure the oil has been changed frequently and that antifreeze has been maintained. The unit is long-lived if looked after, but the key is to search for signs of previous overheating – which can scrap an engine.

TRANSMISSION

The autos featured a Borg Warner transmission until 1977, then XJ12s received a GM400. Some Series I autos were clunky when new, but later cars should be smooth. Even if all seems well it's worth inspecting the fluid for colour, level and condition. If it's black and smells foul, a rebuild is on the cards, at £850-plus. The manual 'box is strong and is usually fitted with overdrive. If this is slow to engage, the oil probably needs changing or topping up; wear is unusual. Differentials are tough but can leak oil over the inboard rear discs. Repairs are at least £1200; the seal often leaks because the brakes have overheated, so a full rebuild might be needed.

STEERING & SUSPENSION

All XJs have power steering, which is generally reliable, but check for leaks. If the fluid isn't topped up, the car probably hasn't been cherished. Worn suspension and rear subframe bushes are usual so make sure they've not split; worn front tyres point to perished bushes in the suspension, knocking out the geometry. There are a huge number of bushes throughout the car and if they all need renewing it's a costly, involved exercise. Inspect the dampers as they can leak, which is an automatic MoT failure. Replacements cost £45 upwards apiece, so do a bounce test and make sure the car quickly settles.

TIMELINE

1968
XJ6 introduced to replace S-type, 420, 420G and Mk2

1969
Daimler Sovereign goes on sale

1972
XJ12 and Daimler Double-Six join range

1973
Production of SWB models ceases

1974
Series II XJ arrives and XJ coupé reaches showrooms. Final 2.8-litre cars are built

1975
XJ6 3.4 and Daimler Vanden Plas 4.2 arrive

1977
The final coupés are built

1979
Series III arrives and six-cylinder cars gain a five-speed option

1981
V12s are now in HE (High Efficiency) spec

1982
Six-cylinder cars get a BW66 auto

1987
Final XJ6 is built

1989
V12s can now officially use unleaded

1990
Anti-lock brakes now standard

1991
Last XJ12 is built

1992
Last Daimler Double-Six is produced

SPECIALISTS

David Marks
www.davidmarksgarages.co.uk

Alan Lloyd
www.jaguar-specialists.com

Aldridge Trimming
www.aldridge.co.uk

David Manners
www.jagspares.co.uk

Knowles-Wilkins Engineering
www.kwejaguar.co.uk

Martin Robey
www.martinrobey.com

SNG Barratt
www.sngbarratt.com

CLUBS

Jaguar Enthusiasts' Club
www.jec.org.uk

Jaguar Drivers' Club
http://jaguardriver.co.uk

BOOKS

Original Jaguar XJ
by Nigel Thorley. Bay View Books
ISBN 1 901432 11 4

Jaguar XJ, the Complete Companion
by Nigel Thorley. Bay View Books
ISBN 1 870979 22 2 (OOP)

Left
Series II models like this had similar rear styling to the Series I's.

Thanks to David Marks of David Marks Garages for his help with this feature.

BRAKES & WHEELS

The rear brake discs are mounted inboard and as a result they often get neglected or covered in oil from a leaking differential. They also sometimes rust, so check their condition as replacing the various bits is fiddly and time consuming – although at least it's all work that you can do yourself, without any special skills. The handbrake is frequently poorly maintained as it isn't very accessible; it has its own calipers and pads, which can seize up. Make sure the car can be held on a hill using just the handbrake, as fixing this can be a pain.

ELECTRICS

Series II XJs suffered all sorts of electrical gremlins; Series Is and IIIs are generally better but you still must check everything carefully. Switchgear on earlier cars could be unreliable and the powered window buttons are usually the first thing to pack up. Everything is available to put things right, but some bits are costly so be prepared for big bills if there are lots of problems. XJ looms tend to be quite complex and faults can be tricky to pin down, so look for evidence of bodgery such as modern stereos and alarms being spliced in; sorting these can be a nightmare.

'Mint examples are cheap – but they can be hard to find, so you'll have to search to find the car that's right for you'

TRIM

Much of the XJ's appeal lies in its cabin, which is as luxurious an interior as you'll find. Most XJs feature leather trim, but the 3.4 was introduced for the fleet market so it often came with cloth. Any interior that's seen better days could cost big money to fix – as much as £3000 if all the trim needs TLC. Then there are the carpets and maybe the wood, too; the potential for serious expenditure shouldn't be underestimated. Also make sure all the exterior brightwork is there and in good condition; most XJs came with lots of bodywork trim and some of it is hard to revive.

CONCLUSION

Nowhere are *Grace, Space and Pace* more readily available than here; all three are offered in abundance. Even better, mint examples are cheap – but they can be hard to find, so you'll have to search to find the car that's right for you. Tread carefully if you're considering a restoration project, because costs can quickly escalate. There's a surprising amount you can do yourself but these cars are complex in places and experts will be essential for some jobs. That's why you need to weigh up exactly what's needed if you're buying a car that needs work of any kind.

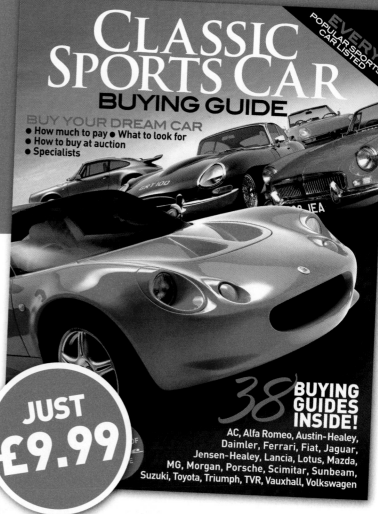

JAGUAR XJ-S

With a 21-year production run, there are plenty of XJ-S coupés to choose from. Consider your choice carefully, buy the right one and you won't regret it
Words: Simon Goldsworthy

Go on, treat yourself. You know you deserve it. For the cost of a service on the Ferrari, you could go out and buy the kind of power that you can't even begin to justify with a straight face, packaged with such sensual grace that it leaves a deliciously-guilty feeling every time you run a hand over the panels. Yes, the XJ-S has the lot. But can you make a case for using one as a daily driver?

In part, that comes down to what kind of driving you do every day. The XJ-S was conceived as a true Grand Tourer, capable of devouring huge distances while cocooning the occupants in the utmost luxury. Which, to be quite honest, couldn't be more different from the average school run or office commute.

But stay with it for a moment. Just because the run to work is dull, that doesn't mean you want it to be uncomfortable. Surely borrowing a little glamour from an imaginary cross-continental jaunt can only leave your energy levels higher when Monday morning rolls around? And if the school run is an integral part of your morning, then it stands to reason that most of your passengers will be rather short in stature and so ideal for the pint-sized plus-two seating out back.

But every indulgence comes at a price, and there is no getting away from that dreaded Jaguar thirst. The XJ-S was more aerodynamic than the E-type, but the very first cars struggled to get into double figures under all but the gentlest of use. That's hardly surprising when you consider the long, wide and very sturdy bodywork sitting on a modified version of the XJ6C floorpan. Combine this with a lusty 5.3-litre V12 engine and, although driving a car with so much torque that it can accelerate to over 140mph from rest in top gear alone may get addictive, paying for the privilege at the pumps on a daily basis will always be painful.

Fortunately, there are ways of mitigating this problem. The most obvious is to buy a post-1981 car with a 5.3HE tag on the back. That stands for High Efficiency, and refers to the adaptation of Michael May's

'BUY ONE THAT IS SOUND AND HAS BEEN REGULARLY SERVICED. LEAVE SOME MONEY OVER FOR THE OCCASIONAL HEFTY REPAIR BILL THEN RELAX AND ENJOY THE EXPERIENCE'

head design for the combustion chambers. Combine this with the fuel injection and you get the same power, a torque curve that comes in usefully lower down the rev range and a 20% improvement in economy. Heck, with that you can even push towards 16mpg.

Or, if you are confident enough in your own abilities not to need the reassurance of twelve cylinders, go for the 3590cc AJ6-engined models that arrived in 1983. They'll still do 142mph thanks in part to the five-speed Getrag gearbox, but can squeeze up to the psychological 20mpg barrier. With either of these later cars, you'll also get facelifted interiors with the

wood paneling that the cars' elegance somehow seems to demand.

There were subtle but extensive changes to the panelwork in 1991, but those distinctive flying buttresses remained. If you really can't live with them, there is always the Convertible option available from 1988. But whichever you choose, don't think about trying to run an XJ-S on just loose change – it takes all the fun out of the experience. Buy one that is sound and has been regularly serviced. Leave some money over for the occasional hefty repair bill, then relax and enjoy the experience.

As we said, you deserve it. △

Above
XJ-S's styling was controversial but it followed the seminal E-type and opinions have since mellowed.

JAGUAR: THE FAMILY TREE

Your ultimate guide to Jaguars, classic and modern. From the earliest Lyons-designed Swallow Sidecars to the svelte new XF, they're all here for your enjoyment...

Words: Matthew Hayward

SS1 1931-1936

This is where it all started. The SS1 was William Lyons' first car built on a purpose-built chassis, rather than borrowing someone else's. The Standard Motor Company supplied the underpinnings, who built it especially for SS Cars. Despite its sporting styling, the SS1 was not particularly fast by 1931 standards, although its good looks and low price made up for this.

Power: 55bhp Top Speed: 72mph

SS2 1931-1936

The SS2 was not a replacement for the SS1, but a smaller and cheaper counterpart that was sold alongside, and widened the appeal of Lyons' cars. The SS2 was considerably smaller than the SS1, due to packaging the Standard four-cylinder side-valve engine, but it was well proportioned and looked just as good as its bigger brother.
Power: 27bhp Top Speed: 60mph

SS90 1935

Based on a shortened version of the SS1 chassis, the SS90 was an open-topped sportscar powered by the Standard side-valve engine used in the SS1, but with an uprated alloy cylinder head and twin carburettors. Even with these modifications, the SS90 remained a leisurely drive and a mere 23 were built before switching to the SS100 in 1936.
Power: 70bhp Top Speed: 90mph

SS Jaguar 100 2½-litre 1936-1941

The SS100 was the car the SS90 should always have been, and was a landmark in the development of the marque. The engine was a development of the SS90's, and featured the same upgrades as the 2½-litre saloon's – power output rose from 70bhp to 102bhp, and performance was significantly improved. The SS100 Jaguar was conceived as an image-building exercise; Lyons expecting it to do well in competition circles. In the end, 308 were built, most being sold to road-going enthusiasts. **Power: 102bhp Top Speed: 94mph**

SS Jaguar 1½/2/3½-Litre saloon 1936-1946

This was the first Jaguar saloon that had power to match its looks, paving the way for the company's subsequent legendary big, fast cars. Performance was impressive for the class of 1936, thanks in no small part to the Standard engine getting a boost from twin SU-carburettors and an overhead valve set-up in the range-topping 2½-litre version. From 1938, the bodies were formed from pressed steel rather than hand-beaten aluminium, because demand for their cars had outgrown supply, and production volumes needed to rise significantly.
Power: 102bhp Top Speed: 88mph

Jaguar 2½/3½-litre saloon 1946-1949

After production of the SS cars ceased in 1940, the assembly line was turned over to military use until 1945. Now known by the marque name, Jaguar, Lyons' first post-war car was the handsome 2½-litre saloon. This was basically a light update of the pre-war car, now powered by Jaguar's own engine. In 1947, Jaguar launched the drophead coupe, designed very much with the export drive and American market in mind.
Power: 102bhp Top Speed: 87mph

Jaguar Mark V 1948-1951
Designed as a replacement for the 2½-Litre saloon, the Mark V was Jaguar's first car to feature independent front suspension. This was the last Jaguar powered by the six-cylinder Standard-derived engine that had served the company so well for over 20 years.
Power: 125bhp Top Speed: 91mph

Jaguar XK120 1948-1954
Originally planned to raise marque identity through competition, the XK120 proved such a hit that Lyons put it into mainstream production. The first 240 examples were aluminium bodied, but to meet with demand Jaguar switched to pressed steel bodies in 1950. The remarkable new twin-cam six-cylinder XK engine was a major motivating factor behind the car's success. In 1951 a Fixed Head Coupe XK120 was launched, extending appeal.
Power: 180bhp Top Speed: 125mph

Jaguar Mk VII/VIIM 1951-1957

Jaguar enlisted the help of the Pressed Steel Company to mass-produce body panels for its newest saloon model. The elegant MkVII was powered by the XK engine, lauded for its responsiveness in the XK120; and it gave this car an impressive turn of speed, too. In 1954 the VIIM was launched, with a new high-compression XK engine boosting power from 160bhp to 190bhp.
Power: 160bhp Top Speed: 105mph

Jaguar C-type 1951-1953

Only 53 XK120Cs were ever produced, partially due to the delays in moving to the recently-purchased Browns Lane factory in Coventry. The tubular chassis and aluminium body panels helped the car drop 450kg compared with the standard XK120 roadster, but mechanically they were both very similar. At Le Mans, the C-type won at its first attempt in 1951. The engine was upgraded to and performance was suitably uplifted. **Power: 200bhp Top Speed: 144mph**

Jaguar D-type 1954-1957

The D-type was perhaps *the* competition car of its day; it was never actually designed as a road car. The alloy monocoque body and highly efficient aerodynamic shape resulted in a car that took Le Mans by storm from 1954-57. The car's designer, Malcolm Sayer, moved to Jaguar from Bristol Aeroplanes after the Second World War, and brought with him his considerable aeronautical experience to aid high-speed stability. **Power: 250bhp Top Speed: 170mph**

Jaguar XK140 1954-1957

Replacing the XK120 was never going to be easy, and many existing customers were left feeling disappointed by the XK140. It was bigger and heavier and more powerful, and less of an out-and-out sportscar. The driving experience was blunter, and more relaxed, resulting in a relaxed long distance cruiser perfect for the impending motorway age.
Power: 190bhp Top Speed: 123mph

Jaguar 2.4/3.4 1955-1959

Just like the D-type racer, the Jaguar 2.4 saloon featured unitary construction; the first roadgoing Jaguar to do so. The new car's swooping low-roofed styling set the trend for Jaguars for years to come; and proved a big hit with buyers. Initially the car was offered with the detuned, short stroke 2.4-litre XK engine, but a larger 3.4-litre version was added to the range to satisfy demand in the US.
Power: 112bhp Top Speed: 101mph

Jaguar XKSS 1957

When Jaguar gave up racing the D-type, it was left with a handful of unused, lightweight monocoque chassis. A vestigial windscreen and a fabric roof were added – and the roadgoing XKSS was born. Lyons' plan was to sell the car in the US, and hoped that it would appeal to anyone who wanted to compete in Class C production racing. However, only 16 found homes before the factory fire of 1957 destroyed the remaining cars. **Power: 250bhp Top Speed: 144mph**

Jaguar Mk VIII/IX 1957-1961

Like the VII before it, the MkVIII featured independent front suspension. It resembled the VII in many ways, but was much more luxurious and chrome-laden, and that divided opinions. Despite its bulkiness, the MkVIII was agile to drive, and real fun, even more so in 220bhp MkIX form. Race-proven disc brakes were standard on the later cars, a Jaguar first.
Power: 210bhp Top Speed: 106mph

Jaguar XK150 1957-1961

At 1364kg, the XK150 wasn't exactly a lightweight. Aluminium panels were added to the exterior in an attempt to rein-in the overall weight, but still it tipped the scales at 50kg more than the XK140. The XK150 was the first Jaguar available with all-round disc brakes, and proved an excellent stopper. In 1959, the XK150S was launched, and boasted an impressive 265bhp and a limited-slip differential to handle the extra power.
Power: 190bhp Top Speed: 125mph

Jaguar Mk2 2.4/3.4/3.8 1959-1967

For many, the Mk2 is the definitive classic Jaguar. When new, it was roomy, fast and affordable, and leagues ahead of the opposition. Unsurprisingly, the Mk2 was a massive success, in the UK and USA, with a total of 83,976 examples produced. Dynamically, it was spot on, too. Thanks to various suspension and cosmetic upgrades, it felt so much more than a revised 2.4/3.4 'Mk1'.
Power: 120bhp Top Speed: 96mph

Jaguar E-type 1961-1975

Another landmark Jaguar – and although it's debatable that the first cars were really capable of a *genuine* 150mph, there's no denying it was the fastest car you could buy for the money. As the car grew older, it also became fatter due to US safety and emission regulations. All E-types were fitted with all-round discs and independent suspension. The Series IIIs, introduced in 1975, ushered in the remarkable new V12 engine, Visually, the larger bumpers and a wide chrome grille jarred. **Power: 265bhp Top Speed: 151mph**

Jaguar 420 1966-1969

Jaguar created the 420 by facelifting the S-type, and shoehorning in the 4.2-litre XK engine under the bonnet. In doing so, the ultimate expression of the Mk2 family emerged, although the new front end styling was less elegant. New features such as the Mk X's variable-ratio power steering, made it a very pleasant driving experience indeed.
Power: 245bhp Top Speed: 122mph

Jaguar MkX 3.8/4.2/420G 1961-1970

Serving as Jaguar's flagship for nine years, the MkX was a technological tour de force. They threw in everything they could – unitary body, the independent rear suspension, and an all-round disc brake set-up. As Jaguars went, this one was hard to beat in terms of value for money – and for years was in the *Guinness Book of Records* for being the widest production car available in the UK.
Power: 265bhp Top Speed: 120mph

Jaguar S-type 3.4/3.8 1963-1968

Jaguar created the S-type as an intermediate model to plug the gap between the Mk2 and MkX. Using the smaller car as a starting point, the S-type was created by rummaging through the parts bin. It used the MkX's independent rear suspension, had an extended rear end and an improved interior. The end result was a luxury sports saloon that extended the life of the Mk2 usefully, and which today is cruelly undervalued compared with its illustrious smaller brother.
Power: 210bhp Top Speed: 114mph

Jaguar 240/340 1967-1969

Giving the Jaguar 2.4 engine a modified cylinder head and an improved inlet manifold meant that the Mk2-based 240 could finally top 100mph. The same engine in this car's predecessor never had enough power to push it past the magic ton; a fact that caused Jaguar embarrassment. Production continued long after the arrival of the XJ6, and proved a useful money-spinner for Jaguar.
Power: 133bhp Top Speed: 105mph

Jaguar XJ6/XJ12 S1 1968-1973

This was the first generation of the very successful XJ model range, and introduced a new platform strategy that saw a single range replace the mixed bag of previous models. The Series I XJ6 was not entirely new, but it was designed to reinvent the Jaguar brand; echoing the important values of previous models, but moving the marque forwards. The XJ had independent suspension all-round for a world-beating suspension set-up, as well as the well-travelled XK engine.
Power: 245bhp Top Speed: 124mph

Jaguar XJ-C 1975-1977

Prematurely announced in the summer of 1973, due to delays in development and production engineering it would be a further two years before the 2-door XJ-C finally went on sale. It was worth the wait, though, thanks to successful styling and world-class dynamics. A vinyl roof was fitted to all models, and the frameless windows that caused so much trouble during development were noisy at speed and often leaked. A total of 8373 XJ-Cs were produced.
Power: 167bhp Top Speed: 116mph

Jaguar XJ6/XJ12 SII 1973-1979

Jaguar made many detail improvements to the XJ when creating the Series II. The new heating and ventilation system was welcome, as was the improved fuel economy thanks to the further tweaks the XK engine received. The interior received an upgrade, but the only external differences were the smaller grille and raised front bumpers, to help the XJ meet US safety regulations. The Series II was plagued with poor build quality and reliability issues – a sign of the times.
Power: 167bhp Top Speed: 124mph

Jaguar XJ-S 1975-1996

Based on a shortened XJ6 chassis, the XJ-S was the long awaited replacement for the E-type, that ended up missing the mark with buyers. It wasn't a sporting drive in the way the early E-types were, but a Grand Tourer cast in the Series III mould. The XJ-S was in production for over 20 years and eventually became a financial success for Jaguar, after blooming late in life.
Power: 285bhp Top Speed: 150mph

Jaguar XJ6/XJ12 SIII 1979-1992

With a little help from Pininfarina, the XJ's subtle but effective late-life facelift kept it fresh enough to make it desirable for a further 13 years. in 1981, the V12 version received HE cylinder heads, pushing fuel consumption from the realms of scandalous to merely excessive. The XJ's continuing commercial success was helped by continually improving quality standards during the 1980s.
Power: 285bhp Top Speed: 146mph

Jaguar XJ220 1989-1992

When the XJ220 was unveiled in 1988, its price tag was a cool £361,000. Jaguar took plenty of £50,000 deposits, many of which were placed by speculators hoping to sell for a profit later. However, the market collapsed, and all but a few of the original 240 orders resulted in sales. When the production XJ220 arrived in 1991, many customers cancelled their orders, disappointed that a twin-turbo V6 had replaced the original V12. **Power: 542bhp Top Speed: 212mph**

Jaguar XJ6/12 (XJ40/XJ81) 1986-1994

Development work on the XJ40 started back in 1972, and dragged on so long due to a lack of funding and management direction from BL. When it arrived, the XJ40 embodied the best and worst of contemporary Jaguar – it was technologically ahead of the previous XJ and its rivals, but quality was woefully lacking. The V12's four year delay also limited the model's appeal.
Power: 223bhp Top Speed: 140mph

Jaguar XJR-15 1990

Built by Tom Walkinshaw Racing (TWR) for Jaguar, the XJR-15 was little more than an XJR-9 Le Mans car with an all-new Peter Stevens-designed Kevlar and carbon-fibre body. Unlike the XJ220, it was powered by a normally aspirated V12 engine producing 450bhp. The XJR-15 remains a very raw and unrefined, street-legal race car, which does little to hide its competition roots.
Power: 450bhp Top Speed: 185mph

Jaguar XJ6/XJ8/XJ12 (X300/X305/X308) 1994-2003

Mechanically similar to the XJ40, the more curvaceous frontal styling harked back to the earlier XJ models. The X300 also signalled the entrance of higher-quality Jaguars overseen by Ford. The limited visual upgrades made a huge difference to the X300's overall desirability. Jaguar insisted that it didn't want to share any components with cars from its parent company, and the temptation to dip into Uncle Henry's parts-bin was successfully resisted.
Power: 216bhp Top Speed: 137mph

Jaguar XK8/XKR 1996-2006

The XK8 was styled with the E-type very much in mind; although Jaguar didn't want it to seem too retro. The AJV8 was completely new, designed in-house at Whitley, and was claimed to be one of the most technically advanced power units of its day. However, there was little else in the way of groundbreaking technology to mark out the rest of the car, which shared its underpinnings with the XJ-S. Despite that, the XK8 became the best selling Jaguar sports car to date.
Power: 290bhp Top Speed: 155mph

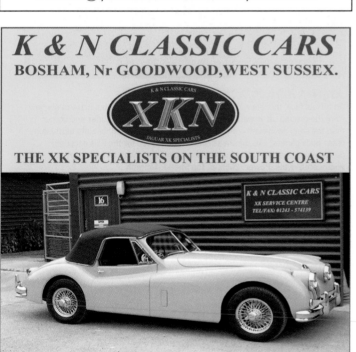

Jaguar S-type 1998-2008

Sharing its platform with the Lincoln LS, early S-types weren't blessed with great handling, but they did offer great value for money. Jaguar worked some of its magic into the later cars, with an improved dynamic package that transformed the S-type. Retro styling split opinions, but it was the company's first car in this sector for over 30 years, making Jaguar ownership a more affordable proposition. **Power: 240bhp Top Speed: 146mph**

Jaguar X-type 2001-date

Jaguar's baby, the X-type, completed the four car model strategy devised by Ford to take the luxury car fight to BMW. Originally available in 4WD form, it struggled in the marketplace, and only picked up with the introduction of the 2- and 2.2-litre diesels. It initially sold well in the USA, but combination of strong competition and an poor exchange rate meant that Jaguar pulled the model from that market in 2007. **Power: 194bhp Top Speed: 135mph**

Jaguar XK8/XKR 2007-2008

The all-aluminium XK shares virtually nothing with the old XK, apart from its AJV8 engine. Although it's no more powerful, lower weight improved body stiffness have radically improved this car. The XKR version, which features a supercharged V8 producing an impressive 420bhp, is now a genuine supercar. **Power: 300bhp Top Speed: 155mph**

Jaguar XJ/XJ6/XJ8/XJR 2003-2008

On the surface, the latest XJ just looks just like the old one, but it's actually new from the ground up. It features an aluminium monocoque, stiffer and lighter than the steel equivalent – and this is complemented by lightweight aluminium outer body panels. This lightness is the main reason for the XJ's excellent performance, handling and fuel economy compared with its more conventionally engineered rivals. **Power: 240bhp Top Speed: 145mph**

Jaguar XF 2008

Based on the show-stopping 2007 C-XF concept, the production XF is a new direction for Jaguar design, and it's a more forward thinking car than any car produced by the compan y since the original XJ . The XF is a direct replacement for the S-type, and actually uses that car's platform. But substantial structural changes have been made, improving safety, stiffness and space efficiency, and the overall result is a vast improvement for the driver.
Power: 235bhp Top Speed: 147mph